W9-CNQ-222

# The Year and Our Children

Also from Sophia Institute Press®
by Mary Reed Newland:

*How to Raise Good Catholic Children*

Mary Reed Newland

# The Year and Our Children

Catholic Family Celebrations for Every Season

SOPHIA INSTITUTE PRESS®
Manchester, New Hampshire

*The Year and Our Children* was originally published by The Firefly Press, San Diego, California, in 1956. This 2007 edition by Sophia Institute Press® includes minor editorial revisions to remove dated material and infelicities in grammar.

Copyright © 2007 Sophia Institute Press®

Printed in the United States of America

All rights reserved

Cover design by Theodore Schluenderfritz

No part of this book may be reproduced, stored in a retrieval system, or transmitted in any form, or by any means, electronic, mechanical, photocopying, or otherwise, without the prior written permission of the publisher, except by a reviewer, who may quote brief passages in a review.

Sophia Institute Press®
Box 5284, Manchester, NH 03108
1-800-888-9344
www.sophiainstitute.com

*Nihil obstat:* Rev. Andrew A. Martin, *Censor Librorum*
*Imprimatur:* + Christopher J. Weldon, Bishop of Springfield
Springfield, Massachusetts, March 7, 1956

**Library of Congress Cataloging-in-Publication Data**

Newland, Mary Reed.
  The year and our children : Catholic family celebrations for every season / Mary Reed Newland.
    p. cm.
  Originally published: San Diego, Calif. : Firefly Press, 1956.
  ISBN 978-1-933184-27-2 (pbk. : alk. paper) 1. Church year.
2. Catholic Church — Customs and practices. 3. Rites and ceremonies.
4. Family — Religious life. I. Title.

BX2170.C55N49 2007
249 — dc22
                                                      2007005194

07 08 09 10 9 8 7 6 5 4 3 2 1

*To*
*Ann Murphy Reed, M.D.,*
*and Catherine Phelan Newland —*
*otherwise known as*
*Grandma and Granny,*
*without whom there would be*
*no we and our children*

# Contents

# Foreword

"Did you always do these things?" people ask when they meet a family that celebrates the feasts of the Church year at home. The answer of our family is, "No, we did not always do these things." We are one of the families that "picked them up."

We were a typical American family stirred by an uneasiness that was hard to define. It had to do with the desire to draw closer to the Church and what she was doing as she moved from one season to another, but we didn't know how to explain it. We loved her, but we weren't close enough to her, and we couldn't tell why. We thought there were many more ways *she* could illumine our lives, but we didn't know what they were. *Stirred* is a good word for it. We were quite stirred up.

Strangely enough, the most important step in the changing of our family life was being stirred up. Afterward, we learned that the Church prays for it again and again during Advent. If it is a real stirring, inevitably you begin to learn — first of all, because God wants you to learn and has stirred you up in the first place, and secondly, because you already possess much of what you want to learn. But you possess it in a kind of disorder, so that you don't re-alize that you possess it. What we were seeking was a new perspective from which to see the treasure we already possessed, and a way to re-assemble it, to put it in order.

Let me explain.

We had the Faith and, in it, sacramental life. We lived the Christian year (at least, we half-lived it: if you go to church, you can't help at least half-living it). We knew much of the doctrine, and we had problems on which to apply it, but there seemed to be a connection missing between the doctrine and the application — as though much of the time we were powerless to see how it applied. We had a number of natural gifts distributed among the lot of us, as all families have — some intelligence, some ingenuity, some imagination — and it seemed that these ought to be used in combination with the other things. Yes, but how?

What we sought was a way to combine all these things harmoniously so that they would make a life for our family that was wholly Christian and would allow us to grow in the knowledge and the love of God in the times in which we live.

To see that the Church lived the year made the difference. To see ourselves as part of the Church, and therefore with a year to live, was the clue. Christ is our life. If we would pattern our life after anything, it should be after His life. But we share His life in the life of the Church. We had the pattern all the time in the daily life of the Mystical Body, and didn't know it.

This is how we started "living the Church year." It began, for us, with an Advent wreath and reading the fine print in the missal; after that, we read everything we could get our hands on that would help us. One by one, the seasons of the Christian year began to shape our prayer and our activity, and shed light on how we were to use the doctrine. We were a long time reaching the point where we fell naturally into the practices we now use to celebrate feasts and keep vigils. Because it was new to us, we were awkward, even embarrassed. This is something we meant with all our hearts: one is afraid to be caught posing at something so precious to us. So it entered us slowly, this "Christening" of our life.

We planned things that never quite came off. We planned things that fell through. Sometimes the family didn't respond, or the order of the day was disturbed by some unexpected event and we celebrated not a thing, except perhaps by way of a passing thought that today was to have been so different — if only it had turned out right. But looking back, some of the most valuable lessons are learned with the failures, because this is a way of life we hope will perfect us in doing God's will, not in having our own. Once St. Gertrude[1] complained to our Lord that He didn't send her the grace to enjoy one of the great feasts as she had hoped to do. He replied that it would have pleased her to enjoy it, but it pleased Him more to have her offer the lack of joy to Him. So sometimes He teaches us best by letting us get nowhere.

Some might protest that this is not really praying with the Church, this making of wreaths, baking of cakes, crowning of kings, dressing of dolls, cutting, pasting, sewing, planting; that this is not prayer of any depth and certainly not the liturgy of the Church. No, but for people who are learning what the liturgy is, and how to follow the prayer of the Church, who are making their first attempts really to pray it, this is the way to learn. We learn to swim in the shallow water before we are able to swim in the deep. These delightful things to see and touch and smell and taste and hear and make and do are by far the best tools there are to teach of the beauty and power of God, and the richness of life in Christ. We provide the natural settings, teach the words, give the ideas, draw the analogies, read the stories, sing the songs, tell the tales, warm all this with our love — and God makes the increase. We are not trying to do His part of the job, only our own — which is to prepare the hearts and minds of our families so that they will respond to Him. If they love the approaches to the knowledge of His

---

[1] St. Gertrude (c. 1256-1302), German mystic.

love and grace, they will be more easily led to the fountains of love and grace.

This book tells of the year and its seasons, their spirits, some of the background and stories that go with them, and things to make and do to celebrate them. Some of the customs are borrowed from beautiful European customs that have so enriched American family life. Some we have made up ourselves because they seemed the best way to communicate certain ideas and joys to an American family. We have used them all; so we know that they are practical. The stories have been written so that they may be read aloud from the book, or retold, if that is your way. We hope everything this book contains will be useful and will serve as a springboard for families who, trying out our ideas, will change them here or there, embellish them, give them their family's personality and flavor, and make their own lasting Christian customs. It is not the customs that are universal, but the liturgy.

From householders there will be the question of cost of materials and the convenience (or inconvenience) of storing them. The materials need never be costly. Most of what does not come from the pantry cupboard, the workbench, the rag-bag, or the "good junk" that all families accumulate may be purchased at the Five-and-Ten.[2] More expensive materials are excellent gift suggestions for aunts and uncles, grandparents, godparents, friends who want to know what to buy a child for his birthday, feast day, Christmas, or Easter. If you have the custom of bringing some sweets home after a shopping trip, as a treat for the family, why not substitute a creative kind of gift — something to add to the family art supplies? The joy to be had from these lasts longer, and it's better for their teeth!

---

[2] Nowadays such materials can be purchased at craft stores, hardware stores, or dollar stores. — ED.

The one expenditure necessary for families who would grow in the love and knowledge of the Church is *books*. These sometimes seem to be entirely out of reach, until we reassess our values and compare how much we spend to feed the bodies, which will one day be dust, and how little to feed the minds, which will live forever. It is worth sacrificing to buy books.

Space is the problem of families in small living quarters. This is one of the reasons television has proven such a successful minder of children. It takes so little room and is never messy — in the tangible way. Creative projects are often messy. Putting up with this is difficult or not, according to how we weigh the value of creative experiences for our children. A certain amount of common sense must operate here, however. It is always best to plan ahead the time and space for the more elaborate projects, not letting ourselves be teased into permitting a soap-carving session a half-hour before company arrives. Good activities for restricted space, for company times, and for especially busy housework days, are the reading aloud (among children), telling stories (mothers can do this as they work after they have mastered enough stories), talking-about, thinking-game, drawing-with-crayons kind of things.

If you are frantic for space and can persuade your landlord to permit it, you might paint one wall of the children's bedroom with blackboard paint (black or green) with the promise that you will paint it an orthodox color before you move. It will keep many children busy for hours at a time and is an ideal way to work out many lessons, stories, and teaching sessions. There is chalk dust, of course — but we can't have everything!

The more cluttery projects give greater play to the imagination, and the exploring and adventure of rich sessions with some great feast and the desire to illustrate it, demonstrate it, describe it in symbols — whatever — is a never-ending journey that leads all the way to eternity. Always conduct these projects (if they are carried out on flat surfaces) on opened newspapers, and the cleaning-up operation is cut to a minimum.

Storing things could be a problem for some. An excellent folio for keeping paper and drawings flat and clean is a paper garment bag cut in two and slid under a bed. Put new paper in one; store drawings in the other. Mayonnaise jars with screw-on tops keep odd trinkets, jewels, buttons, and all the "junk" supplies in assortments out of reach of small hands but in sight on a bit of shelf space. Can someone bear to give up a bureau drawer and go halves with someone else? The family art and make-and-do supplies can go in there. An old suitcase rarely used but needing storage keeps our ribbon and yarn supplies clean and safe and always handy for puppet-making and gift-wrapping. Patterns for cut-outs, stencils, and flat designs needed from time to time are kept in a flat manila envelope taped to the wall. An old orange crate is a file; in addition to correspondence, we keep clippings, pictures, and material of all kinds that will be useful for either home or school projects. One of the nicest Christmas gifts we ever received was a deep tray holding emptied prescription bottles containing paper clips, spread-apart paper fasteners, reinforcements, odd stationery supplies, a hole punch, a box of crayons, colored-paper pads, and so forth. All were vitally important to a family that "makes." (Do put a stapler in someone's stocking next Christmas — very important to a "maker.")

There is also the question of time. Where do you find the time? Like these other questions, the answer is, we can find it if we plan for it. We can find it quite easily by looking to see where we waste it. Not wasting it is not easy, because the habits of time-wasting, although they are harmless, are hard to break — as I know from experience. Mothers have this struggle all to themselves. It involves such things as the radio habit, coffee breaks, cigarette breaks, long telephone conversations, chatting with neighbors, a heavy involvement in outside activities. Somewhere most American women can "find time" to devote to the enriching of their families' spiritual life. The joyous discovery is that once we have struggled and found the time, tasted and seen how sweet are these pursuits together, we begin to gauge all our doings so that there will be time — because we are convinced there must be.

Last of all, personalities. Suppose your family includes some who aren't the procession-type, who don't enjoy doing anything unconventional, who are too much overcome with self-consciousness to take part in any new or different kind of family prayer, feasting, celebration. What then? Then you use your head, and your tact, and your love — and you never force the issue. Perhaps all you can give to such a one is a crumb of interesting information passed along in dinner-table conversation, or the children's amusing report of what they celebrated at their party, or answer questions about the things they have created to help with the celebration of a feast. Adolescents, teenagers, husbands, sometimes wives, relatives living in — it is possible they fail to share the enthusiasm of younger children and mothers. All right. If these customs do not enhance faith and prayer for such ones, it is certainly not good to force their use and precipitate tension. If we are living the year with the Church with the proper love and eagerness to learn of Christ, one of the increases should be in our own patience and understanding, respect for each other as individuals, caution in judgments. We can always pray.

One of the gravest problems of our day is the problem of working mothers. Some mothers must work, but not all. Those who are not obliged to are often driven to by compulsions that appear to be defensive. Is it not possible that one of the reasons they leave their homes is because, aside from daily chores, there seems nothing to do there? No excitement, no adventure, no thrill. Nothing but the drudgery of housework (as it has been called); and no suggestion is given about how to use this except to "offer it up." If only these mothers would discover that they have left their real fortune behind them when they leave their homes daily to make it. Their life with their families offers infinite variety — and opportunity for adventure, riches they have never yet examined, challenges to their minds and their bodies and their hearts — in the living out of one day after another with their Mother, the Church.

For the families who begin to suspect that they have let their lives get too complicated with worldly cares, too much involved in secular values, too materialistic, living through the year with the Church is the stabilizer, the way to keep to first things first.

And for the families who conceal behind their front doors some hardship or cross, whether a suffering shared or inflicted or borne, the tempo of life in Christ as He leads the Church at prayer through the year is calming, enriching; it brings wisdom, sheds light, gives courage.

The families who have discovered the joys of living the year with the Church would be the first to say so — to the families who, we pray, will discover them.

# The Year and Our Children

Chapter 1

The Wreath, The Gift, and The Candle

Christmas is coming — for the children, the most wonderful time of the year. And for the children of Light, it should be the most wonderful, *wonderfull* time of the year, because to the Church, it is the year's beginning. No one but God could have made such a beginning, so full of beauty and glory and sheer magic as this.

But you cannot just walk into such a blaze of glory without preparation, to be ready for that sharp sweet moment when an Infant's cry cut the night "a moment's fall, the last we should know of loneliness." You must creep up to it, think about it, count the days, watch the signs, and prepare. And folly though it seems in a world where all value is counted in material things, a child can never know the whole ecstasy of Christmas unless he knows its meaning; unless he takes its meaning into his own two hands and examines it closely and finds its mystery for himself. It must be made of his own experience and delight and love.

*Making the Advent Wreath*
Advent for children should rightly be a very busy time, starting with the making of the Advent wreath. This is a sacramental in which the whole meaning of Advent is symbolized, and symbols are a language children understand very easily.

If the wreath is to be hung from the ceiling, the frame can be made in a number of ways. It can be wire coat-hangers unshaped and twisted to form a circle (with cross-pieces to brace it); it can be cut from plywood; it can be a cast-off floral-wreath frame; it can be several circles of heavy cardboard cut and taped together and braced with cross-pieces; or it can be (as is ours) the circular wooden frame from an old ash-sifter (which works incredibly well). Any of these ways is all right, so long as you make it. That is the most important point: to make it.

Candleholders, improvised or ready-made if suitable, can be wired to, soldered to, or cut into the frame at the four points of the compass (we made ours of bouillon tins, nailed to the braces and silvered). On a hung wreath, the greens are fastened to show from the bottom rather than the top. It is tied with purple ribbons between the four candles and hung by the ribbons from the ceiling. If purple ribbon is not available for Advent, you can dye white ribbon, and at Christmas you may, if you wish, change the ribbons and candles to red or gold, the colors of divine joy and love.

One year we sprayed our wreath with water glass, an egg preservative purchased at drugstores, but the advantage is debatable. It does not make the wreath nonflammable, although it would burn with difficulty; it does make it dry and crumbly. This may be because we use crow's-foot (an evergreen creeper) and princess pine for our wreaths, and these get dry before the season is over. If you decide to spray your wreath, place it on a wide spread of newspapers on the floor or table so that you won't have water glass all over everything.

The principal protection against fire is to have the candleholders firm and the candles firmly in them. Our bouillon-cube tins provide three or four inches of fireproof candleholder. We never let the candles burn down too far, nor light them unless there is a grown-up present, and we have never had any trouble with our Advent wreaths beyond some soot on the ceiling one year, and one scorch mark because we hung it too high. The candles need not be blessed candles, although the beeswax candles burn the most beautifully and more slowly, and there are plenty of ways to use up the leftover candle stubs.

A table wreath can be a simple wreath of greens resting in a pan of water to keep them fresh, or a large ringmold filled with wet sand, which will keep the greens fresh; or you may put greens in a ringmold filled with wet plaster (of course they do not come out!). Candlesticks are placed on the table inside the wreath. The ribbon may be tied to the candle, or it may bind the wreath or be tied on it in four bows between the candles.

Well, what does it mean?

The circle is a symbol of eternity and the never-endingness of God, and the evergreen is a symbol of eternal life and the never-changingness of God. Tertullian,[3] in the third century, wrote to the Christians of his day, "You are a light of the world; a tree ever green." Children love to learn by symbols.

We wondered one year if the smaller ones remembered. "What does the circle of the wreath mean, dear? Do you remember?"

A small boy thought very hard and then said, "I can't tell you, but I can show you." He hugged himself with both arms and went around and around in a wide circle. "See? God never stops."

"You mean God goes around in circles?"

"No! God doesn't go around in circles. 'God never stops' means 'God never ends.' " He thought. "He never begins, either. Like circles."

It is what the catechism says — only in his words.

*Did God have a beginning? God had no beginning. He always was and always will be.*

---

[3]  Tertullian (c. 160-225), Church Father.

The four candles in the wreath are for the four weeks of Advent. Three candles are white for divine innocence,[4] and one is rose to match the rose vestments permitted on Gaudete Sunday (third Sunday of Advent), reminding us of the shout of joy in that day's entrance antiphon: "Rejoice *(gaudete)* in the Lord always; again I say, rejoice." The rose-colored candle says that the promise is almost fulfilled; come, everyone, rejoice!

The ribbon is purple for penance, but it is a different kind from the penance of Lent. That penance is heavy with sorrow, bitter and painful with the knowledge of our sins. We are sinners in Advent, too, but the emphasis is differently placed. The emphasis is on our longing, our need — not only for the great graces of the feast of His Nativity, for the renewing in our hearts of the mystery of His birth, but our need to be ready for the glorious moment of His Second Coming. This penance is a chastening, a cleansing, a hurrying and a waiting, a longing and an aching that is at the same time both painful and sweet. Like the family waiting for the baby to come, we could all but die with the waiting — for His birthday and His coming again in glory.

The family gathers for the blessing of the wreath on the first Sunday of Advent or on its vigil, with the father or some older member of the family reading the blessing.

BLESSING OF THE ADVENT WREATH

*Leader:* Our help is in the name of the Lord.

*All:* Who hath made heaven and earth.

*Leader:* Let us pray. O God, by whose word all things are sanctified, pour forth Thy blessing upon this

---

[4] Three purple candles, as a reminder that Advent is a time of penance, prayer, and preparation, are typically used nowadays. — ED.

wreath, and grant that we who use it may prepare our hearts for the coming of Christ and may receive from Thee abundant graces. Through Christ our Lord.

All:    Amen. (*Sprinkle wreath with holy water.*)

The father or leader reads the prayer for the first week, then holds up the youngest child to light the first candle, which is also lighted all through the week when the family gathers in the room with the wreath. Two candles are lighted by the oldest child the second week, three are lighted the third week by the mother, and four the fourth week by the father.

In families where there are many children, it is impossible to satisfy all who want to light candles since there are only four Sundays in Advent. We solve this problem in our house by letting the children take turns lighting the candles during the week. They are never lighted unless an adult is present. When there is a guest who asks, "What a pretty wreath. Is it something special, with the candles like that?" the children love to explain: "It's an Advent wreath, and the four candles are for the four weeks of Advent. Every week, we light another candle, you see, and the light around it grows bigger. That means that the birthday of the Light of the World is coming soon. Baby Jesus, you know, and Christmas. It's His birthday and He's the Light of the World."

*Advent Penances, and a Story about a Juggler*
Next, there is the all-important matter of a birthday gift for the Light of the World. If there are to be gifts for others, there must first be a gift for Him. It is His birthday, not ours; and what kind of birthday is it when all the gifts go to the wrong people? What kind of gift would He like?

# The Year and Our Children

There is a story to tell at the beginning of Advent, about someone who had nothing to give. It illustrates best of all for children how the intangible is to God the most tangible, and makes entirely reasonable to them a scale of values one would suppose far over their heads. The story is "The Juggler of our Lady." It is as old as old, but each time it is told, it seems more beautiful.

It is about a monk who had no great talents, who could not illuminate manuscripts or write music or sing songs or paint pictures or compose prayers or do any of the dozens of things the other monks were preparing to do in honor of the Mother of God and her newborn Son. So he made his way to the crypt below the main altar of his abbey church, and there before her statue, he humbly confessed that he had nothing to give. Unless . . . but of course. He had been a tumbler and a juggler in the world. Long ago. He had been a rather brilliant tumbler and juggler, if the truth were known. Might she like to see him juggle and tumble? She was young and happy. She had laughed and clapped her hands. Surely her Child had. Perhaps he could tumble for them, all alone in secret? That is what he would do: give her the only thing he had to give. He would display his talent for the honor and glory of God and the entertainment of the Queen of Heaven.

So he removed his habit down to his tunic, and then he danced. And he leaped and he tumbled and he juggled in the most inspired fashion until finally he fell in a swoon at the feet of his Lady. And while he lay there limp and wet from his efforts, senseless as though he were dead, she stepped down from her pedestal and tenderly wiped the sweat from his brow and sweetly considered the love he had put into this performance for her and her dear Son's sake.

And this happened every day.

Now, there was another monk there who began to notice that the tumbler came not to Matins and kept watch on him because "he blamed him greatly." So he followed closely the movements of the tumbler. One day he followed behind him and carefully hid himself in the recesses of the crypt and witnessed the whole performance. So profoundly was he impressed and inspired that he hied himself straight to the abbot, who prayed God would let him, too, witness this wonder of dancing and juggling for the Mother of God. And he did see not only the dancing and the juggling and the leaping and the capers but also the Queen of Heaven, in the company of angels and archangels, come down and with her own white mantle fan her minstrel and minister to him with much sweetness.

When it came to pass that the abbot made it known to the minstrel that he had been seen — poor minstrel! He fell to his knees to beg forgiveness and plead with them not to send him out from the monastery. Which, of course, they did not do but held him in high esteem until the day he died, and there about his bedside they saw the Mother of God and the angels of Heaven receive his soul and carry it to everlasting glory.

"Think you now that God would have prized his service if that he had not loved Him? By no means, however much he tumbled. . . . God asks not for gold or for silver but only for true love in the hearts of men, and this one loved God truly. And because of this, God prized his services."

This, then, is the pattern for the gift: it must be a giving of *self*.

Our children usually give Him their desserts and treats during Advent except on Sundays, the two feasts, and the two birthdays that we celebrate with special festivities. These days they give Him something else instead. They try to give more willingly than before their bumps and hurts, and (this really hurts) their will in such matters as being first, sitting by the window in the car, licking the bowl, doing the dishes without being asked, or doing homework first instead of last.

*No funnies* (especially no Sunday funnies) makes a beautiful gift for the funnies and comic-book addicts, and no radio for the radio fans. No TV is an excruciatingly difficult gift to make but more beautiful for its being difficult; and the Christ Child has a way of giving back more than you have given Him.

These gifts of self-denial are not quite so hard when you see that you are accomplishing something. Gift boxes chosen at the beginning of Advent receive a bean for each day of enduring self-denial. On Christmas Eve these are wrapped in gay paper and ribbon and put under the tree to await the feast of Epiphany. Another custom is to make a tiny cradle for the Christ Child; a piece of hay or soft yellow yarn or a shred of finely cut tissue paper for each daily self-denial makes Him a soft bed to lie on. Salt boxes, match boxes, cornmeal boxes, lined and covered with pretty papers, make lovely cradles. Then, on Christmas morning, to their great delight, the children find a tiny Baby Jesus wrapped in swaddling clothes, contentedly lying on this soft bed they have so arduously made for Him.

Going without TV, radio, or these other things need not be so difficult as it appears to be — not if we make good substitutes for them. It is far more satisfying to make, to do, to act, or to sing yourself than it is to watch someone else do it. It is a fundamental part of emotional security and self-confidence to know that you are able to do something in your own special way. Many parents worry about the tendency of children to sit vegetating in front of TV sets, becoming by avocation a perpetual audience, but cannot quite discover the secret to shutting off the set and contenting the children without it. Creative activity is one answer. Taking advantage of the great penitential seasons of Advent and Lent, not only to encourage self-denial but also to explore the spiritual meanings of these seasons with creative activities, is almost certain to bear fruit.

# The Wreath, The Gift, and The Candle

Ultimately we must insist on times of quiet, away from the manufactured entertainments of this world, in order to form the habit of recollection. We are supposed to be contemplatives according to the capacity God has given us — which means that we see the world, ourselves, and all that is created in the right relation to God and that we think on these things often with love. Whether we will end up "contemplatives" in cloisters or as contemplatives who are farmers, writers, bus drivers, policemen, dancers, whatever — in order to grow, we must be reaching constantly to God with our minds. We need quiet for the very least of this, for the beginning of meditation. Parents can begin the process for their children with quiet times of creating and conversation together. That is what these conversations are — family meditations. Making a Christ candle during Advent can be such a project and can be, for a child, the beginning of learning how to meditate.

⤳

### The Christ Candle and the Meaning of Christmas

There are various ways to make a Christ candle. (A baptismal candle is decorated the same way, substituting the symbols for Baptism and the form of the baptismal rite.) It is a German custom to decorate a large candle with a *Chi Rho* or another symbol of Christ, place it in a holder, and cover it with a blue silk mantle symbolic of our Lady, who carried the little Christ under her heart before He was born. Lighted Christmas Eve at midnight, the flame is a symbol of Christ, the Light of the World.

We have made our own kind of Christ candle in order to teach the children that the reason for Christmas was the Fall and to help them see the thousands of years the Jews awaited the Messiah as the prologue to the Redemption. They must understand this, or there is no good excuse for Christmas. He did not come down to be born a baby just because it seemed like a lovely idea.

# The Year and Our Children

After rereading the story of Original Sin in Genesis in the Old Testament, we plan figures for our candle that will help us travel in our minds the long corridor leading from the Garden of Eden to Bethlehem.

We use a liturgical candle (at least 51 percent beeswax) about two feet long, which can be purchased in most religious-goods stores. After planning where the designs will be placed on the candle (these designs may be drawn on paper with a soft lead pencil. Reverse them, pencil-side down, against the candle, and transfer by rubbing on back of design), we apply one coat of white shellac to the side of the candle where they will appear. This helps the oil paint to "take." White shellac can be bought at the Five-and-Ten, as can a cheap watercolor or sash brush for applying it. Clean shellac from brushes with rubbing alcohol.

For painting the designs, we use a small pointed brush of good quality, oil paints, a little turpentine for thinning, and a cloth with turpentine for wiping off mistakes (but don't be too fussy — they rarely look like mistakes to anyone but you). After the paint is dry, we shellac the designs again as protection against too much handling.

One does not have to be a fine artist to decorate a candle. Even clumsy attempts are beautiful when finished, and the effect of the whole is rich and colorful. More important than technique is love and enthusiasm. Remember that it is not just the handiwork but the reading and thinking and conversations that go with it that make the completed work valuable.

As for the figures, if you can't draw them "out of your head" you will find many small figures to trace — in this instance, tracing is allowed (rarely otherwise!). Keep them simple, not bothering with fingers, toes, complicated features: stress the action boldly so that they tell their story. Paint in bold, bright colors without fussing: this helps to give the final work crispness if the figures are outlined in dark brown — a sienna or umber. Simple patterns of dots, stripes, little crosses, and bands of decoration add interest and contrast to the garments.

The choice of figures and stories is optional. At the top we have the tree, bright green with red apples, brown trunk, yellow serpent coiling into the tree to recall the reason the Redeemer had to come. Reading in Genesis, we find that God the Father makes the first prophecy of the Messiah immediately after the Fall. In it He points to Bethlehem — to Christmas — because the Woman and her Seed He promises are going to be Mary and her Son.[5]

Next, we have Adam and Eve dressed in animal skins, weeping with their faces in their hands, and drawn in profile because it is easier to depict the action this way. They understand clearly what they have done: disobeyed God, wrought a debt they can never pay, brought sin and death into the world, destroyed the harmony of the universe. Worst of all, they have lost that divine life they shared so intimately with God: sanctifying grace. Jesus was born on Christmas to repay man's debt to His Father, to open the gates of Heaven, to defeat death by purchasing for us eternal life, and to *institute a means by which we might share God's life again, as Adam did.*

While we live here in our exile from Heaven, the object of His birth in the stable in Bethlehem is our oneness of life with Him in His Mystical Body, the Church and, through it, the unbelievable intimacy of our soul's life with the indwelling Father, Son, and Holy Spirit. Thus did Christ restore what Adam lost. Well might

---

[5] Gen. 3:15. Except where otherwise noted, the biblical quotations in these pages are taken from the Douay-Rheims edition of the Old and New Testaments. Where applicable, biblical quotations have been cross-referenced with the differing names and enumeration in the Revised Standard Version, using the following symbol: (RSV =). — Ed.

Adam weep, at the top of our candle. Original Sin was a terrible thing.

Next, we have Noah's ark with the dove and the olive branch on top. Bright yellow ark, with an orange roof, white dove, and bright green olive branch; it is very cheery. This tells us that Noah is a type of Christ. God sent the deluge to destroy all the wicked on earth, but preserved Noah because he was holy, and through him the human race is born again just as through Christ, who from the Cross poured forth grace into His Church, and through His sacraments we are born again to divine life. Noah, sheltering in the ark his family, from whom would spring a new generation (Semites from his son Sem, Gentiles from the others), is a type of Christ sheltering His newborn people in the ark of the Church.

Next, we have Abraham and Isaac walking hand in hand up the mountain to the place of sacrifice. Abraham has a torch for the fire in one hand and a sword for the sacrifice in the other. Isaac has a bundle of sticks on his back. Again we see that they are types: Abraham, chosen by God to be the Father of the Jews, out of whom would come the Messiah, is a type of God the Father leading His Son to sacrifice; Isaac is a type of Christ the Son, the Victim. The sticks are a symbol of the Cross. There is a line in this story of obedience, faith, and sacrifice that pierces to the heart. Isaac asks, "But where is the victim?" And Abraham replies, "God will provide the victim."[6]

For Abraham He provided a ram caught in the brambles; and for us He provided His beloved Son, born in a stable, died on a Cross.

Then comes Jesse in a crimson robe with a golden crown, holding an ancient musical instrument that looks like a cello. Try as we might, we can find no explanation for the cello; it simply appeared

[6]  Cf. Gen. 22:7-8.

with Jesse in an old illuminated manuscript and delighted the children. Jesse is one of our Lord's grandfathers and is familiar to us in the genealogy of our Lady known as the tree of Jesse; she is referred to as springing from the Root of Jesse. There is another interesting thing about Jesse: his grandmother was Ruth, the lovely widow who returned to Bethlehem with her mother-in-law, Naomi, although by birth she was not a Jewess. "Thy people shall be my people; thy God my God," she said.[7] We had never stopped before to think what that meant: our Lord had, among His antecedents, a Gentile grandmother!

Next is the son of Jesse, King David. He sits holding his harp to remind us of his beautiful songs, the Psalms, and wears royal purple and a golden crown. "Jesus, son of David . . ." "Out of the house of David . . ." "Mary and Joseph of the house of David . . ." All these point to Bethlehem, "the city of David." Indeed, the very name *Bethlehem* means "house of bread," which lifts our minds to still another meditation on this "Son of David."

Then — Mary. She is beautiful in a blue mantle with white stars and a gold crown with stars around it. It is easy to see the point of her title "Gate of Heaven." Through her He came, and it is through her that we go to Him.

Eve weeps at the top. Mary rejoices at the bottom. Below Mary, in swaddling bands, a snug white cap on His head, a gold cruciform nimbus behind Him, is Jesus. And at the bottom, in gold, as though it were shouting and singing and dancing, is *Gloria*.

If the children are small, the figures are best painted by the grown-ups with the little ones held firmly at bay. They do jiggle and upset things. It will also help if the candle is lodged firmly in its box and painted there. But the planning, the talking, the awe and wonder of reading and conversation about these great things

---

[7] Ruth 1:16.

are for all the family; and as the children grow older, they can help with the painting, each one doing a bit so that it is really a family affair.

What if it takes all of Advent to do it? It is a beautiful preparation for Christmas. Without once saying, "Christmas isn't all presents, dear; Christmas isn't just Santa Claus," we begin to teach them what Christmas is. The feast of our Lord's birth in the stable at Bethlehem is more than the gladdest and happiest event of the winter. It celebrates the beginning of the Redemption, the story of God's love after man's disobedience, of God's desire that man shall be with Him in Heaven. It contains the seed of all the truths of the Faith, of the doctrines they must learn about the Church, the sacraments, the Mass. It explains how we must love one another, why we must love one another, why we get presents at all on His birthday. The greatest gift of all at Christmas is ours: the Son of God was sent to buy us back with love.

Chapter 2

Saints of Advent

The feast of St. Barbara on December 4 may seem to have no apparent connection with Advent other than the date; but it does connect, as you will see. She is especially important to our children, and they consider it *"de rigueur"* to salute her on her feast day since she is the patroness of those who call for protection against lightning and electrical storms. Frequently during the summer we have brief counsels such as, "Now stop fussing and pray to St. Barbara. She will keep us all safe and sound until the storm is over."

She was the daughter of a pagan, Dioscorus, who (according to the somewhat questionable Acts of St. Barbara) placed her in a high and beautiful tower surrounded by marvelous gardens, and sent philosophers, poets, and scholars to teach her all things. Convinced that polytheism was nonsense, she consulted Origen, one of the most brilliant and controversial of early Christian apologists; he sent her his disciple Valentinium, who forthwith instructed and baptized her. She thereupon threw all the statues of pagan gods and goddesses out a window of her tower, traced the Sign of the Cross everywhere on the walls, and had a third slit of a window cut in honor of the Holy Trinity.

This upset her father no end. He had her dragged out of the tower, but she somehow escaped to the mountains as he was about to slay her. He pursued her and dragged her back by the hair of her head (which is why she is sometimes pictured being dragged about by the hair) and handed her over to Marcian, a master at the art of torturing Christians. She was beaten with rods, torn with iron hooks, and suffered other horrible torments. To finish her off with the nicest of niceties, her father asked for the privilege of striking the final blow. He dragged her out of town and cut off her head with an axe. The best part of the story is that, as she was being carried to Heaven by the angels, her father is supposed to have been struck dead by lightning and "hurried before the judgment seat of God." Hence her concern that we be preserved from lightning and from a sudden and unprovided death. She is also patroness of firemen, mathematicians, firework makers, artillery men, architects, smelters, saltpeter workers, brewers, armorers, hatters, tilers, masons, miners, and carpenters, and she is invoked against final impenitence.

With this to her credit, she is precisely the saint we want supporting us in our brave resolves at the start of Advent. So, on December 4, we sing at the dinner table, "Happy feast day, St. Barbara," and tell her story. At night prayers, we invoke her help in the words of the Collect[8] of her Mass:

> O God, who, among the marvels of Thy power,
> has given the victory of martyrdom even to the
> weaker sex, grant in Thy mercy that we who keep
> the birthday of blessed Barbara, Thy virgin and martyr,
> may, by her example, draw nearer to Thee.
> Through Our Lord Jesus Christ, Thy Son, who
> liveth and reigneth with Thee in the unity of
> the Holy Spirit, God, world without end. Amen.

[8] Collects are brief prayers formerly used in the liturgy before the reading of the Epistle. — ED.

*St. Nicholas versus Santa Claus*

On December 6 comes the feast of the Christmas saint, St. Nicholas, although most of our celebration of this feast comes on his vigil, December 5. We find a puppet show a delightful way to tell his story, explain his relation to the Christ Child, and introduce the hanging of stockings for his feast day.

St. Nicholas was really a Turk born in Asia Minor. For a long time he was Bishop of Myra (near the southern coast of Turkey to the right of the Island of Rhodes — in case you look for it on a map). An orphan, he grew in love of God, became a priest, and made a pilgrimage to the Holy Land to venerate the places of our Lord's life. On the voyage, a terrible storm threatened to sink the ship, but by his prayers all were saved. For this reason he is venerated as patron of boatmen, fishermen, dock workmen, and sailors.

Returning to his native land, he was made a bishop; his generosity and love for the poor and for children, as well as his many miracles, endeared him to Christian people all over the world. He is also venerated as the patron of scholars, coopers and brewers, travelers and pilgrims, those who have unjustly lost a lawsuit, and as patron and annual benefactor of schoolchildren (especially boys), and is invoked against robbers and (in Holland) for protection of seafaring men.

Many legends surround St. Nicholas, among them the one saint story I personally cannot abide: the tale of the three little boys murdered and salted down in a tub is too much.[9] We never tell it.

The story we like best is the well-known tale of the three marriageable daughters who were nevertheless unmarriageable for

---

[9] According to this legend, three boys were murdered by an innkeeper, who put them in a tub of brine, and St. Nicholas found them and restored them to life. — ED.

want of dowries. Hearing of their plight, the saint went silently by their house one night and tossed a bag of gold through the window for the oldest, who not long after found a husband for herself with no trouble at all. Then he crept by a second time and tossed a bag of gold through the window for the second daughter, who likewise was suddenly at no loss for suitors. As he was about to toss the gold through the window for the third daughter, the father of the girls caught sight of him. Throwing himself at his feet, he thanked him, confessed his sins, begged his blessing. Plainly it is from this story that the tradition has grown wherein St. Nicholas is said to leave gifts, candies, and sweets on windowsills, in shoes, and even in the stockings of good little children.

It is the Dutch diminutive *Sinter Klaas* ("Sant Nikolaas") that became, by way of the New Amsterdam Dutch, the familiar American Santa Claus. It is among the Dutch also that we find the appearance of Black Peter, his page, who follows him, distributing switches, coal, straw — whatever — to the naughty children as St. Nicholas gives treats to the good. Black Peter appeared in the Dutch festival after the invasion of Holland by the Spaniards, who brought black servants with them.

"Telling the truth about Santa Claus" need not rob children of their Christmas magic. It adds to it with another feast to celebrate, another saint to know and love, another emphasis gently persuading them to meditate on the coming of the divine Child. And if we really fear to take away that part of it which is surprise, that marvelous moment Christmas morning when the presents are at last mysteriously there, be assured the little ones continue to pretend. Our littlest ones, knowing the truth, continue to pretend that it is all assembled in the most mysterious and magical fashion.

"But — then — who gives us the presents?" children will ask.

"Who loves you most in all the world gives you the presents."

"Who is that?"

"You guess."

They screw up their faces, think hard. Then suddenly all brighten: "You — and Daddy, and Grandma and Granny!"

It is like the circle that never ends. God loves mothers and fathers and gives them children they will love, and they teach the children about God, and the children love God, and since God wants them all with Him in Heaven, He sends His Son who loves them so much that He gives up His life for them, and that is so much love that it pays for their sins and buys back Heaven for them. . . . At Christmas everyone is so happy about all this that we all give each other presents. Shouldn't that be the reason we give and receive presents?

It would be a little embarrassing to be asked, "Don't you think the Christ Child is an adequate substitute for Santa Claus?" and feel you must answer no. He really is and He must become the all of Christmas for families who are going to try to live lives of deep faith. It is not really worth it to toss in this "little white lie" when we are trying so hard to teach children impeccable truthfulness. Probably not all children who discover there is no Santa, when they have been told by their parents that there is, will consider their parents dyed-in-the-wool liars, but there is the danger that they will discount some of every other truth they are taught. This is an age when accuracy and unadorned truthfulness are not particularly in vogue. Yet a concern to speak the utter truth in everything will teach a child better than anything else how to be utterly truthful himself, how to be honest with his own conscience — which is the same thing as being honest with God. Santa Claus is not a serious lie, but St. Nicholas in his rightful place, gazing with us at the Christ Child, is a much lovelier truth.

One thing, however, it is not cricket to do: go about the neighborhood telling all the children who do believe in Santa Claus that "there is none." This kind of revelation is guaranteed to leave nothing but heartache behind. Without proper explanation or background, it is really cheating a child of something he dearly loves. Most children can learn to keep their own counsel about this; where there is disparity on the subject in the neighborhood, with love and tact the mothers can explain and help prevent unpleasant exchanges.

One of the traps into which most parents of goodwill eventually fall before Christmas has arrived is to shout in the heat of some shortness of tempers: "How do you expect to get presents on Christmas if you aren't good now?" No sooner are the words out of your mouth than you could bite off your tongue. But it has been said. The ugly implication is there: you might not get presents for Christmas. St. Nicholas's feast is an ideal time for straightening out this problem of being good and not being good before Christmas. It is true that the issue should have something to do with the end result, but when we threaten this way, we forget that the reason God the Father sent the Christ Child wasn't because everyone had been good, but because they hadn't been good.

To transfer the burden of the "be good or else" problem to St. Nicholas is infinitely more comfortable. Here the threat involves no more than a stockingful of cookies, but it is a prospect sufficiently dreadful to give them pause. It also involves a happy solution to the naughtiness. No good behavior — no cookies. It usually works (I speak from experience). The shock of seeing that you meant what you said, of hearing St. Nicholas warn you the night before and discovering he meant what he said, is most salutary. Most *enfants terribles* will stand dolefully watching the more virtuous munching their cookies and make a superb effort to mend their ways, and yet the event is not of such magnitude that it leaves any permanent scars.

People always ask how we handle the delicate business of sharing should this occasion produce one or two malcontents without cookies. We are all, of course, very sad to see they have no cookies, but if it is a warning and a punishment, then it is a warning and a punishment. Character training is involved, and also your own authority. No cookies — shared or otherwise.

*The Vigil and the Puppet Show*

We have our puppet show on the eve of St. Nicholas's feast. Our puppets are made of socks — a white one for St. Nicholas and a navy blue one for Black Peter (we didn't have brown or black clean that day). St. Nicholas is the toe of a white sock stuffed with cotton batting until there is a firm egg-shaped head. A rubber band is wound several times at the base of this to make the neck. Two slits are cut on each side of the sock under this, close to the neck. The index finger goes up through the rubber band into the head to wag the head; the thumb and third finger go through the two slits to make arms. The anatomy of the puppet is done.

His face can be drawn on with heavy pencil, paint, or even a ballpoint pen; St. Nicholas has pink cheeks and bright blue eyes (although it occurs to us that most Turks have black). White yarn sewed across his mouth from ear to ear makes his full beard; sewed on around a baldpate, it makes his hair, which hangs to his shoulders.

His alb is a white flounce sewed together like a cuff, gathered at the neck and tacked under the chin, and trimmed with odds and ends of lace. His cope is a piece of red velveteen with green braid trim, and his miter is cut from stiff white paper and trimmed with a green braid cross-stitched or glued or painted on. A piece of white braid stitched across the bottom of the miter ties snugly under his hair at the back, holding it in place. Blind sleeves may be put in his garments, but even without them, the two fingers can be managed to give the illusion of arms.

Black Peter has a garment of red lamé cut from an old blouse and worn under a navy blue cape tied with green and red wool tassels. He has sleeves that come through slits in his cape so that he can maneuver his hands better in the play. On his head is a tam-o'shanter of red lamé with a long pheasant feather in it. His merry face is made with white paint for the whites of his eyes and his bright white teeth, and red for a wide-open, laughing mouth. Black Peter may be dressed to suit any fancy, but St. Nicholas always appears in his white alb and miter and red cope.

The puppet stage is made from a three-panel screen. We unhinged the panels and cut a large square window in the top half of the center panel to make the stage. Slipcovers of bright muslin went over the panels; and with an old curtain of flounces and ball fringe we made a curtain for the top and sides of our stage. We rehinged the panels so that the sides would fold back and — presto! — a stage.

Friends of ours sewed two deep flounces like half-curtains to be tacked across the top and middle of a doorway with the space between for the stage. We have also had successful hand-puppet shows staged from behind a chair and from behind a couch. There is no place where a hand-puppet show cannot be staged. No stage is no excuse. The year we made our stage from the screen it was the children's big Christmas gift. Prior to that we had staged impromptu shows anywhere and everywhere.

Everyone assembles after dinner on December 5, the vigil of the feast, and the puppet show begins. First, St. Nicholas appears, bowing with dignity and murmuring, "Thank you, thank you," to the shouts and clapping. He has a Dutch accent (just for merriment), and if your accent isn't all it might be, frequent interpolations of "Ja, ja" convince all present that it is superb.

"Good evening, little children," he says. "I am St. Nicholas. Ja — a real saint I am, in Heaven now, and my feast is celebrated tomorrow. You are going to celebrate my feast? Ja? Good!

"I am not, you know, the reason for Christmas. Although I am sometimes called Santa Claus, I am not the reason for Christmas. Oh, no. Baby Jesus is the reason for Christmas. It is His birthday, Christmas, the day His Father in Heaven gave Him to all of us.

"I am waiting in Heaven, now, like you on earth, for His birthday on Christmas Day. And do you want to know something? That is why I gave gifts to little children when I was on earth! Because I was so grateful to God the Father for giving Jesus to me. That is why we give each other presents on Christmas Day, because we are full of joy and gladness that Jesus came down to be one of us and to die to pay for our sins.

"Now, here is something you may do for my feast, and it pleases me very much. You hang your stockings tonight, and if you are very good children, you will get cookies in them! But if you are bad. . . . Ahhh, if you are bad, you will get — not cookies — but straw! Black Peter will put straw in your stockings."

Up pops Black Peter, giggling and snickering and wagging his hands at the audience, which promptly rolls on the floor and shrieks.

The bishop is grave. "Peter! Peter! Behave yourself, or I will have to use a switch on you! Peter, you are going to put straw in some stockings? Jah?"

Peter looks coy, cocks his head, and makes odd noises that say neither aye nor nay.

"Ah, he will not tell. Peter, be fair now. No straw for the good children, you know. But be honest as well — straw for the naughty ones!"

Peter snickers again, wags at the children, then turns and throws himself on the bishop, arms around his neck, mewing noisily. As the bishop nods his head paternally, Peter slyly turns to the children, waves a free arm and giggles. Then he quickly buries his head in the bishop's shoulder again.

After this you can have Peter sing a song or two, and the bishop can end the play with a hymn and lead the children in a little prayer or two, asking for the grace to be good and to love little Jesus with all their hearts.

Then it is all over. All go rushing about looking for stockings, full of high hopes for cookies — which, of course, they have spent the afternoon helping to make (or seen Mother buy).

The following morning tells the tale, and it is sometimes a mixture of fun and bittersweet. We have a little friend named Teddy who was unable to bear the suspense; so he bade his sister look in his stocking for him. When she reported, "Cookies!" he was so amazed (what with the weight of his past sins pressing so hard upon him) that he gasped, "Are you sure?"

*St. Lucy and Christmas Wheat*

The feast of St. Lucy, December 13, is a favorite among many peoples, especially the Italian and the Swedish. St. Lucy's story is another of the hair-raising tales of martyrdom ending in heavenly triumph, and we make the telling of it the focal point of our feast. We have Americanized somewhat the Swedish custom of the "Lucy Bride," although we have never been able to work it so that the father and mother of this family were served the traditional coffee and sweet rolls in bed that morning. It is agreed, however, that it is a magnificent idea to be saved for the day when there will be fewer small fry to get up and out to the school bus on St. Lucy's day.

Monica is always our St. Lucy, one of the rewards for being the only girl in the house. For her crown, we omit the lighted candles (a trifle dangerous) but have the boys gather fresh princess pine from the woods. This is made into a wreath bound with two colors of ribbons with streamers to hang down her back. It is after she carries in a Swedish coffee ring crowned with a garland of lighted candles for dessert that she tells her story.

She begins by reminding the family that Lucy comes from the Latin word *lux*, which means "light," and since we are preparing for the coming of the Light of the World, it is appropriate that her feast falls in Advent. She also reminds us that St. Gregory the Great placed St. Lucy, together with her patroness St. Agatha,[10] in the Canon of the Mass, and there we ask God to grant us "some part and fellowship" with her.

St. Lucy was born in Sicily. Since her mother was ill four years with a hemorrhage, Lucy reminded her that a woman in the Gospels with the same complaint was cured by our Lord, and suggested that perhaps praying at the tomb of St. Agatha, who died for love of Him, would procure her mother's recovery. They went to the tomb and prayed all night until they fell asleep. St. Agatha appeared to Lucy in a vision, called her "sister," and foretold her martyrdom. Her mother was instantly cured, and as a thanksgiving she gave away most of her money and goods to the poor. She then permitted Lucy to give away all her money and goods to the poor, as well as take a vow of virginity. (Once, at a retelling of this story, one of our boys observed that probably her mother didn't give away all her goods and money, because someone had to support Lucy.)

Refusing to marry her suitor because she had given herself to Christ, she was denounced by him as a Christian, tried in the praetorium and convicted, then sentenced to be despoiled in a house of ill-fame. (This can be adapted for children by saying she was sentenced to work in slavery with wicked people who were

[10] St. Gregory the Great (d. 604), Pope from 590, writer, and Doctor; St. Agatha (d. c. 251), virgin martyred in Sicily during persecution of emperor Decius.

not pure of heart.) But when they tried to drag her off, she would not budge. They brought a yoke of oxen to drag her, but even they could not make her budge. Raging, her persecutors poured pitch, oil, and resin over her and ignited it, only to see her stand amid the flames as cool as a cucumber.

"How is it you do not burn?" they screamed. She replied that it was by the power of her Lord Jesus Christ that she was saved, in order that she might be a witness to Him. With that they plunged a dagger into her throat, and she finally died and went straight to Heaven.

A legend that has grown up around St. Lucy has to do with her gouging out her eyes in order to destroy their beauty, which had attracted so many admirers. This explains a statue we saw not long ago showing Lucy, sweet-faced and crowned, sedately offering us her eyes on a silver platter. Thank you, no, dear St. Lucy — and I don't believe you ever did it in the first place.[11]

She is invoked, however, for assistance with diseases of the eyes, with dysentery, and with hemorrhages; she is the patron saint of Sicily, especially the city of Syracuse, and apparently the Swedish people fell in love with her when her plucky story was carried north by the early Christian missionaries, and she became their patron saint of schoolgirls. Among the invocations to include in night prayers on her feast is: "Please, dear St. Lucy, help us to love purity."

A beautiful Hungarian custom on the feast of St. Lucy is to plant the "Christmas wheat." Pressed gently into a pot of garden soil, watered, and kept in a moderately warm room, the wheat will be sprouted soft green by Christmas. Then the children may carry it to the crèche as a gift for the Child Jesus, symbolic of the

[11] According to some legends, it was St. Lucy's persecutors who ordered her eyes to be gouged out. — ED.

Eucharistic bread by which He feeds our souls at the altar, as well as of the staff of life by which His Father keeps life in our bodies. For families living in the country where wheat is grown, saving a handful of seed for this custom might be an annual event.

⌒

### The Feast of Lights

At about this time in December, the Jewish people celebrate their Feast of Dedication, or *Hanukkah (Chanukah)*, called by them the Feast of Lights. It is good to know something about this feast since our Lord celebrated it when He was here. St. John mentions our Lord's being in Jerusalem in the Temple for the Feast of Dedication.[12] It celebrates the victory of Judah Maccabee over the Syrians, who had coerced many of the Israelites to idol worship and to abandoning the one God, and who had laid waste the Holy City. It is exciting reading in the Old Testament (First Book of Maccabees), especially for boys who like accounts of wars and battles.

Following their victory, the Jews set about purifying and refurbishing the Temple, which had been despoiled and stripped of its furnishings, and it is the solemnity of the Dedication of the Temple which is celebrated with this feast. An ancient Jewish tradition tells that, on returning to the Temple, the Jews found only one small jar of holy oil left behind for the sacred lamps, but it burned miraculously for eight days until new oil could be made. This is a joyful feast lasting eight days. Its name, "Feast of Lights," comes from the custom of lighting eight candles, a new one each day, for the duration of the feast

There is a connection between many feasts of the Old Law and many feasts of the New. Out of the Old Testament Christ came,

---

[12] John 10:22.

and these are the feasts and stories of His people. The Temple that was despoiled, then regained by the Maccabees and rededicated, was the Temple of our God as well as theirs, and the saints of the New Law, such as St. Barbara, St. Nicholas, and St. Lucy, are witnesses to the Son of their God as well as ours.

We have a book of photographs of the marvelous stone figures in the Bamberg Cathedral, and among them all, our favorites are sculptures titled *Synagogue* and *Ecclesia* (church). They are beautiful, and they teach us this great lesson: that the Church came forth out of the Jews. *Synagogue* is blindfolded, but she seems to be pregnant.

In our preparation for the birthday of the Christ Child, we must not forget His desire for His own people, His flesh and blood. He came for them first, and then for us. We should remember to pray during Advent that soon they will receive Him.

Chapter 3

⁊

# The Immaculate Conception and Gift-Giving

There is a special dearness about Christmas gifts that are made. Even when they are clumsily made, they are lovely because the loveliness that goes into them is from the heart and the mind and the hands: hours and days of tacking and tying, fitting and pasting, stitching and hammering, chiseling and modeling — all of it with a permeation of love and effort that cannot be priced. The making of gifts should be a special part of Advent; an outpouring of self into something we make for someone we love, entirely in the spirit of the remaking of our hearts for Christ, for receiving the gift Someone who loves us made for us.

With this making go long evenings of work together, wonderful conversations, meditations, and evening prayers. We need only work together to have an early dinner, clear away the dishes, tidy the kitchen, get the littlest ones off to bed, keep the TV and radio turned off, and there — we have a long evening before us. Perhaps it is not possible to do this every night, but much can be accomplished in even two nights a week when the family works together and talks together. They will soon discover that this kind of creative recreation grows on them.

The making of gifts has a counterpart in the greatest of the Advent feasts: the feast of the Immaculate Conception on December 8, and we learn from this feast with what infinite pains God prepared the Gift He gave to us. God always knew our Lady just as He always knew us. It is easy for a child to learn this and understand it. You simply tell him, and he knows. You know in your mind what you are going to do before you do it; so, God knew us all in His mind before He made us.

One Advent, a six-year-old of our acquaintance asked, "Mother, was I in Heaven with God before I was in you?"

"No, dear."

"Oh, that's right. But I was in His mind, wasn't I?"

He settled back on the couch contentedly. If someone has told you this, you know that you're important to God. There's no fear He is going to forget you when He has had you in His mind since forever.

Thus, He also knew our Lady since forever. In her humanness, she was to be like ourselves, but in another way she would be different.

When God knew us in His mind before He made us, He knew that we would be conceived and born with Original Sin on our souls. But when He knew our Lady in His mind before He made her, He knew she would be conceived without Original Sin. He was going to make her to be the Mother of our Lord; so He would make her perfect. Even though she would be one of the children of Adam and Eve, she would not inherit Original Sin like the rest of us, nor any weakness that might lead her to commit sin.

Now, it is not necessary for God to give any reason for this except that it pleased Him. He is God. Surely He may do as He wants. And, of course, it is easy for us to understand that the Mother of God should be perfect, the most holy and beautiful of all creatures. But we like to know that things are "fair," that things fit together like the pieces of a puzzle; and this great privilege of our Lady's is not only God's right and her due, but it is also "fair" — in another word, just.

# The Immaculate Conception and Gift-Giving

$\backsim$

*The Reason for Christmas Presents*

Why are we making gifts for each other two, three, four weeks ahead of time? Working as hard as we can to make something beautiful? To wrap it beautifully? To tie it beautifully? To think of something full of love to write on the card that goes with it? Because we know that Christmas is coming. That Jesus should become man and save us from our sins is more than good reason to prepare, to anticipate. We want everything to be perfect for Jesus and for our beloveds when Christmas comes.

Just so, God the Father prepared for the coming of Jesus. He prepared for His divine Son a perfect Mother through whom He could come into the world. This is how He prepared: God the Father knew that when the time came, from our Lord's death on the Cross would flow graces that would never end, that would make it possible for Godlike powers to be given to men. For example, He knew that our Lord would institute a sacrament through which grace would come to wash away the Original Sin inherited from Adam and Eve, and to fill the soul with marvelous beauty where God Himself could dwell.

In creating a Mother for His Son, God used *this grace ahead of time* — not to wash away Original Sin but *to make a Mother whose soul was untouched by Original Sin*. This is what we mean when we speak of Mary's Immaculate Conception, the name she used for herself when at last she told St. Bernadette[13] who she was.

God does not live in time. He invented time for us so that we could keep track of ourselves, but He has no need of it, and in the foreverness of Heaven, He used all the magnificent graces His

---

[13] St. Bernadette (1844-1879), Sister of Notre Dame who, in 1858, received eighteen apparitions of the Blessed Virgin Mary at Lourdes, France.

divine Son poured forth from His death on the Cross in time to merit for our Lady a perfect soul from the instant He breathed it into being.

That is why, when Gabriel came to her in Nazareth, he could say, "Hail, full of grace. . . ."

That is why, when Mary went to visit Elizabeth, Elizabeth could cry out, "Blessed art thou among women. . . ."

This does not mean that our Lady was conceived in a miraculous manner, as her divine Son was conceived. She was born of the lawful union of Joachim and Anne, loving husband and wife. It does mean that at the moment the seed of life that was to become our Lady was united to her immortal soul, it was to a soul God had created perfect.

Our Lady was made immaculate so that when the time came for the plan of the Redemption to unfold, her pure and holy body would be a perfect resting place wherein the love of God — His Holy Spirit — would breathe and His divine Son would begin to live. This beautiful doctrine explained to the children on the vigil of her feast will help form the spirit in which the entire family will assist at the Mass in her honor and receive Holy Communion.

The great Advent mysteries in the life of our Lady relate in many ways to the knowledge we must give our children about their bodies. Now we see again why we must have reverence and awe for our bodies. They are made for great and holy things. All the little girls in the world who will grow up to discover that God's will for them is to be wives and mothers will, as mothers, carry their babies the way our Lady carried her baby. Every mother we see who is expecting a baby can remind us of our Lady.

It is so good of God to have His Son come to us this way, and so sanctify the bearing of babies. He could have come in thunder and lightning. He could have come like a wild storm riding the sun, driving the moon and the stars before Him. But, loving us in our littleness and our struggles and our pains and worries, He chose to be like us in all things save sin, so that we would always know that God knows what it is like to be a man.

If we have children for whom it is time to learn something of the way babies are born, Advent is an especially appropriate time to continue with that part of sex instruction. This carrying of babies within the mother's body, is it not beautiful? This is how our Lady carried her Baby, close to her heart, protected and sheltered there by her own pure body. This delivering of babies, as we call it — the emergence of the baby from his mother's body — is it not wonderful? It is God's way. He decided it was to be like this. If there were a finer way for it to be, He would have it be that way. "Let us pray tonight and ask our Lady to help us have reverence for our bodies, and for the bodies of others, and never to do anything with them God does not want us to do."

These things and a host of others relating to the meaning and spirit of Advent make beautiful, rich, prayerful conversations that go with the making of gifts. Some are for parent and child alone, some for the group; both ways, the treasury to explore is inexhaustible.

⌒

### Gifts from Hands and Hearts

A gift that is fun to make is a Christmas Surprise Ball, and it is not so demanding that we need cease all conversation while we make it. It is adapted from a custom invented by German mothers to help dispel the boredom and discouragement that go with learning to knit. It is made with narrow streamers of crepe paper cut about one-half inch wide from a package of crepe paper. We like to start winding the paper in a Christmas Ball around a tiny figure of the Christ Child, an especially nice medal, or perhaps a small rosary. As the ball grows larger, other things are wound in: a thimble, a pretty button, a gilded acorn, or tiny trinkets or charms, especially those symbolic of a patron saint or some Christmas legend.

The hard sugar decorations for birthday cakes are charming as well as sweet, and they may represent the virtues as well as symbols of our Lady under her titles in the Litany. A little girl named Rose, or one named for Mary the Mystical Rose — Mary, or Virginia, or Regina, or Loretta — would like a sugar rose in hers; a sugar violet is a symbol of humility. A white sugar dove reminds us of the Holy Spirit or of the doves that flew over Mother Cabrini's[14] house when she was born. All little girls named Frances would like that. There are sugar letters for initials and to spell out a child's name or the names of Jesus and Mary and Joseph, and there are sugar numbers for a child's age. It is a gift that is not only colorful and easily made and fun to receive, but one that is rich in meditation material.

A gift mothers like is a little bottle decorated with the *Chi Rho* or the symbol for Baptism in Christ (a scallop shell with water flowing), and fitted with a sprinkler top for sprinkling holy water on the new-made loaves of bread or the Advent wreath, for the blessing of the garden on Rogation days, the blessing of herbs and flowers on the Assumption, and many more occasions. It would be a far happier dispenser of holy water than our mason jar with its water cloudy and a trifle grey from having so many floured fingers dipped into it for the blessing of loaves of bread.

A little girl who has learned to sew might make an apron with a pocket and a rosary buttoned in the pocket for mothers and grannies and very special aunts who are forever misplacing their rosaries and wishing they had them while they stir the sauce for a

---

[14] St. Frances Xavier Cabrini (1850-1917), Italian-born foundress of the Missionary Sisters of the Sacred Heart at Codogno in Lombardy and of orphanages and hospitals in North and South America; first United States citizen to be canonized.

casserole, or wait for a batch of cookies to brown or a load of clothes to come out of the washer.

Coffee cakes, cookies, candies, fruits, and nuts — all the goodies prepared in a busy kitchen, wrapped and sent with Christmas love — these are not the least of the presents. We remind our friends that these are holy, too, if we send them with a gift card we have designed with this in mind. A pleasant addition to our good wishes for a happy and holy Christmas is the text to the blessing of whatever food it is we give.

From a *Blessing of Bread and Cakes* comes this prayer, which we use when we give Christmas coffee cakes (taken from Rev. Philip I Weller's English translation of the Roman Ritual):

> *Lord Jesus Christ, Thou the bread of angels, Thou the*
> *living bread of eternal life, graciously deign to bless this bread*
> *as Thou didst bless the five loaves in the desert: that all who*
> *partake of it may have health of body and soul.*
> *Who livest and reignest forever. Amen.*

The *Blessing of Cheese or Butter* for those who give cheeses for Christmas:

> *Vouchsafe, O Lord, God Almighty, to bless and sanctify*
> *this cheese [or butter], which by Thy power has been formed*
> *from the fat of animals. May Thy faithful people who eat it*
> *be filled with Thy grace, Thy blessing, and all good things.*
> *Through Christ our Lord. Amen.*

And for those who give gifts of fresh fruit, the *Blessing of New Produce* (sometimes called the *Blessing of Fresh Fruits*):

> *Bless, O Lord, these new fruits, and grant that all who*
> *eat of them in Thy holy name may obtain health of body*
> *and soul. Through Christ our Lord. Amen.*

To go in the Christmas wallet for a father is a special gift — a nice print of St. Joseph, Patron of Fathers and Families. This will be a great comfort when he is fishing for the wherewithal to pay the family bills. Devotion to St. Joseph is guaranteed to keep many a father from losing heart over the difficulties of feeding and clothing and housing a family.

For boys there is a set of cut-out puzzles to be made with construction paper and paste. These wrapped with a package of colored construction paper and a pair of scissors hint at the things one can do with paper and scissors. We have made games using symbols and events in the lives of the saints. For example, mounted on a piece of forest green there is a rough cross in light blue, a yellow beehive, a large yellow bee or locust, a cinnamon-colored sword and a platter, and a blue shoe with untied laces mounted on a yellow nimbus. These are cut silhouette-fashion with no embellishment with paint or pencil. Some are authentic liturgical symbols; others are clues to the saint's life. Part of the fun is tracking down unfamiliar clues in Holy Scripture, the lives of the saints, or even the library encyclopedia.

Any guesses? St. John the Baptist. The bee or locust and the beehive, because Scripture says he ate locusts and wild honey in the desert; the sword and platter for the manner of his martyrdom; the shoe with untied laces and the nimbus because he said, "One is to come after me who is mightier than I so that I am not worthy to bend down and untie the strap of His shoes. I have baptized you with water: He will baptize you with the Holy Spirit."[15]

The rough cross is one of the symbols of St. John the Baptist (it looks rather like a staff) always seen in pictures and statues of him.

Another is a series of clues arranged on bright red. A blue boat with a white sail, a green fish, a yellow key, and a brown rock with

[15] Luke 3:16 (cf. Knox translation).

a white church atop. St. Peter. We were tempted to put a sword and an ear on this one, but — next time.

Four of these, after they have been identified and used to puzzle others, can be arranged in a decorative panel over a boy's bed and their symbols will push his mind to what they represent, as well as remind him that the saints were far more virile than a lot of their pictures *en nightgown* suggest. Besides, they are excellent teaching mediums. Such texts as "Thou art Peter and upon this rock I will build my Church," and "Whatever you shall bind on earth shall be bound in heaven, and whatever you shall loose on earth shall be loosed in heaven"[16] — specific doctrines straight from our Lord — are more easily learned when one must repeat the exact words and explain them in order to give the right due.

*Paper and Plastic Saints*

Using the same kind of cut-outs, children can make the Christmas saints for pasting on a special window in a procession that grows in length as the days pass. There is St. Barbara on December 4, St. Nicholas and a schoolboy on December 6, our Lady as the Immaculate Conception on December 8, St. Lucy and a schoolgirl on December 13, St. Elizabeth and St. Zechariah and St. John the Baptist during Ember Week,[17] the Holy Family and the shepherds on Christmas Eve.

---

[16] Matt. 16:17, 18.

[17] Ember days are the days at the beginning of the seasons of fast and abstinence: the Wednesday, Friday, and Saturday after December 13, after Ash Wednesday, after Pentecost, and after September 14, the Exaltation of the Cross. Besides being days of fasting, Ember days were meant to thank God for the gifts of nature, to teach men to make use of them in moderation, and to assist the needy.

# The Year and Our Children

On December 26 comes St. Stephen and on December 27, St. John the Evangelist; on December 28 a few of the Holy Innocents, very happy with martyrs' palms and crowns because they are the first of all the martyrs; and on December 29, St. Thomas à Becket.[18] On January 1 in golden letters is the lovely name *Jesus*. This was the day of His circumcision and the day He received His holy name.[19] On January 6 come the Magi with their camels and gifts and the star, and following them, on the Sunday after Epiphany, is the feast of the Holy Family.[20] We like to have Joseph holding the Christ Child this time, with Mary standing by admiring them.

Shadow boxes are easy to make and help thoughts stay close to the Christmas story. We have made them of old Kleenex boxes, macaroni cartons with their tiny windows, and picture frames to which we have fastened boxes, hanging them on the wall as shrines. The very littlest children can have a shadow box made with an old Christmas card pasted to the back of a macaroni box with its magic peephole. If these are hugged to death with too much enthusiasm, they are quickly replaced with another by even the busiest of mothers.

Older children can use plasticene figures they have modeled, or clay figures, or cut-out silhouette figures, leaving a generous flap at the bottom of these to insert through slits in the bottom of the box. Experimenting with lamplight, sunlight, and candlelight is dramatic and meditative as well.

---

[18] St. Thomas à Becket (1118-1170), Archbishop of Canterbury and martyr.

[19] In the old liturgy, the feast of the Lord's Circumcision was celebrated on January 1. — ED.

[20] The feast of the Holy Family is now celebrated on the Sunday after Christmas and Epiphany on the second Sunday after Christmas. — ED.

# The Immaculate Conception and Gift-Giving

Window boxes or plants in large pots are wonderful settings for tiny figures of the Christmas story modeled or cut from colored papers. Gold paper angels and a gold star are lovely when hung by a thread from the branches of a favorite potted geranium or ivy. Things in miniature have a great fascination for small children. There is something snug and secret and comfortable about a very little scene.

Water clay, which dries hard without firing, is an excellent medium for Advent meditations, and the figures modeled are often fine enough to be given — painted or plain — as gifts. We need not always buy our statues. It is quite proper and fitting to model our own. Let the children consider this, not so much with the object of casting aspersions on manufactured things as such, but to help them see the greater integrity in hand-crafted things. Most of the statues priced so that we can buy them are made by machines. A mold is made and into it is poured paper or plastic, and after this is repeated hundreds and thousands of times by the machine there are a thousand replicas of our Lady and St. Joseph and the Christ Child turned out, packed in boxes, sent to stores, and heaped on counters.

There is a great difference between this and taking the clay in your own hands, thinking about what you will make, praying to the Holy Spirit for help, and then lovingly shaping it this way and that, taking some off, adding some, until you have a creation of your own. Then it is not the work of a machine but of a boy or girl whose mother and father love them beyond all reckoning and who will treasure always something that was made by them.

One Advent, just for fun, Michael F. started to model the crèche figures — but he was sure "they wouldn't be any good." When he was finished, they were so beautiful in their dull green plasticene that his mother, who has impeccable taste, used them in a little stable she arranged of old wood with beautiful fir and pine, with cones and dried weeds and berries; and that was their family crèche.

Dressing dolls as the Holy Family is rich and imaginative play for little girls all during Advent. Every journey into the stable at Bethlehem in your imagination makes it that much more familiar and real; and daily play at these things is a kind of prayer on the part of children.

There are Advent calendars for keeping track of the days, little doors that open on pictures and symbols and Scriptural texts noted by chapter and verse; these read aloud in the evening can be part of night prayers. Or we can choose our own Old Testament texts, perhaps those we read to accompany the figures on our Christ candle, and make our own Advent calendar for keeping track of them. Or perhaps we will want to make one to keep track of the daily Advent mortifications. Cut from dark-green construction paper like a great Christmas tree, the decorations are bright-colored balls, birds, fruits, ornaments of all kinds pasted on, one for each day. This works out very well in a classroom.

All these things gradually prepare our minds for piercing deeper and deeper the reality of that night. The stable, the few shepherds, the star all focused on the figures of a man and a woman and a tiny, tiny Child.

❦

## A Christmas Field Trip

Advent was drawing toward its close, and we were discussing it all over again and suddenly one of the children said, as though really hearing it for the first time, "But — barns are so smelly!"

Yes, aren't they? He was in a sheep cave where, in rainy weather, the shepherds brought their sheep to shelter. Sheepfolds are not the most fragrant places in the world. There is the smell of dung, the mustiness, the heavy oily smell of wool; and these caves were infested with vermin. The child pondered this thought often and deeply. Later, at a catechism lesson, her answer to "Where was Jesus born?" was truly anguished: "In a dirty old, smelly old barn!"

Suppose our baby were to be born in a barn? They were beside themselves. No — never! The bitterness of it all: little Lord Jesus born in a barn . . . They had penetrated the sweet coating on the story and tasted the sharp suffering beneath. That He should come to us this way . . . incredible!

Hay is not so soft as we think. We would see, if we were to take our children to the countryside where there may be sheepfolds, cows in stalls, hay in barns. The sounds and smells of barns, the steamy breaths of animals, the never-ending munching — this is no place for a baby.

We have spent our energy on far less appropriate trips. Trips to see Santa, trips to see Toyland, trips to movies and theaters and entertainments, all because it is Christmas, divert our time. These are diversions but not the true joy of Christmas.

Such a strange custom, celebrating Christmas and not knowing why. Much of the world does not know why — and that is very sad. There is only one reason in all the world to feast and be merry at Christmas: because we are redeemed, and Christmas is the feast of the beginning of our Redemption. In this bewilderingly beautiful season, in a most mysterious and beautiful way, God became a Baby.

*Christmas Novena*

Closer and closer comes the day, the day the Lord hath made. December 16 is the day to begin the Christmas novena, so mark an X on the calendar for this day. The following is a novena in honor of the Infant Jesus that can be used at any time, but is usually made during the nine days preceding Christmas, to prepare for the coming of Christ into our hearts and to obtain some particular favor. We ask especially for a spiritual favor.

Since it is customary to kneel before an altar or picture of the Nativity of our Lord for the reciting of these prayers, the children might contribute simple shadow boxes (as described on page 40) from emptied paper napkin boxes. One kind is white with blue and green and orange polkadots, and is lined with soft blue. Masking the label, the children have made a beautiful shadow box with a Christmas-card reproduction of one of the fine old Nativity scenes.

### A NOVENA TO THE INFANT JESUS

Being fully recollected in spirit, and respectfully kneeling before an altar or picture of the Nativity of our Lord, we address the following petition to our Blessed Lady and St. Joseph, beginning with the Sign of the Cross.

#### *Petition*

*O most holy Virgin, and blessed St. Joseph,*
*obtain for us the grace to perform this novena*
*with such attention, devotion, and ardent charity*
*as will entitle us to join the angels in*
*rendering glory to God. Amen.*

Let us say twelve times the Hail Mary, in remembrance of the care and solicitude shown by our Blessed Lady toward the Infant Jesus until His twelfth year.

Let us make three aspirations, to incline the Infant Jesus to turn His favorable attention on us.

*O Divine Infant of Bethlehem, whom we adore*
*and acknowledge to be our sovereign Lord,*
*come and take birth in our hearts. Amen.*

# The Immaculate Conception and Gift-Giving

*O Infant Jesus, grant that each moment of our lives,*
*we may pay homage to that moment in which Thou*
*didst begin the work of our salvation. Amen.*

*O holy Mother of our Infant Savior, obtain that*
*we may so prepare for His coming, as not to be*
*separated from Him for all eternity. Amen.*

*Let us pray.*

*Most holy Infant Jesus, true God and true man,*
*our Savior and Redeemer; with all earnestness and respect,*
*we beseech Thee, by that charity, humility, and bounty which*
*Thou didst display in Thy Infancy, graciously undertaken for*
*love of us, that Thou vouchsafe to grant us the favor we now*
*beg, if it be for the honor of God and our salvation. Amen.*

Here each one will beg in spirit the particular favor desired.
Pause for a short time.

*O most amiable Infant Jesus, we are most unworthy to be*
*heard in this our petition; but Thy holy Mother, the Virgin*
*Mary, and the great St. Joseph, Thy foster-father while on*
*earth, are worthy to be heard soliciting in our behalf. Then,*
*O divine Infant, being mindful of their most sublime merits,*
*especially those they acquired during the time they served*
*Thee in Thy infancy in Bethlehem, Thy flight into Egypt,*
*and Thy childhood at Nazareth, vouchsafe to grant our*
*request, and give us grace to promote the honor of Thy*
*omnipotent infancy, to serve Thee with fidelity, as domestic*
*servants, all the days of our lives, and to obtain a happy*
*death, assisted in that last hour by the Blessed Virgin and*
*St. Joseph, whose zeal for Thy honor will lead us to praise*
*and bless Thy divine mercies forever and ever. Amen.*

*Anthem*
*Whilst deep silence dwelt on all things below, and*
*the night was in the midst of its course, the almighty*
*Word came down from its throne. Alleluia.*

*Let us pray.*

*O Lord Jesus, who didst, for the love of us, vouchsafe*
*to reduce Thy incarnated divinity and most divine humanity*
*to the humiliating state of birth and infancy; grant that we,*
*acknowledging Thy infinite wisdom in Thy infancy,*
*Thy power in Thy weakness, and Thy majesty in Thy little-*
*ness, may adore Thee, a little one on earth, and behold Thee*
*great in heaven; who livest and reignest with God the Father,*
*in unity with the Holy Spirit, world without end. Amen.*

*The Jesse Tree and Its Blessing*

The idea of the Jesse Tree is somewhat the same as the decoration of our Christ candle described in chapter 1, except that with a Christmas tree there is room for more things. Every symbol known or invented, every story, the Gospel and Advent figures — as many things as are suitable — compose the decorations for the tree. Using time-honored techniques for making Christmas-tree decorations, we have cut, pasted, twisted, tied, painted, baked, and invented many decorations, and the attendant searching through Scripture for ideas and decorations would do a religion teacher's heart good.

First we made an apple of red paper (one year it was a cookie) with green leaves and two bites out of it. Then Lucifer, a bright-yellow serpent cut from a circle with the cut circling inward so that he hangs like a spring. Our Lady is there, a lily piercing the serpent with its stalk — as she was prophesied in the beginning, there in the Garden. The ark is bright, and the dove with the olive branch pacific. Noah hangs, with a thread through his handsome beard, and Abraham walks with the sword and the fire, one in each hand. Isaac carries his bundle of sticks, like Christ His Cross, and Jacob is there with his ladder, a folded paper ladder that spans from one branch to another as from Heaven to earth, while golden angels hanging from branches above seem to ascend and descend, somewhat stubbornly refusing to put their feet on the ladder. St. Joseph is there in the carpenter's symbols, and the donkey that carried Mary so faithfully is there. The manger is surmounted by a *Chi Rho*, and a trumpeter angel is there; a great star, and a crown with twelve stars around it, and little shepherds and their sheep. Then there are secret symbols of their patron saints that each child has prepared, to be guessed by the others; these saints are among the most important because, born in Original Sin like all the children of Adam, they were redeemed by the Babe of Bethlehem, who died on the Cross and grafted them by the Incarnation not only to His family tree, but to Himself in the Mystical Body by Baptism. Among these are our very good friends, the Advent and Christmas saints.

Some of our decorations are cookies, some are paper, some are odd combinations of pipe cleaner, foil, glitter, ribbon, wire — whatever we have saved because we were sure we ought not to throw it out. Tiny odd-shaped boxes, the cardboard forms ribbons come on — such things painted or covered with bright paper always suggest some symbol for a Jesse tree. For all those people who absolutely cannot draw a straight line (most probably can but haven't tried), the figures of the saints, angels, and prophets may be cut from old Christmas cards, illustrations, or wherever a likely figure appears, mounted on stiff paper and substituted for the figures done "out of your head." But do try them out of your head first. You'll be surprised to see what you can do.

A tiny house made from a box is our Lady's house at Loreto, and there is a rose for the Christmas rose, a harp for David (we have a little harp from Ireland), and a gilded cross of twigs for St. John the Baptist, with a piece of chalk for Zechariah (who had to write on his tablet, "His name shall be John"[21]). Some are not legitimate Jesse-tree ornaments, but they still bear on this story, which begins our Redemption; as such, they have a place on our tree.

A round white disk like the Host and a tiny loaf of real bread remind us of both daily breads for which we ever pray.

Then there are the things from the fields and woods that are beautiful as they are, or sometimes painted or gilded; and there is popcorn on strings and cranberry garlands and gingerbread boys with long skirts to appear as prophets. Added to these are our traditional ornaments. One has not the heart to part with these, nor is it necessary — now that we know what a Christmas tree should do, what a Christmas tree should be.

On Christmas Eve, the father of the house or some older member of the family reads the "Blessing of a Tree," and we all think about the meaning of the ornaments, a shining forth of joy and gladness telling that a Savior has been born.

BLESSING OF A TREE

*Leader:* Our help is in the name of the Lord.

*All:* Who hath made heaven and earth.

*All:* All the trees of the wood shout for joy before the Lord, for He comes.

*Psalm* 95[22] (*divide the group and alternate reading the lines*). (This Psalm begs us to praise the Lord and sings of His coming at the end

---

[21] Cf. Luke 1:63.

[22] RSV = Ps. 96.

of time. In the Gospel for the first Sunday in Advent, our Lord warned us to watch for the signs of His Second Coming. We add to this, this night, our anticipation of another celebration of His first coming.)

*Sing to the Lord a new song, sing to the Lord,*
*all you lands: Sing to the Lord, bless His name,*
*announce His salvation, day after day:*

*Among the heathen tell His glory,*
*His marvels to every people.*

*Great is the Lord and greatly to be praised,*
*to be feared more than all the gods:*

*The gods of the heathen are nothings,*
*but the Lord — He made the heaven.*

*Glory and majesty stand before Him,*
*strength and splendor are in His sanctuary.*

*Declare to the Lord, you families of nations,*
*declare to the Lord His glory and strength.*
*Declare to the Lord the glory of His name:*

*Offer sacrifice and come into His courts:*
*worship the Lord in holy attire,*

*Tremble before Him, all the earth!*
*Say among the nations:*
*The Lord is King.*

*He has set the earth firm, not to be moved,*
*He rules the peoples with justice.*

*Let the heavens be glad and the earth rejoice,*
*the sea thunder with all its waves:*

*Let the fields be glad, and all their creatures,*
*all the trees of the wood shout for joy*

*Before the Lord, for He comes,*
*for He comes to rule the earth:*
*He will judge the world with justice,*
*and the peoples with His truth.*

*All:* All the trees of the wood shout for joy before the Lord, for He comes.

*Lesson from the Prophet Ezekiel, 17:22-24 (leader):* Thus said the Lord God: I myself will take the top of the high cedar, and will set it; I will crop off a tender twig from the top of the branches thereof, and I will plant it on a mountain high and eminent. On the high mountains of Israel will I plant it, and it shall shoot forth into branches, and shall bear fruit, and it shall become a great cedar; and all the birds shall dwell under it, and every fowl shall make its nest under the shadow of the branches thereof, and all the trees of the country shall know that I the Lord have brought down the high tree, and exalted the low tree, and have dried up the green tree, and have caused the dry tree to flourish. I the Lord have spoken and have done it.

*All:* Thanks be to God.
*Leader:* And there shall come forth a shoot.
*All:* Out of the root of Jesse.
*Leader:* In Him was life.
*All:* And the life was the light of men.
*Leader:* O Lord hear my prayer.
*All:* And let my cry come unto Thee.
*Leader:* The Lord be with you.
*All:* And with thy spirit.

*Let us pray.* Holy Lord, Father almighty, eternal God, who hast caused Thy Son, our Lord Jesus Christ, to be planted like a tree of life in Thy Church, by being born of the most Holy Virgin Mary, bless, we beseech Thee, this tree, that all who see it may be filled with a holy desire to be ingrafted as living branches into the same Jesus Christ, our Lord, who liveth and reigneth with Thee, in the unity of the Holy Spirit, God, world without end.

*All:*   Amen. (*Sprinkle tree with holy water.*)

Then we sing a song. The great carol rehearsal has always been a part of our Advent, even after we learned that Christmas carols are not proper, but only Advent carols, during the four weeks. We did not cling to our old ways to be perverse, but because we knew only one Advent carol, "The Cherry Tree Carol," and so few Advent songs. We are glad to discover more of them in the kind of notation we can read (after a fashion), to discover the two Advent songs included in *"The Story of the Redemption for Children,"* to see that the difficult *"Rorate Coeli"* ("Drop Down Dew") and O *Antiphons* are not so difficult and may even be within our reach.

Not so long ago, we did not even know that they existed; so even to know of them is to make some progress. It is slow learning if you have no one to teach you, and so far, most of the Catholics in America have no one to teach them. Sometimes when there is someone to teach them, they are indifferent about learning. It is too bad either way, because this music is so beautiful and they would sing it well if they could but know it. Our own small experience — and it is very small — has taught us this. The timid, self-conscious starts with the *Salve Regina* in English gave place a long time ago to sweet singing, and Granny Newland, saying her third Rosary of an evening off in her room, will remark, "It's like the angels." It really is.

One thing more for the mothers, who set the pace for the last week of Advent: let us try to be prepared by *the day before the day before Christmas*. If all mothers prayed for this for all other mothers, we could do it.

The Christmas cards have finally been sent (could be), and the makings of them put away for another year. Prints of each one hang on the tree, showing their greetings — *Alleluia!* and *Gloria! Gloria! Gloria!* The little boxes containing the invisible gifts for the Christ Child are tied and hung on the tree. The presents have been wrapped. The carol sing in our country community is over. Michael, the goose, has been fed, not plucked, and Helen, the mother goat, is milked and fed. Schwanli, her daughter, looks surprised and expectant, but that is because this is her first Christmas. It is time to bless the crib and eat our Christmas Eve supper.

BLESSING OF A CRIB

*Leader:*  Our help is in the name of the Lord.
   *All:*  Who hath made heaven and earth.
   *All:*  O great mystery and wonderful sign, dumb beasts
         saw the newborn Lord lying in a crib.

*The Magnificat (divide group and alternate reading the lines)*

*My soul doth magnify the Lord.*
*And my spirit doth rejoice in God my Savior.*

*For He hath regarded the humility of His handmaid;*
*for behold from henceforth all generations shall call me blessed.*

*Because He that is mighty hath done*
*great things to me; and holy is His name.*

*And His mercy is from generation unto*
*generation, to them that fear Him.*

*He hath showed might in His arm:*
*He hath scattered the proud in the conceit of their heart.*

*He hath put down the mighty from their seat,*
*and hath exalted the humble.*

*He hath filled the hungry with good things:*
*and the rich He hath sent empty away.*

*He hath received Israel His servant,*
*being mindful of His mercy:*

*As He spoke to our fathers,*
*to Abraham and to His seed forever.*

*Glory be to the Father and to the Son and*
*to the Holy Spirit. As it was in the beginning, is now,*
*and ever shall be, world without end. Amen.*

*All:* O great mystery and wonderful sign, dumb beasts saw
the newborn Lord lying in a crib.

*Reader (perhaps the oldest child): The Holy Gospel according to*
*St. Luke, chapter 2, verses 15 through 20:* At that time, the
shepherds said one to another: Let us go over to Bethlehem,
and let us see this word that is come to pass, which the Lord
hath showed us. And they came with haste; and they found
Mary and Joseph, and the Infant lying in the manger. And
seeing, they understood the word that was spoken to them
concerning this child. And all that heard wondered: and at
those things that were told them by the shepherds. But
Mary kept all these words, pondering them in her heart.
And the shepherds returned, glorifying and praising God
for all the things they had heard and seen, as it was told
unto them.

> *All:*    Praise be to Thee, O Christ.
> *Leader:*  The Word was made flesh. *Alleluia.*
> *All:*    And dwelt among us. *Alleluia.*
> *Leader:*  O Lord, hear my prayer.
> *All:*    And let my cry come unto Thee.
> *Leader:*  The Lord be with you.
> *All:*    And with thy spirit.

*Let us pray.* Bless, we beseech Thee, Almighty God, this crib which we have prepared in honor of the new birth in the flesh of Thine only begotten Son, that all who devoutly contemplate in this image the mystery of His Incarnation may be filled with the light of His glory, who with Thee liveth and reigneth in the unity of the Holy Spirit, God, world without end. Amen. (*The crib is sprinkled with holy water.*)

This is the most solemn vigil of the year. Self-denial at supper is to remind us that this night Mary and Joseph sought lodging in a sheep cave, prayed, and waited. Then it happened. In the dark silent cavern in the side of the hill, the Savior of the world was born, hidden from men by God and the earth He had come to redeem.

### Oplatek: An Old Polish Custom

We have adopted a custom from the Polish for Christmas Eve. At their Christmas Eve meal, after spreading hay under the cloth and (in times past) on the floor of the room, the Polish family stands together, and the father breaks off a piece of the *Oplatek* (pronounced *opwatek*), the blessed Christmas wafer, and passes it on. This is a thin bread pressed in oblong irons in the convents, and on it in relief is the Nativity scene. Made like the host, it is a reminder of our daily bread and the Bread of Life who was born a man tonight. The father passes it to the next member of the family, who breaks off a piece and passes it, until all the family has shared it. It is to remind them what this night is, who comes to us, why, and what it makes us, one to another. An extra place at table tells the little Christ and His Mother that they would be welcome in this "inn" should they knock at our door.

In the past, the *Oplatek* was given us by our Polish friends. Now we use this holy symbolism with bread we bake ourselves — and mixing it is a beautiful meditation for a mother. It is baked as rolls in a round tin, round like the circle of eternity and like the everlastingness of God. After the *Blessing of Bread*, the father or an older member of the family sprinkles the bread with holy water, breaks off a roll and passes it to the person on his right, who breaks a roll from it for himself and passes it. It is our own custom, in terms significant to us. The father or ranking member of the family reads the *Blessing of Bread* in the third chapter.

A story was told us by a woman whose family is still in Poland. Every Christmas their family had *Oplatek*. When some migrated to America, those in Poland sent *Oplatek* to America and those in America sent *Oplatek* to Poland. Came the Russians with their persecution and espionage, and the family in Poland learned to conform, withdraw, carry their religion in their hearts and write between the lines of their letters.

When it was time to send the *Oplatek*, they determined to find a way. That year the family in America received a conventional card on which was pasted a red paper-like disk with a conventional greeting. The censor never suspected that it was *Oplatek*, properly blessed, cut in a circle like a host, painted red for Divine Love, not for Communism, and sent as a salute from one part of the Mystical Body to another half a world away. They were reminding each other that they share the same Body, eat the same Flesh.

It is the end of Advent. So much of it we have understood better by signs and symbols. The first Gospel warned us to watch the signs and prepare. Our Lord spoke of His Second Coming, saying there would be signs in the sun and the moon and the stars. Now we are again on the threshold of the feast of His First Coming. Holy Church is so good. She has us prepare every year, prepare and prepare and prepare. She will keep us ready.

Chapter 4

☞

# The Twelve Days of Christmas

*On the twelve days of Christmas my True Love sent to me the feast of St. Stephen and the story of King Wenceslaus, the feasts of St. John the Evangelist and the Holy Innocents, the feasts of the Circumcision and the Holy Name of Jesus, and the feast of the Epiphany.*

And on through the feast of the Holy Family and the commemoration of the Baptism of Christ. If you are loath to bid farewell to Christmas even then, you may continue it without interruption until Candlemas Day, February 2. However you keep it, long or short, it is a far longer season for the Christian child than the world understands. For him festivity is not officially over with the last wrapping torn off the last gift, or the last nut retrieved from the last toe in the last stocking. The Church would have us enjoy this season now that it is here, and celebrate the feasts that follow.

In order to indulge exhausted parents already drained of their grandest efforts for Christmas, this family keeps Christmas-week feast days simply, using Christmas treats for desserts, and storytelling, reading aloud, and charades for entertainments.

☞

## St. Stephen, First Martyr

The day after Christmas is the feast of St. Stephen, deacon and martyr, and an important day for us, as we have a boy named for him. Mass and Holy Communion are the perfect way to celebrate every day, but when this is not possible, the Mass prayers honoring a child's saint are a beautiful addition to night prayers. We honor a saint's child by lighting his baptismal candle at dinner and telling his saint's story.

The story of St. Stephen and his martyrdom occurs in the Acts of the Apostles, chapters 6 and 7. After Pentecost, when the disciples had increased rapidly, there arose a dispute in which the Greek converts accused the Hebrew converts of being unfair to their widows and orphans. So the twelve Apostles called a council and agreed that it was not practical for them to stop preaching in order to "bestow care on tables" (one of the tasks of deacons was to serve meals as well as preach and baptize); and they therefore chose seven men full of the Holy Spirit "to put in charge of this business." Among the seven was Stephen.

Now, Stephen was very holy and performed great miracles, defending the Faith brilliantly against learned Jews from all over, until finally they began to whisper against him, saying that he blasphemed of Moses and of God. These men stirred up the people and the elders and scribes until they waylaid Stephen and carried him bodily to the Sanhedrin to be tried, charging he said that Jesus of Nazareth had claimed He would destroy the Temple and alter the holy law of Moses. "And all those who sat there in the council fastened their eyes on him and saw his face looking like the face of an angel."

Then the High Priest asked whether the charges were true, and to answer him, Stephen told the story of the Jews. This law of Moses they loved so much, he pointed out, was not always such a clear-cut issue nor so dearly loved by their fathers as they liked to imagine.

Abraham was the father to Isaac and Isaac to Jacob and Jacob to Joseph and his eleven brothers: the twelve patriarchs whom they called their "fathers." Did not the eleven brothers sell Joseph into slavery in Egypt? Stephen implied it was not unlike their treatment of Christ. Even so, Joseph sent for them to take refuge in Egypt when their land was afflicted by famine.

There came a time when, long after, these Jews in Egypt and their families had multiplied, and under another ruler they were not treated so well. They were forced to leave their children to die of exposure, and it was then that Moses was discovered by Pharaoh's daughter and taken to be raised as her son.

In his fortieth year, Moses had a longing to know his brethren dwelling in Egypt; so he went out. Seeing an Egyptian cruelly abusing a Jew, he killed him; and he expected they would see that it was a sign of his role of deliverer to them. But they did not.

The next day he came upon two of the children of Israel quarreling. When he tried to make peace between them, they turned and asked, "Who made thee ruler and judge over us?" Again they did not understand.

It was God, Stephen reminded the Sanhedrin, who spoke to Moses from the burning bush and told him to be ruler and deliverer to the people who had asked, "Who made thee a ruler and a judge over us?" Moses told his people, "The Lord your God will raise up for you a prophet like myself from among your own brethren; to him you must listen." And he meant Christ. Their rejection of Christ was a rejection of Moses.

It was Moses, said Stephen, who received from God their holy law. Despite this, the children of Israel became disobedient to the law, disowned Moses, and went so far as to carry about with them the tent of Moloch and the star of the god Rempham, worshiping them.

As for the Temple, when they were in the wilderness, they had no temple; their fathers had the tabernacle with them there. Not until after David did Solomon finally build the Temple where they worshiped daily, but they were not to assume that God was contained only by temples. The prophet Isaiah had said (as our Lord said many different ways), "Heaven is my throne and the earth is my footstool. What home will you build for me? What place can be my resting place? Was it not my hands that made all this?"

Then bitterly Stephen accused them: "Stiff-necked race, your heart and ears still uncircumcised, you are forever resisting the Holy Spirit, just as your fathers did. There was not one of the prophets they did not persecute; it was death to foretell the coming of that just man whom you in these times have betrayed and murdered; you, who received the law dictated by angels and did not keep it." Stephen was saying that circumcision was a symbol and the dedication and loyalty to God it symbolized reached deep into the heart so that one marked by circumcision as a member of a blessed race would hear the word of God and do it.

Infuriated, they began to gnash their teeth. But Stephen was filled with the Holy Spirit and, looking to Heaven, saw there the glory of God and Jesus standing at God's right hand. "I see heaven opening," he said, "and the Son of Man standing at the right hand of God." This was too much. They put their fingers in their ears to deafen this latest blasphemy and fell upon him, dragging him out of the city, "and the witnesses put down their clothes at the feet of a young man named Saul." As they stoned Stephen, he, meanwhile, was praying, "Lord Jesus, receive my spirit!" And kneeling down, he cried aloud, "Lord, do not count this sin against them." With that, he fell asleep in the Lord.

Saul was one of those "who gave their voices for his murder."

Everyone is in this story: Abraham and all the prophets and Christ and His followers and His enemies and Stephen and Saul, and we are in it, too. We can look up at our Christ candle with its flame a symbol of the divine life we share, and remember that Stephen and Paul and we ourselves are all one in Christ. We are in the Church Militant. They are in the Church Triumphant. With the members of the Church Suffering in Purgatory, we are all members of the same Mystical Body, because the Head, who is Christ, and the members, who are we, are the Church. It is no play on words to say that we are part of Christ.

St. Stephen is the patron of smelters and, of course, stonecutters.

⌒

### Good King Wenceslaus

This is also the day to sing the carol about "Good King Wenceslaus," who went out on the feast of Stephen. St. Wenceslaus has a feast on September 28, but the carol has so attached him to Christmas that we hardly remember him otherwise. He is a hero for boys, although his story is rarely told.

His mother, Drahomira, was a pagan of particularly horrible bent. When her husband, Wratislaus, Duke of Bohemia, died and left her regent, she persecuted the Christians viciously. It was her mother-in-law, the saintly Duchess Ludmilla, who taught Wenceslaus his religion; and as a boy, he practiced the Faith and received the sacraments secretly at night. (This should certainly make St. Ludmilla one of the patrons of mothers-in-law, grandmothers, and duchesses.)

When he was eighteen, Wenceslaus claimed his right over a large part of his kingdom and ruled it as an exemplary king. He built churches, recalled priests from exile, opened the frontiers to Christian missionaries. He was tenderly devoted to the Holy Eucharist and is said to have prepared with his own hands the altar breads and the wines made from wheat and grapes he planted himself. (This should certainly make St. Wenceslaus a patron of millers, wine pressers, kings, and sacristans.)

He had a horror of bloodshed; once, in a desperate attempt to end a bloody war without further loss of life, he challenged an invading duke to single combat and is said to have vanquished him by the Sign of the Cross. (He would be a good patron for the United Nations.) He eventually effected a reconciliation with his mother and his pagan brother Boleslaus and invited him to a banquet on the feast of SS. Cosmas and Damian, September 27. The following morning, as he was on his way to Mass, his brother repaid the compliment by having him murdered — which is why his feast falls on the twenty-eighth. Two years before that, his mother had had his grandmother Ludmilla strangled to death by hired assassins.

The carol tells about a miracle said to have happened on December 26, wherein the good king sees a poor man gathering wood for his fire. Learning from his page where the man lives, he bids the page:

> *Bring me flesh and bring me wine;*
> *Bring me pine logs hither;*
> *Thou and I shall see him dine*
> *When we bear them thither.*

And without ado, he tucked his royal robes into his boots and trudged through the cold to the hut underneath the mountain.

This spirit of serving is one of the things that needs to be restored to our society. Money is needed, and the needy are thankful for it; but the givers of the money need to do more for their own spirits than sign checks. Like King Wenceslaus, they would refresh their vision of Christ by the experience of serving, by the experience of looking into Christ's face in His poor and feeding Him, changing His sheets, bathing His sick body, shopping at the grocer's for His food. And for every act done with love for Him, He repays a hundredfold.

So this day the children may imitate both St. Stephen the deacon, who served, and St. Wenceslaus the king, who served, and set aside some of their Christmas toys or dollars to take to other little Christs less fortunate than themselves. This is hard, but there is an inner joy that children as well need to experience if they would know what we mean when we talk of serving. It is one thing to hear your parents talk about the blessedness of giving. It is quite another to part with something you do not very much want to part with, and then taste the peace and joy and contentment that come to the souls who have given up their own will for love of Christ.

This act of serving was hard for the little page, too, but the carol tells what a marvelous reward was his:

> *In his master's steps he trod,*
> *Where the snow lay dinted.*
> *Heat was in the very sod*
> *That the saint had printed.*

Children love especially to sing this carol while walking out-doors in the snow. If there are enough who know it (do help them learn all the verses: it makes no sense otherwise), they can take parts, one being king, one page, one the poor man, the rest "voices." And afterward bid them remember, whenever they see footprints in the snow, the saint-king who journeyed to the poor man on the feast of St. Stephen, and bid them help someone that day in imitation of him.

### St. John the Evangelist

December 27 is the feast of St. John the Evangelist, another patron in our family. The Roman Ritual tells that it is customary to bless wine on this day, and many a family has had spiced St. John's wine to drink his heavenly health. For families with little children, cider or fruit juice served mulled and hot is a treat — especially when there is a long stick of cinnamon for stirring.

BLESSING OF WINE

*Bless and consecrate, O Lord God, this vessel of wine
through the merits of St. John, Apostle and Evangelist.
Bestow benediction and protection upon all who drink of this
cup. For as the blessed John partook of the poisoned potion
without any hurt, so may any who on this day drink of the
blessed wine to the honor of St. John, be freed by him from
poisoning and similar harmful things. And as they offer
themselves soul and body to Thee, O Lord, give them
absolution and pardon. Through Christ our Lord. Amen.*

St. John the Evangelist was one of the three — Peter, James, and John — who were with Jesus on so many special occasions. He saw the raising of Jairus's daughter, and he was there at the Transfiguration. He never mentioned himself by name in his Gospel but used "the disciple Jesus loved" instead. It was he who put his head on Jesus' breast at the Last Supper to ask who was the traitor, and our Lord answered him by dipping bread and offering it to Judas. He went to the Garden and saw the agony, and he fell asleep and woke to meet the soldiers and see our Lord arrested. He ran away with the others, too, then came back to follow after our Lord. It was probably St. John who gained Peter entrance into the High Priest's house, heard him swear to the portress that he "knew not the man." And then he heard the cock crow and saw Peter's face. He saw Peter, weeping, run away. John stayed, and followed our Lord and watched the trial and the Passion and the Crucifixion. He stood with our Lady at the Cross, and heard our Lord state the doctrine of the Mystical Body: "Son, behold thy Mother."[23]

"The Mother of the Head would be the Mother of the members. The Mother of the Vine would be the Mother of the branches,"

---

[23] Cf. John 19:27.

our Holy Father[24] has said. He couldn't have said it more simply. We are part of Christ in His Mystical Body.

There is something else about St. John we love to remember this night, and that is what happened when the holy women returned from the tomb to tell the Apostles that our Lord had risen. Peter and John started to run to the tomb to see for themselves, and John, so much younger, ran faster than Peter and got there first. But he waited for Peter to enter before him because Peter was head of the Church and John was beneath him. St. John teaches small boys named John (others as well) respect and obedience as well as love. These difficulties come easily if you love enough.

St. John is the patron of theologians and is invoked against burns and poisons, and (this is nice) for good friendships. The reason he is invoked against burns is because he is said to have been miraculously preserved when plunged by the Romans into a vat of boiling oil. This is commemorated on the feast of St. John Before the Latin Gate, May 6.

We think the most beautiful addition of all to night prayers on his feast is the beginning of his Gospel. It is something quite easily memorized, and its beauty is of such purity and simplicity that one may ponder it for many years and still it seems unendingly new. He wrote his Gospel that "you may believe that Jesus is the Christ, the Son of God, and that believing you may have life in His name."[25]

*Please, St. John the Evangelist, help us to love like you.*

⌒

## The Holy Innocents

December 28 is the feast of the Holy Innocents, the feast for all babies. In our own baby is imaged the babes of that dreadful

[24] Pope Pius XII.
[25] John 20:31.

slaughter, and no parent can look at his own baby this day, remember the Innocents, and fail to know the anguish of their parents. It is the Innocents' parents one remembers when standing over the bed of a fevered child, keeping a night's vigil.

Little ones have always held the center of the stage on the feast of the Holy Innocents, some crowned as kings, some as boy bishops, some in convent schools as superiors; there were processions and games and feasts all to their choosing. Perhaps we know someone who has no baby and would like to borrow a "holy innocent." Big families with their wealth of babies might lend one to reign over childless households for a day.

In some places, children were spanked to remind them of the sufferings of the Innocents. We do not do this, but we do tell the story of their martyrdom and the madman Herod who valued life so lightly that he could order the slaying of his whole family, even his three sons. So why not the sons of others? Why not, if necessary, the Son of God? There was a saying: *It is better to be Herod's pig than his son.* As a Jew, he could not eat pork; so he would not kill his pig.

Dom Chapman wrote with gentle humor, "I drank milk all day in honor of the Holy Innocents."

Charles Péguy writes in his *Holy Innocents:* "That name for which they died, they did not know. . . ." And after many more lines, plunging new thoughts about them, he says, "These Innocents that simply picked up in the scuffle the kingdom of God and eternal life . . ."

If you do not as yet have the custom, this is the day to begin the beautiful practice of blessing your children. There is a traditional *Blessing of Children* given by the priest in church on this day. If it is not a custom in your parish, perhaps it could become one if enough parents inquired about it. This is the way it reads in the new English Ritual:

BLESSING OF CHILDREN

*O Lord, Jesus Christ, who didst embrace and lay Thy hands
upon the little children when they came to Thee, and didst say to
them, "Suffer little children to come unto me, and forbid them
not, for the kingdom of Heaven is theirs, and their angels always
see the face of my Father": look with a Father's eye upon the innocence of these children and their parents' devotion, and bless
them this day through our ministry. By Thy grace and goodness,
let them make progress in desiring, loving, and fearing Thee, obey-
ing Thy commandments, thus coming to their destined home,
through Thee, Savior of the world, who, with the Father and the
Holy Spirit, livest and reignest, God, forever and ever. Amen.*

For parents there is the beautiful blessing of children for use at
home: "Bless you, my child, in the name of the Father, and of the
Son, and of the Holy Spirit." It is a custom to add some loving petition such as "and may you have a sweet sleep"; or if a child is sick,
"and may you be better by morning"; or if a child is anticipating a
special occasion, something like "and may you have a lovely feast
day tomorrow." The parent places one hand on each side of the
child's head as the words are said and accompanies the invocation
of the Trinity by making the Sign of the Cross with the right thumb
on the child's forehead. It makes a beautiful end to a day and is an
added source of confidence when starting on a journey, off to
school, before exams, to the doctor, to the dentist — anywhere.

*New Year's Eve, a Party, and Some Resolutions*
New Year's Eve is the eve of the feast of the Circumcision[26] as
well as the night of the turning of the year. Even to the unchurched,

---

[26] January 1 is now the feast of Mary, the Mother of God. — ED.

# The Year and Our Children

New Year's Eve is a waiting to start all over again. It is good to gather together to wait for the time of starting again, but sad to see so many make such a poor start. The reason the Church made it a holy day of obligation was to attempt to counteract the excesses of the pagan celebration. In the early centuries, she kept the eve of the New Year and the day following in prayer and quiet.

In order to form our children in customs that celebrate a happy and holy New Year's Eve, we can reverse the custom of "going out," and stay in. A party for our family, and other families if possible, can celebrate with food and fun and a time of "watch," all the things we want to celebrate this night. To bed for the children at ten o'clock or thereabouts, and as the new year rings in, parents walk through their bedrooms ringing a bell to wake the sleepy celebrants so that they may call out, "Happy New Year!"

If there is a parish Mass or Holy Hour, the grown-ups can arrange the rest of the evening so that some may attend while babysitters prepare a festive breakfast at home.

A party for such a group should include a game of thanks. Each brings some token symbolizing a blessing; and after a supper that includes all the things children envy the grown-ups at their parties, everyone tries to guess the meaning of the tokens.

A doll: someone is thankful for baby. Three have dolls: thrice thankful for baby. A tiny car? This year we have a car! A Red Cross swimming certificate: one boy is thankful that at last he learned to swim. A book? A slow reader is slow no longer and reading is a joy. Three heads of wheat (guess two thank-yous for this): bread on our tables, and the Bread on our altar. Two candy hearts? Hearts mean love. Two kinds of love? Love of God and family. Of all things — a bag of peanuts! All the children shout, "The trip to the zoo!" There is so much to be thankful for.

Now for a silly game (no point to it except having fun): Gumdrop on a String. You need a ball of string, a needle with a large eye, and a bag of large gumdrops. For every pair at the party, thread a string about three feet long into the needle and draw it through the gumdrop, placing the gumdrop in the center. Have a pair of participants each put one end of the string into their mouths, and at the word *go*, start to "chew the string." The winner gobbles to the gumdrop first, and of course gets to eat it for his pains. If you prepare enough strings, you can have a play-off and a champion. It is probably the most hysterical game in all the world.

How about regrets — the failings of the past year and the resolutions to begin anew?

Almost everyone knows — or if they don't, it is easily learned — the tune to the spiritual "I Want to Be Ready," an appropriate sentiment for the New Year, which, after all, might be our last year. Knowing from past experience that it is much easier to own up to our failings and laugh at them together, at this party everyone gets a slip of paper with two lines written out for him to sing when his turn comes in this song. These have been worked out ahead of time.

The song properly goes like this: "I want to be ready / I want to be ready / I want to be ready / To walk in Jerusalem just like John." Then follow various verses such as:

*Solo:* John said that Jerusalem was foursquare.
*Refrain (all):* Walk in Jerusalem, just like John.
*Solo:* I hope, good Lord, I'll meet You there.
*Refrain (all):* Walk in Jerusalem, just like John.

We change the solo lines and the names in the lines sung by all. Great hilarity is the result. Here are some of the lines we sing in our family:

*Monica:* To pray the prayer of Tidy-and-Neat will earn me a fine gold front-row seat.

*Jamie:* If I obey and never once pout, in Heaven I'll sing and dance and shout.

*John:* If I give up my old self-pity, I'll live forever in the heavenly city.

*Peter:* If I work hard and give up sloth, in Heaven there'll be no work to loathe.

*Mommy:* If I keep calm, be patient and good, I'll be forever in a heavenly mood.

*Daddy:* If I don't shout or roar or groan, I'll sing forever in a heavenly tone.

*Granny:* If I don't fuss or feather or fume, I'll sing forever in a heavenly tune.

*Grandma:* If I don't wag my finger and scold, I'll sing forever in the heavenly fold.

This song and many more are found in the inexpensive song booklets available at book shops and music stores. Usually the difference between getting people to sing and not getting them to sing is having the words at hand.

The time for prayers must be gauged so that it will not tire or bore the children. This is extremely important. The objective of this celebration, if it is to be repeated every year, is to form in them a concept of New Year's Eve that combines joy with prayer, and the time of prayer must be as enjoyable as the entertainment. For most American families, adding a time of prayer to a New Year's Eve party would be an innovation; so it is wise to make it short the first time and familiar rather than strange. A leader keeps things going along well and can explain the various parts beforehand.

"Come, Holy Ghost" is an excellent hymn to begin with, for even families not familiar with liturgical music know this. Then follows the *Confiteor*, recited aloud together, because we want to acknowledge our sins seriously as well as in fun and ask for the grace to begin again. Next, one of the older children can read from the Gospel of St. Luke, including the passage in the feast-day Mass on the morrow. This passage (2:8-21) tells of the joy of the shepherds, the Gloria of the angels, and how the little Lord Jesus was taken to the Temple on the eighth day to be circumcised and given His holy name.

Then, a Psalm that is especially delightful to children, with many thoughts and word pictures they will love to ponder. The group may be divided for the reading of Psalm 97,[27] and the leader may wish to explain any words that are difficult for the children.

After a few minutes of silence to think carefully of the needs of our families and the families of nations all over the world, we may use the Collect from the Mass of the Circumcision for our prayer of petition.

*Leader:* O God, who, through the fruitful virginity of blessed Mary, didst secure for mankind the reward of eternal salvation, grant, we beseech Thee, that we may experience her intercession for us, through whom we have been made worthy to receive the Author of life, our Lord Jesus Christ, Thy Son, who, with Thee, liveth and reigneth in the unity of the Holy Spirit, God, world without end. Amen.

Then, beautiful and familiar and comforting, the Our Father aloud, everyone together. And finally, a closing hymn. If everyone knows the melody to the *Laudate Dominum*, it is a lovely ending sung in English.

*Praise the Lord, all ye nations:*
*praise Him, all ye people.*

[27] RSV = Ps. 98.

*Because His mercy is confirmed upon us:*
*and the truth of the Lord remaineth for ever.*
*Glory be to the Father, and to the Son,*
*and to the Holy Spirit.*
*As it was in the beginning, is now,*
*and ever shall be, world without end. Amen.*

If the group does not know this, then "Holy God, We Praise Thy Name" or another of the familiar anthems would be suitable for closing. A parental blessing completes each child's sharing of New Year's Eve with his parents.

*Feast of the Circumcision*

The next day is the feast of the Circumcision. "But what does it mean — circumcision?"

If there are babies in the family who have been circumcised, it has probably already been explained when the children have seen their mother change the dressing on the newborn's circumcision. If not, and the child who asks is old enough to understand, this is a good time for the father to explain circumcision, using the story of Abraham (Genesis, chapters 12-25). Explaining it this way is especially suitable because the occasion is the feast and the rite, and attention is not focused on some familiar boy. When all the children are girls, it might be better for the mother to explain, although it is not impossible for the father to do so.

God chose Abraham to be the father of the Jews, the race that would produce the Messiah. Circumcision would mark them as His people.

Then God said to Abraham, "This is the covenant you shall keep with me, thou and thine; every male child of yours shall be circumcised; you shall circumcise the flesh of your foreskins, in token of the covenant between me and you. Generation after generation, every male child shall be circumcised when it is eight days old.... So my covenant shall have its seal in your flesh....[28]

This meant that the organ which makes a boy's body different from a girl's would have a tiny bit of skin called the foreskin cut away. It was the law for the Jews. Now, if this was done to mark them as the race from which would come the Messiah, it was hardly necessary that it be done to Jesus. He *was the Messiah*. But in obedience to the law, He submitted to the rite when He was eight days old, and the pain and blood He shed prefigured in the tiny Christ Child the terrible suffering of the Cross.

If the children ask, circumcision among Gentiles helps to keep boy babies clean. "It makes bathing easier for little boys, helps keep them nice and clean." Young children are serious and interested, and so it helps them to see a mother bathe a boy baby. The solicitude of the mother as she shows them what a circumcision is and comments on it will help their attitude to be wholesome and good, while if questions are left unanswered or shrouded in mystery, the children are likely to dwell on the idea and develop an unwholesome curiosity.

A New Year's Day custom that might well flourish again is to entertain or visit godparents, or, if godparents are too far away, to send a letter or small gift, a snapshot of the godchild and an account of his doings. These will help to remind us all of the seriousness of the role of godparent, the blessedness of the baptized child.

The day the Jewish boy baby was circumcised was also the day he received his name. The feast of the Holy Name of Jesus is celebrated either on January 2 or on a day soon after.

[28] Cf. Gen. 17:10-13.

Once the father of ten was telling about their Polish family customs, among them the greeting, "Praised be Jesus Christ," when they return to their house after a journey. The first person through the door calls out the greeting, and the rest of the family respond, "And may He bless all here." We repeated this to our children and waited for comments. One boy said, "But wouldn't you feel kind of funny? I mean, if you weren't used to saying it and if nobody you knew ever said it?"

"I wouldn't feel funny," said another. "I'd say it. I think it's a nice thing to say."

"It's not that I don't think it's a nice thing to say," said the first. "It's just that . . ." He couldn't quite explain.

I had an idea. "How many times have you felt funny when you heard Mr. N. say, 'Jesus Christ!' when he was angry?"

They looked at one another. That's right. He says it all the time. They don't approve, and they say to themselves, "My Jesus, mercy," the way Sister told them to at catechism class. But they'd *feel funny*, or maybe just afraid, to tell someone that big not to say it. They were beginning to turn over in their minds the inconsistency of our attitude toward God's name. Making a public greeting of it, as a doxology, causes us discomfort; yet we are so accustomed to hearing it used in blasphemy that we are no longer as outraged as we should be.

"Thy name is from eternity." For so long His name was God's secret. For so long Gabriel knew it before he told it to our Lady. And she kept it a secret in her heart. Even St. Elizabeth did not learn His name from the Holy Spirit when He enlightened her at the Visitation. She learned who He was but not that He was to be called Jesus.

"Such a beautiful sound. Let's think about it for a moment and then say it out loud together, very lovingly."

*Je-sus.*

Do your children like to memorize poems? It is a long time since I have heard of any children who were asked to memorize fine poetry, as we were in school. Maybe once or twice in an English course they will commit something to memory, but on the whole, it is little done. There is a lovely anonymous poem, easy to memorize, called "May the Sweet Name of Jesus." It is really a prayer, and a worthy prayer on this feast of the Holy Name of Jesus.

*May the sweet name of Jesus*
*Be lovingly graven*
*In my heart's inmost haven.*

*O Mary, blest Mother,*
*Be Jesus my Brother*
*And I Jesu's lover.*

*A binding of love*
*That no distance can sever,*
*Be between us for ever,*
*Yea, O my Savior,*
*For ever and ever.*

*The Epiphany and Some Blessings*

January 6 is the feast of the Epiphany,[29] the celebration of the Three Kings' journey to Bethlehem with their gifts; the day the children of the household journey to Bethlehem to take Him the gifts they have made during Advent, and the day the tiny kings join the rest of the Nativity figures in the crèche. They have been slowly inching their way across the mantel with their camel train, nearer each day. We bake a delicious Crown cake for the

---

[29] The Epiphany is now celebrated on the second Sunday after Christmas. — ED.

evening. Crown cake, King's cake, Epiphany cake — any name you wish to give it — is baked in a tube pan so that it looks like a crown. We have borrowed Mrs. Berger's icing from *Cooking for Christ*, fluffy white and decorated with gumdrop jewels. From the French we borrow the custom of baking a bean and a pea in the cake, as well as assorted objects of our own inspiration that have symbolisms, entirely invented.

The bean and pea were supposed to fall to the king and queen for the night, but we have the bean portend a trip to Boston and the pea tells that you are a princess (secretly, of course). A button means you will be a bachelor; a thimble, a seamstress. A penny means that you are going to be poor, and a dime, rich. A ring? You'll be married for sure. A raisin — I hate to tell you — you'll be wrinkled. A chocolate bit? You're *sweet*. You got nothing? That is to remind you that God loves you. Remember what our Lord said, "Blessed are those who believe and yet do not see."[30]

These things have only one purpose — fun. One caution: chew carefully.

Next the crowns are cut from aluminum foil or leftover Christmas wrappings. Where there are more than three children, the limited number would seem to pose a problem; but happily there is a possibility that there were more than three kings! Some say it was assumed that the kings were three because the gifts were three; and some say it is because in Psalm 71, used in the Epiphany Mass, it is stated, "The kings of Tharsis and the Islands shall offer presents: the kings of the Arabians and of Saba shall bring gifts." They were probably not kings as we think of kings, for "Magi were Persian pseudo-scientists devoted especially to astrology and medicine." The Jews of the Dispersion who had been captured in wars or had migrated to foreign ports to trade had kept their faith, and

[30] Cf. John 20:29.

it was undoubtedly from these that the Magi knew of the expected Messiah.

In the Middle Ages, the kings were given the familiar names Caspar, Melchior, and Balthasar. The Fathers of the Church interpreted their gifts mystically as symbols of Christ's kingship (gold), His divinity (frankincense, because it was used for worship in the temple), and His mortal humanity (myrrh, because it was used in the burial of the dead).

As for the attempts of modern astronomers to identify the star as a juncture of comets or as Halley's or another comet, they have entirely ignored the miraculous nature of the Star of Bethlehem, its appearance, movement, and disappearance.

This may seem to complicate the celebration of the feast of the three kings — who were not kings, nor three. But if not kings by rank, they were kings by faith and noble bearing and persevering determination. So we arrange crowns for the heads of as many kings as we must crown (visiting kings as well).

*Epiphany* means "manifestation": this is the feast of God's showing His Son to the world. One week after Epiphany we will celebrate another manifestation: when our Lord was baptized by St. John the Baptist, and God the Father spoke from Heaven, identifying Him. And the second Sunday after Epiphany we celebrate the third great manifestation, heralding the beginning of His public life: the miracle at the wedding feast at Cana, where our Lord showed openly His divine power.

Many blessings are given traditionally on the Epiphany: the *Blessing of Chalk*; the *Blessing of Gold and Frankincense*; the *Blessing of Bread, of Eggs, and of Salt*; and the *Blessing of Homes*.

There is a difference between blessings given by a priest and the same blessings read by the father or some older member of the family when it is not possible to have the priest present. But it is a mistake to consider them without efficacy when the layman reads them. By our Baptism we have a share in Christ's Priesthood. If we are part of Christ in His Mystical Body, and He is High Priest, we share this with Him. Ours is not the same as the power of the consecrated priest, but it is our right and privilege to ask God's blessing on the things we use in daily life, and we should exercise this privilege often. The *Blessing of Chalk* is usually given by a priest at church. The chalk is then distributed to the people, who take it home to use after the *Blessing of the Home*.

BLESSING OF CHALK

*Leader:*  Our help is in the name of the Lord.
   *All:*  Who made heaven and earth.
*Leader:*  The Lord be with you.
   *All:*  And with your spirit.

Bless, O Lord God, this creature chalk to render it helpful to men. Grant that they who use it in faith and with it inscribe upon the entrance of their homes the names of thy saints, Caspar, Melchior, and Balthasar, may, through their merits and intercession, enjoy health of body and protection of soul. Through Christ our Lord. Amen. (*Sprinkle chalk with holy water.*)

If this blessing is not ordinarily given at church, perhaps it could be if enough parishioners requested it; at any rate, it may be read by the father or one of the grown-ups at home. In some parishes, it is a custom for the pastor to bless the homes of the parish from the church doorway, the people reading the words of the blessing at the same hour in their homes, and going in procession from room to room, sprinkling the house with holy water. At the end of this procession, the father or another grown-up writes over the front door with the blessed chalk the year and the initials of the three kings, separated by crosses; for instance, 19 + C + B + M + 56.

BLESSING OF HOMES ON EPIPHANY

*Leader:* Peace be to this house.

*All:* And to all that dwell herein.

*All:* From the East, the Magi came to Bethlehem to adore the Lord; and opening their treasures, they offered costly gifts: gold to the great King, incense to the true God, and myrrh in symbol of His burial. Alleluia.

Now follows the reading of the *Magnificat* (Luke 1:46-55). The home is sprinkled with holy water, and following the *Magnificat* the antiphon is repeated: From the East . . . Then the Our Father, silently.

*Leader:* And lead us not into temptation.

*All:* But deliver us from evil.

*Leader:* Many shall come from Saba.

*All:* Bearing gold and incense.

*Leader:* O Lord, hear my prayer.

*All:* And let my cry come unto thee.

*Leader:* The Lord be with you.

*All:* And with thy spirit. *Let us pray.* O God, who, by the guidance of a star, didst this day reveal Thy sole-begotten Son to the Gentiles, grant that we who now know Thee by faith may be brought to the contemplation of Thy heavenly majesty. Through the same Jesus Christ, Thy Son, our Lord, who liveth and reigneth with Thee in the unity of the Holy Spirit, God, forever and ever. Amen.

*All:* Be enlightened and shine forth, O Jerusalem, for thy light is come, and upon thee is risen the glory of the Lord, Jesus Christ, born of the Virgin Mary.

> *Leader:* Nations shall walk in Thy light, and kings in the splendor of Thy birth.
>
> *All:* And the glory of the Lord is risen upon thee. Let us pray. Bless, O Lord, almighty God, this home that it be the shelter of health, chastity, self-conquest, humility, goodness, mildness, obedience to the commandments, and thanksgiving to God the Father, Son, and Holy Spirit. May blessing remain for all time upon this dwelling and them that live herein. Through Christ our Lord. Amen.

The *Blessing of Bread* is found in chapter 3. The *Blessing of Any Victual* may be used for the salt:

### BLESSING OF ANY VICTUAL

*Let us pray.* Bless, O Lord, this creature salt, so that it be a saving help to humankind; and grant that, by calling on Thy holy name, all who eat of it may experience health of body and protection of soul. Through Christ our Lord. Amen. *(Sprinkle salt with holy water.)*

Last, there is the:

### BLESSING OF THE EGGS

*Let us pray.* Let Thy blessing, Lord, come upon these eggs, that they be salutary food for the faithful who eat them in thanksgiving for the Resurrection of Jesus Christ, our Lord, who liveth and reigneth with Thee forever and ever. Amen. *(Sprinkle eggs with holy water.)*

We have neither gold nor frankincense to bless this day, alas, unless we include our "Magi's Gold" when we bless the food. This is nothing more than candied orange peel made with the rinds of the Christmas oranges (navel oranges are best, but watch out that the children don't peel them in little scraps and throw the peel away). Packed in small tin boxes with gilt paper and gilt bows, they are lovely gifts for friends. All cookbooks have recipes for candied orange peel. Be sure to sprinkle the peel with granulated sugar (not all include this) because it gives it a beautiful jeweled look. Save the sugar that falls off for the tops of cookies.

⌒

### Enacting the Epiphany Story

Now for our evening's celebration of Epiphany. With celebrations such as this, it is important to understand that, as years go by, some of the kings will grow up. Some will begin to feel too big to be crowned, to indulge in the same play as the little ones. These can move on to roles as planners of the party, designers of crowns, bakers and decorators of cakes, superintendents of caravans, and so forth. These feasts must be a joy for all, and it is not difficult for the parents to adapt them as the family grows. Eventually the delights of these feasts will be almost entirely intellectual and spiritual, but one grows up to this. Remember how St. Paul said he did?

Some of our growing children discovered an intriguing aspect of the paintings of the Adoration of the Magi this year — something they had not noticed before: too many people. Great crowds were pouring into the pictures from the horizon, winding up and down hills, clambering about the stable and underfoot everywhere. It seemed not to be quite according to Scripture, yet there they were — in paintings by Fra Angelico, Fra Lippo Lippi, Botticelli, Hugo Van der Goes, Breughel, painters who were such sticklers for scriptural detail. We wondered if they would stoop to inaccuracy for the sake of mere effect.

Then we discovered that their interpretations were entirely accurate from a liturgical, symbolic point of view, for the manifestation to the Magi on Epiphany is symbolic of Christ's manifestation to the Gentiles, and these crowds pouring into the pictures from the wide world beyond are symbols of all men seeking Christ in His Church. We can add this to our discussion of the simple procession at home, and add to our prayers on Epiphany and every day the petition that for all men searching out Christ there will be *safe home*.

Night falls and the stars are out, God willing (if not, we pretend that they are), and the kings take themselves off to the farthest bedroom — or the attic, if there is one — to begin. Finding the star out the window, they start their journey, carrying their gifts and caroling:

> *Then entered in there Wise Men three,*
> *Full reverently on bended knee. . . .*
> *(from "The First Nowell")*

Making their way through the rooms of the house, they arrive in the dining room to enlist the aid of Herod, who sits enthroned, and bearing a striking resemblance to Father. (It is a horrid trick to make Father enact Herod every year; but he is the biggest man in the house and, if we do say so, he makes a magnificent Herod. He insists it is his naturally horrible — or did he say horribly natural? — disposition, but we are as sure that it is his gift for the drama of the thing. He is hardly at all like Herod.) The kings ask Herod where they may find the newborn King of the Jews. Herod is startled (it says so in Scripture) but controls his alarm nicely, and calls the scribes. These resemble Mother, and this role calls for no such talent as the role of Herod. Reading from Micah 5:2, they (she) discover He is to be born in Bethlehem:

And thou, Bethlehem of the land of Judah, art by no means least among the princes of Judah; for from thee shall come forth a leader who shall rule my people Israel.

The kings bow and depart as Herod assures them with an oily smile that if there is a newborn King, of course he will want to pay tribute also, and they will come back and tell him, won't they?

Ha for you, Herod!

Then at last, Bethlehem. They arrive and kneel, presenting their gifts and adoring. They say the sweet things children say about this most beautiful Baby in the world and His most beautiful Mother. Then suddenly there is a hush. One points to an invisible being off in the comer.

Ah. An angel. He is advising them to go home by another route. Herod wants only to kill the Child. The kings nod excitedly and whisper, "Okay." Up they scramble as silent as mice and tiptoe out the other door. Herod sits in the dining room scuffling his feet and growling about the irresponsibility of foreigners who pass themselves off as kings and make promises and never keep them.

Then all at once there is great giggling in the hall, and the episode is over. They pile back into the living room and arrange themselves in front of the fire, where Herod, out of character at last (thank goodness!), is welcomed to eat Crown cake and open Epiphany presents (which are merely a few Christmas presents saved for Epiphany). Incidentally, for parents who deplore satiation with gifts on Christmas Day and haven't found yet a remedy for it, this is most practical. It makes an additional surprise; it is like the children in so many lands who get their presents at Epiphany — "little Christmas" — and it frees the children to enjoy wholly a few toys or gifts at a time rather than to try to play with too many at once.

☙

### The Feast of the Holy Family

The feast of the Holy Family, kept on the Sunday after Epiphany, has one of our family's favorite letters and Gospels. The letter is that of St. Paul to the Colossians, 3:12-17, the one that has the putting on of the "cloak of kindness" in it. We make a charade out of this for the feast of the Conversion of St. Paul, January 25. This day he sums up all we have learned through this beautiful season in a lesson for our family to help us in our imitation of the Holy Family. And in the Gospel we find the Boy Christ, no longer the Baby, going down with Mary and Joseph from the Temple to "be subject to them."[31]

That is such a great mystery — that God should be subject to them. This is the way of the Holy Family, the way to be a holy family: parents in authority, children subject to them, and in their midst — Christ. In the midst of the family is Love, who makes all holy in Him.

[31] Luke 2:51.

Chapter 5

⁊

# The Conversion of St. Paul

On January 25 comes the feast of the Conversion of St. Paul, apostle for apostles, missionary for missionaries, and if we are looking for heroes for boys and girls, little or big, there is none better.

St. Paul never even knew Christ in the literal sense of the word. He was born in another part of their world, he was about fifteen years younger, and the closest he came to the Body of Christ was his continual hunting down of His followers. In that sense only, up to the time of his conversion, did he trade blows with the living Christ. But there were crossings of their paths long centuries earlier in their family lines.

⁊

*Paul's Family Tree*

Far back, long-removed grandfathers to Christ and St. Paul were brothers. Judah and Benjamin were two of the brothers of Joseph, who was sold into captivity and turned up later in Egypt interpreting the dreams of Pharaoh. After the affairs of Joseph and his brothers were somewhat settled and they married and began to raise families, as the hundreds of years rolled by, the families came to be known as tribes.

The meeting that concerns us here took place when King Saul, of the tribe of Benjamin, sat brooding in his tent one day, rankling over the insults of Goliath. An officer came to announce that a shepherd boy at the front, visiting his brothers, was insisting that he could vanquish Goliath.

"Bring him here."

So the boy David, of the tribe of Judah, was brought in, and he persuaded the king that he could do it. For families who have not read it, there is a delightful surprise waiting for them in David's conversations with Saul and Goliath.[32]

First, David was armed with brass helmet, coat of mail, sword, spear, all the rest. Then David said he was sorry, but he couldn't move around in all that armor; so he took it off. (I daresay this episode was quite noisy.) Then he went over to a brook running through the camp and chose five smooth stones to put into his purse. At this point it is supposed by some that Saul and his men exchanged glances and asked one another, "Whose idea was this, anyway?"

David reassured them. Once he was attacked by a lion, and once by a bear who came to steal his sheep, but with the help of the Lord God, he slew them both. Should he doubt God's help now? And he added with the marvelous wisdom of the young and full of faith: "Who is this uncircumcised Philistine who hath dared to curse the army of the living God?"

The rest of the story you know. Goliath thought David was a great joke, and it turned out that he wasn't. One stone and one swing, and that was the end of Goliath.

There is a contrast between David and King Saul much like the contrast between Christ and Paul. Saul the warrior calling for conquest by the sword, and David the stripling vanquishing with faith and the power of God, are like Paul the murderer (still called Saul)

[32] 1 Kings 17 (RSV = 1 Sam. 17).

chasing his enemies down Damascus road and being overcome by Christ, the meek, in whom is all power in Heaven and on earth.

◠

*Saul the Pharisee*

Saul was a Jew and a Pharisee, so proud of both that he wrote of himself, "Hebrew, son of Hebrews . . . Pharisee, son of Pharisees; according to the strictest sect of our religion I lived a Pharisee."[33] And as a Pharisee he was educated well and painstakingly in all the exactness of the law. It was said that ten thousand regulations had been appended to the Law of Moses. The strange thing about the Pharisees, even the best of them, was that, for all their religion, they had little humility, and it went against their grain to think that the Messiah would come in any but the most fashionable manner. So when Jesus of Nazareth arrived and with His followers began to preach a New Law that would be the crown and fulfillment of the Old, it was men like Saul who set out to put a stop to the thing and quickly. The first sight we catch of Saul in the New Testament is in that scene where he stands over Stephen, holding the coats of the men who had stoned him to death (Acts 7). That done and approved, he sought permission to follow the Christian Jews who had fled to Damascus, and here is the scene of this feast.

It was 180 miles to Damascus, and ordinarily it would take men on horseback about seven days to make it. But Saul was in a passion, and he would have none of the ordinary pace; both men and horses drove themselves to the breaking point. High noon that day, they were riding wildly when suddenly a light brighter than the sun fell upon them. Their horses screamed in fear, rose in the air, and Saul was dashed, blind, to the ground. Where he had been

[33] Cf. Acts 26:5.

scanning the distance to Damascus there was blackness, and he heard for the first time the voice of his Enemy.

"Saul, Saul, why dost thou persecute me?"

Imagine the terrible impact of the fall, horror of sounds, stamping, fright, cries, gritty dirt in his mouth, blood on his tongue, all shattering the driving, driving, driving toward murder. Like a child, he must have whimpered when he asked, "Who art Thou, Lord?"

"I am Jesus, whom thou art persecuting."

And there is the doctrine of the Mystical Body again. It cannot be said too often or with too much emphasis that the lesson of this feast is our Lord teaching this doctrine Himself. Christ had ascended into Heaven. Paul knew that. He was chasing Christians, and Christ said to him, "Why dost thou persecute me?" We are part of Christ in His Mystical Body, the Church, and when Saul hunted Christians, he hunted Christ.

This is his first meeting with the doctrine that as St. Paul he would preach so eloquently, with so much love. He was biting the dirt when the knowledge came to him. Our Lord added, "It is hard for thee to kick against the goad." It was a tender rebuke, one we might imitate — or try to, when we rebuke our children, and there is a lesson for children in it, too.

It would be easier for them to understand it if we said, "It is hard for you to pull against the bit." Little children who know about horses know about bits; the more a horse pulls away from the direction his master wants him to go, the more cruelly is his mouth cut by the bit. He explained things in such simple ways, our Lord did. And He knew so well about anger. It is evil, and the more we give in to it, the uglier and more evil we grow inside, and all the time miserable, until finally we are hating everyone and the world as well, and we go about kicking things and taking our meanness out on people who have done us no wrong.

Surely Saul, who loved the Law, could hardly have forgotten, "Thou shalt not kill." But his sense of propriety had been offended to hear the Apostles preach from every street corner that Jesus, the stable-born One, was King of the Jews. He became angrier and angrier until his temper was wild and he risked his soul on an errand steeped in murder.

Now he knew. Blind and helpless, he whispered, "Lord, what wilt Thou have me do?"

We must use this feast to teach our children that submission to God's will is not weakness, but a chance to begin again. In one flash of light, Paul's life was undone, his works rubble. Not knowing how he was to take one step and follow it by another, now he waited to be told what to do. Paul teaches the little boy who defies authority that it is not worth it to continue to scream and save face. Give in, turn back, be sorry — and there will be forgiveness and love and help. He teaches the adolescent girl who balks parental cautions that there is wisdom in obedience and love beneath the intolerable restrictions.

So many lessons for the whole family to learn from Paul. . . .

But back to that day. He was given a mysterious direction. "Arise, and go into the city, and it will be told thee what thou must do."

So they made their stunned way into Damascus, leading by the hand the one who had always been so sure. For three days he waited without food or water, and prayed.

Now, there lived in Damascus a disciple named Ananias. As our Lord spoke to Saul, He also appeared to Ananias and told him about Saul waiting in the house on Strait Street. But Ananias was doubtful. He recalled Saul's reputation, and then our Lord told Ananias something of the future of this violent ugly little man — that he would go to preach His name "before Gentiles, and kings, and the children of Israel."

### Saul into Paul

That was enough. Ananias went right out to find him. Entering the house where he waited, he laid his hands on Saul's head and restored his sight. Far more wonderful, he baptized him. Saul, stopping only long enough to break his fast, rushed (he always rushed) out to the steps of the synagogue and started to preach Christ crucified.

The people were dumbfounded. Here was the man always so full of hate suddenly so full of love. It didn't take them long to gather their wits, however, and soon it was whispered that men lay in wait for Saul to kill him before he could slip through the city gates. But God had plans.

One night when the city was sleeping and the enemy keeping watch by the gate, a silent group of men made their way to the city wall carrying a rope and a large basket (perhaps some good wife's clothes-basket). They climbed to the top, tied the rope to the basket, tucked someone in, and then — as in *Peter and the Wolf* — they "carefully lowered it down" and saw him land safely and scurry off in the direction of Jerusalem.

Maybe one day later on, a message arrived from the city: *All comes out in the wash.* Who knows? It was the kind of thing the early Christians did. They were not above using code messages and symbols, cryptograms and signs to communicate right under the noses of their enemy.

There is more to the story of St. Paul, but this is the beginning and the episode we celebrate with this feast. The children must know, in addition to all this, that he was a tent maker by trade, and why, if he was named Saul, he is called St. Paul. Tarsus was a city governed by Roman law, and Paul was as proud of being a Roman citizen by birth as he was of being a Jew. *Paulus* was the Roman (Latin) for Saul, and he liked to be known by that name.

*A Paul Charade*

Now for the fun. This is a charade that works equally well at home and in a classroom with the story familiar and well reviewed. One set of charades will describe who Paul was. Another set will describe three details of his conversion. Three excerpts from his letters will introduce the children to some important things he said.

- *We describe him as a Jew.* Boy wearing beanie (like the "Yarmulke," the cap worn by boys and men in the synagogue) and imitation prayer shawl sits before audience reading from prayer book. (These articles of wearing apparel are explained beforehand.)

- *We describe him as a Pharisee.* Girl stands before group of children with arms piled high with books. She says sternly, shaking finger at them, "Woe to those who do not keep the Law! And its ten thousand regulations!"

- *We describe him as a Roman.* Boy stands before group holding sign on which is printed, "WHEN IN _____ DO AS THE _____ DO." He says loudly, "I live in one of the oldest cities in the world. It is called the Eternal City." ("Eternal City" is a name the Christians have given to Rome.)

- *We describe him as a tent maker.* Boy drapes sheet over two chairs, then pantomimes sewing tent seams with imaginary needle and thread. Finished, he crawls inside tent, peers out, saying, "This is my home, and I made it myself."

- *We describe him under his Jewish name, Saul.* Boy seated on floor with crown on his head, deep in thought. He looks worried, then says, "Who will come forth to fight the giant

Goliath?" This, of course, is King Saul, of the tribe of Benjamin, after whom Saul of Tarsus was named.

Now we describe three scenes from his conversion.

• *The ride to Damascus.* Boy sits astraddle chair or stool as though riding a horse at full gallop. Suddenly sees light in the sky, covers eyes, falls to floor. (This charade is no trouble to cast, as all local cowboys eagerly volunteer. Great success always.)

• *We have Ananias and Paul at Paul's Baptism.* Boy with eyes closed to suggest blindness kneels on floor with hands folded in prayer. Girl answers knock at door, leads second boy into room. He places hands on head of blind one, latter opens eyes. Girl brings cup (pretending water) and two boys pantomime Baptism.

• *The escape from Damascus.* Boys enter with clothes-basket, rope, and sheet. Mount three chairs placed together, or low table or bench, tie rope to basket, which is set on floor. Boy playing part of Paul gets down in basket, and others cover with sheet. Pantomime slowly letting rope out as if lowering basket over wall. (No clowns need apply for parts in this.)

Now we come to the letters. These should be discussed during the preparation for the feast, as well as frequently when circumstances suggest them. All appeal especially to children.

• *Run the race as though there were only one prize* (1 Cor. 9:24). Boy crouches down in position of runner about to start race. Second boy holds crown and says, "Run your best; there is only one prize!" (You have explained this previously in terms of life, death, and eternity.)

• *If I . . . have not charity, I am become as sounding brass or a tinkling cymbal* (1 Cor. 13:1). Boy stands before audience and says, "I have great faith. I have great hope. I possess many gifts." Girl asks, "And do you not have charity, *which means love?*" Boy scowls and says, "No!" Girl brings two pot lids from behind her back and clangs them together as cymbals.

• *Put ye on therefore . . . the cloak of mercy, kindness, humility, modesty, patience* (Col. 3:12). (In some translations, you will find *soul* for *cloak* and *benignity* for *kindness*. It is quite proper to make the above substitutions.) Girl stands before audience, and boy lays across her shoulders a cape made from an old sheet on which is lettered KINDNESS. (This text has tremendous appeal for children, especially as they start for school each morning. Putting on daily your cloak of kindness is a beautiful thing to do.)

These charades are lots of fun, and they teach. Some of them may be simplified for very small children, but strive always to give them more rather than less. Make them reach with their minds. They will if you keep coaxing. They have a surprising capacity for really big ideas.

The Collect from St. Paul's Mass may be used as part of evening prayers this night:

> God our Father, You taught the gospel to all
> the world through the preaching of Paul Your apostle.
> May we who celebrate his conversion to the Faith
> follow him in bearing witness to Your truth.
> We ask this through our Lord Jesus Christ,
> Your Son, who lives and reigns with You and the
> Holy Spirit one God, forever and ever. Amen.

And have one of the children compose a little prayer asking Paul to help us see Christ in each other, and love the Christ we see in each other. When a child expresses these ideas in his own words, he learns them all the better.

Then, after they are in bed with their heads full of Christ and St. Paul, you can turn to this saint with the groan of the well-spent parent (or Sister) and say, "You boasted of being all things to all men: very well, they are your children, too. Please help us to make them apostles. Please help us to make them saints."

Chapter 6

✑

# Candlemas and St. Blaise

Candlemas, on February 2, celebrates the feast of the Purification of our Lady and the Presentation of our Lord in the Temple, both of which rites were obliged by Jewish law. To prepare for this feast, it is necessary to go back as far as Exodus — that is, if you are the curious kind who wants to know why these were part of the Law.

The night before the Exodus, God gave the Jews instructions concerning the Paschal Lamb. Not only were they to slay, roast, and consume it, but they were to dip hyssop in its blood and smear the lintels of their doors so that when He passed over Egypt slaying the firstborn males among the Egyptians, He would spare the firstborn of the Jews. And because He would not have them forget the heavy price paid for their freedom, He laid down the law concerning firstborn sons.

There is a rich scriptural background for this feast, and the family's preparation might include these passages from the Old Testament. When we take the trouble to go back to the Old Testament to help shed light on the events in the New, we are helping our children see that the two are interdependent, part of a whole.

Chapter 13 of Exodus, verses 1-3, tells what He did to ensure their remembering:

And the Lord spoke to Moses, saying: Sanctify unto me every firstborn that openeth the womb among the children of Israel, as well of men as of beasts: for they are all mine.

And Moses said to the people (verses 11-13):

When the Lord shall have brought thee into the land of the Canaanite, as He swore to thee and thy fathers, and shall give it to thee, thou shalt set apart all that openeth the womb for the Lord, and all that is first brought forth of thy cattle. Whatsoever thou shalt have of the male sex, thou shalt consecrate to the Lord — and every firstborn of men thou shalt redeem with a price.

(A brief run-through beforehand helps parents to see what words might need changing for smaller children.)

In verses 14-17, He gives the reason for this consecration of firstborn to Him:

And when thy son shall ask thee tomorrow, saying: "What is this?" thou shalt answer him: With a strong hand did the Lord bring us forth out of the land of Egypt, out of the house of bondage. For when Pharaoh was hardened, and would not let us go, the Lord slew every firstborn in the land of Egypt, from the firstborn of men to the firstborn of beasts: therefore, I sacrifice to the Lord all that openeth the womb of the male sex, and all the firstborn of my sons I redeem. And it shall be as a sign in thy hand, and as a thing hung between thy eyes, for a remembrance, because the Lord hath brought us forth out of Egypt by a strong hand.

So this is why Jesus was called Mary's firstborn Son: because there was an obligation attached to it, whether the child be the first of many children or the only Son.

These firstborn belonging to God were to be priests and serve at the sacrifices. Not long after this, however, God appointed Aaron and his sons, of the tribe of Levi, to be priests, and out of their line from that time on were to come His priests. This would seem to release the firstborn of the other tribes, but God said no, not yet. Not until a ransom had been paid for them could they be released from His service to return to their families; and then they were to serve Him in a special way in their lay life, dedicated to doing His will. At the time of our Lord, the ransom for a firstborn son was five shekels — about five dollars in our money.

⁓

### The Meaning of the Purification

In chapter 12 of Leviticus (so called because it gives the laws of worship entrusted to the tribe of Levi) is the law concerning the purification of women. The fortieth day after the birth of her son, the mother should appear at the door of the tabernacle of the testimony bringing a lamb yearling for a holocaust and a young pigeon or a turtledove for a sin offering. Accepting these, the priest would offer them before the Lord and pray for her and she would be cleansed:

> And if her hand find not sufficiency, and she is not able to offer a lamb, she shall take two turtledoves or two young pigeons, one for a holocaust, and another for sin: and the priest shall pray for her and so she shall be cleansed.

Mary offered what was known as "the poor woman's offering."

This purification of women is almost always a puzzle to modern mothers. Why were these Jewish mothers considered unclean? To bear a child was matter for rejoicing among the Jews; it was barrenness that was the disgrace. Why should they consider the fruitful mother unclean? None of the assurances that this was only a legal stain satisfied me until Franz Michel William's *Mary, the Mother of Jesus* explained it this way:

> This law of purification seems strange to us in these modern times. But if we read the history of ancient peoples we find that those who lived close to nature observed certain religious practices at the time of pregnancy and childbirth. The law of Levitical purification is to be accepted in the same sense. It was a question of a ceremonial uncleanness, not of any sin, and the offering at the end of the prescribed period signified that the person was leaving a condition in which he was conscious of his own weakness and his utter dependence on God.

But even the "ceremonial uncleanness" did not touch our Lady. Far from claiming exemption from the Law, however, she chose willingly to submit. It was an incomparable moment. She who was conceived without sin went to the Temple for purification and bore in her arms a Child born to ransom men; offered Him to God and to His service and ransomed Him for five shekels that He might return home with them to begin the life that would end this law and the priesthood of this Temple. Strange: as a Baby He was ransomed in obedience to the Law, yet He had come as ransom that men would be free; and as a man the price paid to Judas for His head was thirty pieces of silver, the price the Law put on the life of a slave.[34]

*Candlemas and Light*

But something else happened before they left for home. As the ceremony ended, the old priest Simeon came forward, guided by

---

[34] Exod. 21:32.

the Holy Spirit. Speaking his canticle, the *Nunc Dimittis*, he provided the theme for this feast:

> *Now Thou dost dismiss Thy servant, O Lord,*
> *According to Thy word in peace;*
> *Because my eyes have seen Thy salvation,*
> *Which Thou hast prepared before the face*
>    *of all peoples:*
> *A Light to the revelation of the Gentiles,*
> *And the glory of Thy people Israel.*

And Anna, the old prophetess, tottered off to announce Him
to all who awaited the redemption of Israel, while they probably
nudged one another and agreed that she was crazy in the head.

"A light of revelation to the Gentiles . . ." All the ceremonies
preceding this Mass, and the Mass itself, speak of Light. It is the
day the candles are blessed for use in the church and in the homes
of the people throughout the year; hence, "Candle-mass." First
comes the blessing of the candles, then their distribution to the
people, then the procession around the church with lighted candles, and finally the Mass. It is not always possible to have the
distribution and procession, but one can arrive at church early
enough to put the family candles with the rest for the blessing,
then take them home and have a family procession in the evening.

"In Christian tradition the clean wax of the candles is symbolic
of the pure flesh of Christ, the wick the image of the soul of Christ,
and the flame a figure of the Divine personality of the Word made
Flesh."

The *Blessing of the Candles* included in the missal preceding the
Mass is very beautiful. Its first prayer makes reverent mention of
the substance of the candle: "This liquid to come by the labor of
bees to the perfection of wax"; and those for whom the candle will
be used: "That Thou wouldst vouchsafe to bless and sanctify these

candles for the use of men, and the health of bodies and souls whether upon the earth, or on the waters . . ."

The lesson in the Mass of the Purification is taken from the minor prophet Malachi, whose name means "Angel of the Lord" and who was the last of the prophets, coming some four hundred years before Christ. In it he foretells that our Lord will come like "a refining fire, and like the fuller's herb."[35] To my dismay, I discover there are two fuller's herbs, one being teasel and the other, after several translations from Hebrew to Latin to English, being a type of saltwort. Having written once upon a time on the subject of teasel and its symbolism in this passage, now I must admit the error of the piece and correctly identify Malachi's fuller's herb as saltwort (it is sometimes translated fuller's soap). Saltwort is a family of plants that, in biblical days, were burned for their alkaline salts and made into soap; the symbolism implied in the prophecy is taken from the use of soap for cleansing wool before it is woven. The wool is sorted, soaked, and washed several times with soap to remove dirt, oil, and any trash it has picked up from sheep to fuller; hence, its application to the feast of the Purification.

It makes an eloquent meditation for mothers and wives, occupied so constantly with washing, whether their laundry or their children, their dishes or their floors. These are purifications. Malachi has said that Christ will purify us the same way, refining us by the fire of our trials, purifying us of self-love by the washing of our wills. He would have us in wedding garments, clean and bright.

☙

### A Shadow-Box Show and a Procession

On Candlemas night at our feast-day dinner, there are two tiny white sugar doves on the cake. After dinner the children tell the

---

[35] Mal. 3:2.

story of the Purification and the Presentation and present it in their shadow-box theater.

A shadow-box theater is easily made from a grocery carton, some tissue paper, gummed tape, and cardboard. Our present theater is made from a box about 11 by 11 by 15 inches. Take the flaps off, and set it on its side. On what was originally the bottom of the box, cut a stage opening about an inch in from sides and floor of theater, with a swag-like cut across the top like a theater curtain drawn up. Tape tissue paper over this opening, leaving enough lap on all four sides to tape it to the sides of the box. Cover the entire box with fabric, wallpaper, or whatever suits your fancy.

The *dramatis personae* in this case are Mary, Joseph, Simeon holding the Child Jesus, and Anna the prophetess. These are cut from stiff paper in silhouette. They must be generous in length as they are inserted in slits in the floor of the stage, and part of their shadow is lost crossing the stage floor. The action of the figures must be simple and distinct so that the silhouette will tell clearly what they are doing. If you cannot draw, you can find figures to trace in religious coloring books, cut-out books, stories of the lives of the saints, or the life of Christ for children.

We have Simeon holding the Child up in his arms and gazing to Heaven as he says his *Nunc Dimittis*. Anna, bent over with age, has a prominent nose and chin to distinguish her age, and both arms are extended in awe. Joseph stands serenely with his hand on his staff, and in front of him stands our Lady, straight and lovely, with her hands together in prayer. All the figures are in profile.

The theater is lighted by a candle stump in a saucer set a foot or so behind the theater (this is variable), and it is best displayed in a darkened room. This is one of the loveliest of all forms of dramatization for children, for the effect achieved with such crude materials simply and quickly put together, is truly magical. They are always speechless to see it finally lighted with its shadow figures so lifelike. They always say, "Ohhhhhhhhh." It is an especially easy medium for learning the mysteries of the Rosary, because once it is put together, all that needs changing are the figures.

This night, after the story is told and the theater is alight, we say the Joyful Mysteries of the Rosary while we meditate on this scene.

Then we have our family procession with lighted candles. Small paper cuffs keep the wax from dripping on hands. The babies have their candles alight in candlesticks on the mantel. All through the downstairs we walk, with a grown-up reading the Antiphons for the procession of the morning and the children joining in hymns. We sing *Salve Regina* in English, and *O Sanctissima*, and the familiar "Hail Holy Queen, Enthroned Above." Families who know chant well have a large repertoire of songs to choose from, and for those who are eager to add to their repertoire or improve it, the *Pius X Hymnal* is an excellent investment. We have just been given one by a holy friend who is eager that we improve our repertoire. Bless her!

⌒

### A Mother's Thanksgiving

The *Blessing after Childbirth* is often confused as a modern version of our Lady's Purification, but it has no such meaning. The Church intends this blessing as a thanksgiving (as indeed one of the ceremonies over our Lady that day was a thanksgiving) for the safe delivery of the mother and the precious new life brought forth from her. There is, however, another blessing that should precede this: the *Blessing before Childbirth*. These together surround the mother with heavenly protection both before and after her delivery.

The *Blessing before Childbirth* is given shortly before delivery, or if the mother is ill and in danger, and of course always by a priest. It contains such comforting petitions as these for the expectant mother:

> *Receive the sacrifice of the contrite heart and the ardent desire*
> *of Thy servant . . . who humbly asks Thee for the welfare of*
> *the child which Thou didst grant her to conceive. Guard the*
> *work which is Thine, and defend it from all the deceit and*
> *harm of our bitter Enemy, so that the hand of Thy mercy may*
> *assist her delivery and her child may come to the light of day*
> *without harm, be kept safe for the holy birth of Baptism, serve*
> *Thee always in all things, and attain to everlasting life.*

In another prayer it asks these great comforts:

> *Visit, we pray Thee, O Lord, this house, and drive far from*
> *it and from this Thy servant N., the Enemy with all his plots.*
> *May Thy holy angels dwell here to keep her and her child in*
> *peace, and may Thy blessing be always upon her. Save them,*
> *O almighty God, and grant them Thy unfailing light.*

The *Blessing after Childbirth* is given as soon as the mother is able to attend Mass again or any time thereafter. After reading the *Magnificat* of the Blessed Virgin Mary, the priest prays:

> *Almighty, everlasting God, who, by the childbearing of the*
> *Blessed Virgin Mary, has for Thy faithful turned the pains of*
> *childbearing into joy, look with kindness on this Thy servant,*
> *who comes rejoicing to Thy holy temple to give thanks to Thee,*
> *and grant that after this life, she and her child may, by the*
> *merits and intercession of the Blessed Virgin Mary, attain*
> *to joys of everlasting life. Through Christ our Lord.*

If the mother has her infant with her, there is also at this time a blessing for the infant. It is like the prayer used for the *Blessing of Children* (see page 67).

*St. Blaise and Blessing Throats*

The feast of St. Blaise, February 3, is the day to receive the *Blessing of Throats*. St. Blaise was a physician who was made Bishop of Sebaste in Armenia. Bishop or not, he withdrew to a cave and soon had a reputation for curing both men and beasts. It is told that if the animals found him at prayer, they would wait patiently for him to finish. Under the Emperor Licinius, Agricola, governor of Cappadocia, came to Sebaste to persecute the Christians. Sending his hunters out in quest of wild beasts for the arena, they were startled to find at the mouth of the cave on Mount Argeus, wolves, tigers, bears, and lions waiting for Blaise to finish his prayers. They promptly arrested him and tried without success to make him apostatize.

While he was in prison, the poor, the sick, and the lame continued to come to him. The most familiar of the events surrounding him appear to have happened at this time. He returned to a poor woman a pig that a wolf had stolen, and he cured a little child with a fish bone caught in his throat, from which miracle grew his great reputation as a healer of throats. According to the *Acts* of his martyrdom (considered somewhat legendary), after horrible torments, he was thrown into a lake, upon which he proceeded to walk, inviting his tormentors to join him. I wish I could have seen that. They took up the challenge and were drowned to the last man, ha-*ha!* Told by an angel to return to dry land and receive martyrdom, he did and was promptly beheaded on the shore. Went right to Heaven.

Special candles are blessed to be used for the *Blessing of Throats*. In this blessing of candles, we find mention of his power of healing throats, granted him at his request as he was dying, it is said:

> *In virtue of which, among other gifts, Thou didst bestow on him this prerogative — of healing all ailments of the throat.*

*Thus we beg Thy Majesty that, overlooking our guilt, and*
*considering only his merits and intercession, Thou wouldst*
*deign to bless and sanctify and bestow Thy grace on these*
*candles. Let all Christians of good faith whose necks are*
*touched with them be healed of every malady of the throat,*
*and being restored in health and cheer, let them return thanks*
*in Thy holy Church, and give praise to Thy wondrous name,*
*which is blessed forever. Through our Lord Jesus Christ,*
*Thy Son, who liveth and reigneth with Thee in unity*
*of the Holy Spirit, God, eternally. Amen.*

When we go to church to have our throats blessed, this is what
the priest says as he touches our throats with the crossed candles:

*Through the intercession of Saint Blaise, Bishop and*
*Martyr, may God deliver you from sickness of the throat,*
*and from every other evil; in the name of the Father,*
*and of the Son, and of the Holy Spirit.*

St. Blaise is one of the Fourteen Holy Helpers[36] or Auxiliary
Saints, the others being St. George, St. Erasmus, St. Pantaleon,
St. Vitus, St. Christopher, St. Denis, St. Cyriac, St. Achatius, St.
Eustache, St. Giles, St. Margaret, St. Barbara, and St. Catherine.
So we greet him on his feast day and give thanks to God for his
blessing. And I don't suppose he'd be cross if we said that really
and truly this *Blessing of Throats* might well be termed the liturgi-
cal antibiotic.

---

[36] These saints are invoked as a group because of their efficacious intercession in adversity or difficulties. — ED.

Chapter 7

⤳

# St. Valentine's Day

St. Valentine's Day is not one of the major feasts of February, but it has the peculiar distinction of being celebrated by almost everyone for reasons known to almost no one. Because it is most of all celebrated by children in school, we ought to know more about it.

There are three Saints Valentine listed in early martyrologies for the date of February 14. That their feasts should end up united to a celebration in honor of lovers seems to have been more an accident than a design, although there are interesting complications that conspired to make this so.

Long ago the Romans celebrated the eve of their Lupercalia on February 14. This being a time of great festivity, it is thought by some that the martyrdom of the saints on this day was merely an added attraction to the pagan celebration. Still another possibility connects with this feast the Roman celebration in honor of Juno. The drawing of partners for the festival by maidens and youths oftentimes degenerated into extreme improprieties, and it is thought the desire to redeem the day suggested to the Christians that they fix it as the date of the martyrs' feasts. Pope Gelasius appointed it an official feast in the fifth century and named St. Valentine the patron saint of lovers.

Add to this the widespread belief during the Middle Ages that February 14 was the time of the mating of birds; so it is no wonder that from it all evolved the custom of consecrating it to lovers as a proper day to exchange notes and poems and lovers' tokens. In Chaucer's *Parliament of Foules* there are lines spoken by Nature thus:

> Ye knowe wel, how on Saint Valentines day,
> By my statute, and through my governance,
> Ye do chese your makes, and after flie away.

The third line, I have discovered, translates "Ye do choose your mates."

The legend that one of the Saints Valentine left a note in his cell the morning of his execution, into which he "cut curious devices" and wrote "pious exhortations and assurances of love to the keeper's daughter, signing them 'your Valentine,' " is of doubtful origin but accounts for the lacy paper and the signature which are (or used to be) part of all valentines. All this makes quite a potpourri of things that have contrived to make a great to-do about valentines, although only a little to do with the Valentines. And they are not without relevance on a day consecrated to lovers. When love is so lightly abused and profaned, the petition in the Collect for their Mass seems especially apropos:

> Grant, we pray, almighty God, that we who celebrate the
> birthday of the blessed martyr Valentine, may in virtue of
> his intercession be freed from all the evils that threaten us.
> [The "birthday," the children must understand, which
> a saint's feast celebrates, is his birthday into Heaven —
> except in the case of our Lady and St. John the Baptist.]

"Now here is a sour note," some sentimental soul will comment, "consigning love to the category of evils that threaten us and begging that from these we be freed. I, for one, am all for love, and I'll thank St. Valentine to free me not." Nor did the Saints

Valentine deplore the business of love; else they would not be saints. Rather did they love to the limit of folly and end up losing their heads for love. It is the difference in loves and manners of loving that is the issue here: there is love that is holy and love that is not, and if you are celebrating this day as a Christian with the Church who is Christ's own True Love, a requirement implicit is that you make yours a feast of holy love.

On this feast we celebrate the kind of love that leads men to shed their blood, die in prison, burn at stakes, or part with their heads for love of Him who is All Love. If we use the graces of the feast well, perhaps we can translate this in terms of the love required by our vocation. We may not presently be called to violent death for the love of God, but with grace we may daily slay a little of the self-love that is between us and God, trying harder to love the people in our lives who are not so easy to love.

### A Question of Valentines (Three)

But we should start with the stories of the Saints Valentines — as well as we can discover them (most of what is known is taken from a thirteenth-century collection of legendary lives of the saints).

One St. Valentine is said to have been a Roman priest living in the third century. He was arrested and called before the emperor Claudius the Goth to give testimony of his faith, and having stubbornly declared himself a Christian, he was commanded to expound his opinions of the gods Jupiter and Mercury. Since neither of these was reputed to excel in morals or integrity, Valentine dismissed them tartly as "shameless and contemptible characters." So saying, he was committed to a magistrate named Asterius who was appointed to pronounce sentence. Turning the tables by restoring the sight of the magistrate's blind adopted daughter, Valentine converted the magistrate and his family and was rewarded for his pains by being beaten and decapitated. This is apparently the Valentine who is supposed to have left the note signed, "Your Valentine."

The second Valentine was said to be an Umbrian bishop in the same century and had adventures much like the first except that he was more cautious. He promised to cure the son of a pagan philosopher in Rome if the philosopher and his family became Christians — which they did, together with three of the philosopher's disciples. The boy was cured, and the enraged prefect Abundias had this Valentine beheaded.

About the third nothing is known, except that he and his companions are supposed to have died in Africa, early in the history of the Church.

This is "love stuff" of the kind that interests even small boys who are temporarily convinced that girls are old things, and it certainly puts a new meaning on the well-worn "Be my valentine." What if we turned that about so that it read from up to down instead of right to left — from God to man, that is? This makes "Be my valentine" rich with possibilities. Could it be that Christ has been saying this to us all these years on this feast and we have missed the point? Perhaps it means "Be my martyr. Be my saint."

### A Valentine Game

A good valentine game to play at a party or in a classroom on this feast is patterned on "Who am I?" but it is called "What valentine am I?" Each child uses his patron saint, gives brief hints about his life, and if possible, shows symbolic clues. For example, Elizabeth, Betty, Betsy, or Bess can use any of St. Elizabeth's lines at the Visitation (after some profitable research into the Gospel to find exactly what they were) or could wear a crown or carry a basket of bread or roses for St. Elizabeth, Queen of Hungary. If she were a mother and had one, she could merely point to "my son John." A girl named Mary has countless Mary symbols she might use, or she can repeat that meaningful line of our Lady at the marriage feast at Cana: "Do whatever He tells you." It sums up everything our Lady has to say. A girl named Ann can wear a crown and hold a doll wearing a crown, because St. Ann is often shown crowned in the statues venerated at her great shrines. Another symbol of St. Ann is a cradle with a child in it representing the Blessed Virgin. The question "What valentine am I?" translates, in this game: "What lover of Christ am I?" It is a good question.

The Austrian custom of baking valentines is a happy solution for mothers forced by local custom to supply valentines for an entire classroom, although I personally rebel loudly at this custom. I like baking the cookies because I want to, but not because I must. Ginger cookie dough is spread quite thin and cut into hearts, baked and decorated with liturgical symbols telling of God's love (confectioner's frosting for these). Even when shapelessly formed, these symbols of divine love are joyful and eloquent. For special gifts for special people, we cut the hearts very large, freehand, and wrap them in red tissue with lace paper frills tied in the bows.

Most fun of all is making valentines at home. The materials cost little or nothing if you keep a supply of construction papers, pastes, and other such items on hand, and the work provides many opportunities for mothers and children to discuss the differences between friendship and love and the lamentable forcing of the boyfriend issue in the first grade. It is not always the children who are at fault. Abetted by the teasing of grown-ups, children little more than babes make the unfortunate conclusion that boy must meet girl and be boyfriend and girlfriend at six years of age; they never do learn that it is possible to be that rare and wonderful creature: a friend who happens to be a boy. The same parents who wring their hands over high-school children determined to go steady are the ones who encourage puppy love in the kindergarten.

꿈

*Friendships among Children*

Friendship is an art. When we ignore the fact that childhood crushes in the young are merely an awkward way of trying to be special friends, we do them no favors. Of course children get crushes, and of course girls become boy-conscious, with vice becoming versa; but they need not be shoved and pushed so hard. One of the most excruciating trials of youngsters who believe themselves to be in love these days is restraining their impulses of affection. Very few children deliberately set out in their first encounters with crushes to commit any sins of impurity. In their innocence of experience, they do not know exactly how such sins can be, or if they know the theory, they do not know the fact. It is the task of Christian parents to convince them that these impulses must be held in check. Held in check they are good, they are manifestations of sincere and genuine affection, but they can so easily be transformed into something that is not good. The reason it has become such a delicate and difficult task (although I suppose it always was a worry for parents) is not because this restraint is impossible but because so few today seem to practice it. The example of promiscuous contemporaries is a powerful thing.

It rarely helps to start lecturing on the subject once children reach high school; it does not help at all to pooh-pooh love or schoolgirl crushes or the boyfriend business once it begins for a son or daughter growing up. But such occasions as St. Valentine's Day (with innumerable opportunities all year round, of course) open this subject for discussion in a pleasant way. We may use the evenings spent making valentines to have our own open forum on the subject of *love* and the *making of love* and how it is that people fall in love, and how it is all related to *God's love*.

Such Christian concepts as respect for girls and women, respect for our bodies and the bodies of others, the propriety and impropriety of kissing — whom and when — right judgment about the movies, their ads and their love-making, many other things can be formed at a very early age. We must use all our talent and love and conviction to form them in our children. We are foolish if we think that our children, because they are *nice* children, are automatically safe. In the movie ads and posters they see, the newsstand magazines and comics, the covers of the paperbacks, slicks, and in a hundred ways promiscuity is preached to them — and it is not preached to what is nice in them but to the deplorable weakness left in human nature by the inheritance of Original Sin.

We can work to form in them the conviction that *making love* is something positive and beautiful that belongs with marriage, and this concept can exist even for the small ones without, as we might fear, any undertones of s-e-x. Demonstrations of affection they can automatically connect with mommies and daddies, as well as with relatives and friends. When there are things to denounce, such as this week's ad showing a movie siren and lover wrestling on the beach, we can make our denunciations more convincing if we avoid panic but rather express regret that some people persist in distorting out of its sacramental context what should be the beauty of human love.

There are many facets of this subject for parents to ponder. Each can adapt best the teaching for his children, but let us emphasize while they are still little that it is *friendship* that holds the joys of companionship for them.

I suppose the free use of the word *boyfriend* has made it almost a synonym for *friend*, but not quite. It may be a losing battle, but we continue to explain the difference. "Your *friend*, dear — your *friend* who is a girl. Little boys in second grade have friends, not girlfriends. Yes, I know — they tease and say you have a girlfriend, and that is too bad, because it is necessary that you love everyone with much more love than the word *girlfriend* intends. You must try to love them as our Lord loves them, and you must try to see our Lord in them. If you like someone especially well, better than others, that is all right. Then they are among your special friends. Be glad and be careful of your friendship. Friendship is a beautiful, holy thing if you keep it that way."

⌒

### To Buy or to Make?

Understanding how we are supposed to love betrays the glaring imbalance of the customary classroom exchanging of valentines. It is brutally discriminative. Suppose one of your darlings were not pretty. Suppose you had, as someone I know, a dearly beloved little one with a harelip. Suppose one of yours were, as another I know, lamentably fat. Suppose one son has a crossed eye, or a tantalizing stutter. The struggle to teach that beauty of mind and soul is far more important than curly hair or limpid eyes is not made easier when a child's small harvest of classroom valentines proves that to have a pretty face, to be whole and well-built, to be lively and attractive is what counts most after all. I am all for valentines in the classroom but with the emphasis on what this feast of St. Valentine teaches: love, not the deciding of popularity contests. It is good neither for the child who gets the most valentines, nor for the child who gets the fewest.

The answer to this seems, therefore, to have every child buy valentines for every other child, but this is as inadvisable as the alternative, because love bought by the bushel at the paper-store counter is not love at all. Love is thoughtful and considerate, and takes pains to give the loveliest.

One solution that is fair and fun is to have the children draw names, say, of six other children, and, starting two or three weeks ahead of time, make the valentines to be given to these six. Then every child in the room gets six lovingly wrought valentines, an art project has been worked out, and a lesson in the intrinsic value of a thing made with care and given with love is learned.

A delightful book for parents and teachers is *Appolonia's Valentine,* by Katherine Milhous, a story of some children in a schoolroom who made their valentines, with a poignant exchange of truly loving valentines between a little Pennsylvania Dutch girl and a little boy in France. The illustrations suggest numerous variations of valentines.

Our experience with homemade valentines has taught us many lessons. Since such valentines are not the custom where our children go to school, it has happened that St. Valentine's Day found them with lovingly but somewhat clumsily made greetings that, of course, did not begin to measure up to the polish and print of the commercial items.

Some of their teachers have commented approvingly when they made their valentines, but sometimes other children have opened them, sniffed, and put them in the wastebasket. Suspecting that this would happen, we wondered how to handle what would be the inevitable hurt feelings. The answer is not (if you feel this strongly about these things) to surrender the idea of making things with love. To buy inexpensive valentines and then sit up most of the night addressing envelopes is a capitulation we do not make easily. Anyway, when you begin to have four or five or more children in school, the cost of all those inexpensive valentines adds up.

As we suspected, one of them especially was hurt by the discovery that the lovingly given handiwork had been dismissed as crude and unacceptable. I admit I didn't think much of my chances of convincing her that it didn't make any difference. "I know, dear, and I suppose it isn't surprising," I began. "You can't really see their true beauty unless you understand how the person who made them felt. The children who threw them away should not have done it because it was ungracious and impolite, really not nice at all — but then you can forgive them because they do not know any better. No one has explained to them how much better handmade things are. It takes no pains to walk into the stationery store and buy inexpensive valentines from that mountain of valentines showing pigs and ducks and chickens and horses and donkeys all saying *Be my valentine*. If they are the only valentines available, and if the children haven't thought about making them, that is all they can do. And of course you must accept their valentines graciously because they have given you the best they could find.

"Your valentines took time and care; you cut and pasted and made ladders for them, lettered them, and made envelopes. All this work you put in them gives them real value. And knowing what the feast of St. Valentine means, you know how right it is to give valentines you have made.

"I cannot comfort you by saying that the children did not mean to throw away your valentines. But I can ask you this: did you not love making them? Wasn't it fun? Didn't we do it as part of our prayers, and we prayed for the children and tried to think about how our Lord would have us love them? Well, lots of times loving is going to be like that: you will love people and they will not recognize it as love at all, or value it. It is important, though, that you go on loving. Do not blame the children. They did not understand. Be glad you had a happy time making them, and ask God to help them understand about true love."

She said, "Yes, I guess so," that sadly smiling way children have of trying to agree to something you tell them when they don't agree at all. And I thought: It's all very well for me to talk, but you do want your gifts appreciated just the same.

But we are always underestimating grace. She came back at the end of the day. "You know what? I just figured it out. They don't understand about Valentine's Day the way they don't understand about Christmas. Christmas isn't just all toys and presents either — but they don't understand."

*O thank You, Lord Jesus.* We cannot always coax them to hold out. They will make compromises with popular custom. As long as they do not compromise with sin, it is safe to watch and say nothing and see if, in the afterward of the compromising, their own good sense and judgment don't finally clarify the values we have tried to give them.

But it is important that we define our values. The reason many people do not understand the value of carefully wrought craftsmanship is because the issues have never been explored for them. Poor taste and mediocrity are so often the only face of things some people have ever seen. To be cross about it is not the answer. To explain with love will change more, faster.

*Some Valentine-Making Ideas*

To make valentines is truly a joy — but they must be started a week or two ahead of time. It is an excruciating ordeal if you start too late.

Red construction paper, lace-paper doilies, wallpaper-sample books, leftovers of wallpaper, flower-seed catalogues in color, cast-off magazines, watercolors, poster paints, inks, glitter, floral stickers, white typing paper, ribbons, and many odds and ends may be used. We make some mobile with ladders — two-inch strips of paper folded in three steps for mounting decorations.

For children who know their patron saints, we use their symbols. "Happy Valentine's Day to Theresa" should certainly be surrounded by flowers, and do tell little Theresa (if she doesn't know already) that the "Little Flower" was a name St. Thérèse[37] gave to herself because she was one of God's little ones, not because she was one of God's pretty ones.

Martins can have coats sliced in half on theirs like the coat St. Martin of Tours[38] shared with the beggar, or they can have little rats to suggest St. Martin de Porres,[39] who had to scold his rats for nibbling the altar linens so that they moved straightaway to the garden.

Boys named Frank can have animals on theirs, for St. Francis.[40] And boys named Joseph can have carpenter's tools on theirs for St. Joseph of Nazareth, or lambs or birds for St. Joseph of Cupertino,[41] who once had lambs for Vespers and gave the nuns he served a little bird to sing in choir with them.

Kevin should have a blackbird on his for St. Kevin,[42] who prayed with his arms outstretched through the tiny hut window. When a blackbird came and made her nest in his hand, he stayed there until her eggs were hatched — or so the legend goes.

Margarets and Margaret Marys should surely have hearts with flames for St. Margaret Mary[43] and her Beloved, the Sacred Heart. These are nicest if they are of cut paper with the flames cut to dart out from the center fold.

---

[37] St. Thérèse of Lisieux (1873-1897), Carmelite nun and Doctor known for her "little way" of holiness.

[38] St. Martin of Tours (c. 316-397), bishop.

[39] St. Martin de Porres (1579-1639), Dominican brother devoted to the poor.

[40] St. Francis of Assisi (1182-1226), founder of the Franciscan Order.

[41] St. Joseph of Cupertino (1603-1663), Franciscan tertiary.

[42] St. Kevin (c. 498-618), hermit and abbot.

[43] St. Margaret Mary Alacoque (1647-1690), Visitation nun who promoted devotion to the Sacred Heart of Jesus.

If there are many valentines to be made and simplicity and time are of the essence, we make lacy cut-outs, mount them on ladders, and paste them on various lovely papers. The smaller these are, the more intriguing. Although very little children cannot use small scissors too well, they can make ladders, and paste and mount the hearts that their older brothers or sisters or mothers make for them.

A simple technique for enhancing cut-out valentines is known as pinprick. It appears on the early Pennsylvania Dutch and German valentines. A hat pin or darning needle is used to prick designs or names or words through the folds of the cut-out before it is opened. The folded valentine should be pricked over a newspaper so the table beneath will not be marred.

Another type is the folded valentine. The trick with these is to refold them correctly after they have been opened. We use a piece of white typing paper cut square. First fold the four corners so that they touch each other in the center, thus making a smaller square (this is the way bandages are sometimes folded). Fold the four corners of this square, making another square; if there is room, fold still another square. We end up with a tiny square folded note pasted shut with a heart sticker that "breaks" when it is opened. A design decorates the bottom of it, and inside it is decorated and inscribed with messages and symbols.

Another fold goes thus: a square piece of paper is folded diagonally, making a triangle. Fold it in half, making a smaller triangle. Take one of the end corners and fold it in to touch the apex of the triangle. Fold the other corner the same way, getting a square. Now fold the four corners of the square to the center and seal it with a heart sticker. These folded valentines are a nice way for children to give their parents or their teacher a spiritual bouquet for Valentine's Day, as there is plenty of room on them for all the writing.

Another kind of valentine message can be made of a *rebus*, one of those messages where the words are broken into syllables and the syllables pictorialized. For example, "I love you" would be a drawing of an eye, a heart, and a capital letter *U*.

An acrostic is still another way of recording a message:

> *Much she loves thee*
> *And tenderly.*
> *Read up and down;*
> *Your name has she.*

Still another intriguing design is what was called "an endless knot of love." It is an interwoven ribbon such as seen often on illuminated manuscripts, or resembling one of the more complicated of the sea scout's knots illustrated in rope-tying manuals.

Perhaps some of the homemade valentines will lack the slickness and polish of the "boughten" ones, but we can compensate with variety and the many intriguing ways of putting them together. Many a conversation piece will result. Most of all, we want them to speak of true Christian love; and it is worth the time and effort and mussing up to help our children to think about this and about ways to express it. We can use St. Valentine's Day to learn more about love, and to teach our children that love is serious, that it is beautiful, and that it is commanded of us. "A new commandment I give unto you: that you love one another, as I have loved you."[44] In the end it will be our love that is our measure.

[44] John 13:34.

Chapter 8

⟜

# St. Patrick

The feast of St. Patrick as popularly celebrated is badly in need of surgery. In an attempt to rid the occasion of indignities and restore to this saint some of his due, we have had recourse to the *Confession of St. Patrick*, an inspiring read-aloud for this night. It has been called by Oliver St. John Gogarty, in his *I Follow St. Patrick*, "the oldest and perhaps the most important document in British history."

More accurately called a *testimony* than a confession, it is too long to reproduce in full here (although actually not a very long document); so we have used the most exciting and interesting parts. Discussed as it is read, it will help give the family a right understanding of the greatness of this saint, his humility, his trials, his boyhood and manhood, and will discover for them, in this long-ago writing by St. Patrick, doctrines we are teaching our children today.

⟜

*Here Begin the Books of St. Patrick the Bishop*

1. I, Patrick, sinner, am the most illiterate and inconsiderable of all the faithful, and am despised in the hearts of many.

I had for father Calpumius, a deacon, one of the sons of Potitus, a presbyter, who belonged to the village of Bannavem Taberniae; for he owned a small farm hard by, where I was made captive.

121

The Year and Our Children

At the time I was about sixteen years old. I had no knowledge of the True God, and I was led to Ireland in captivity with many thousand others, according to our deserts, because we departed from God and did not keep His commandments, and we were not obedient to our priests, who were wont to admonish us for our salvation. And the Lord poured upon us the fury of His anger, and scattered us among many gentile nations, even unto the ends of the earth, where now my littleness may be seen among stranger folk. *[It is supposed that in describing his own sins he has been a bit hard on himself; that perhaps he was, first, an unenlightened Christian as compared with, later, a tremendously inspired one.]*

2. And there the Lord opened the understanding of my unbelief, so that although late, I might summon my faults to mind and turn with all my heart to the Lord my God, who regarded my low estate, and pitied my ignorance and youth, and kept watch over me before I knew Him or had attained discernment or could distinguish good from evil, and fortified me and comforted me as a father his son. *[There follows a long passage, very touching, wherein he acknowledges and apologizes for his lack of learning. It was an embarrassment he never shook off, although he was hardly what we would call uneducated. His early education had ended at fifteen; later, at around twenty-two, when he decided he wanted to be a priest, there arose his unalterable sense of inferiority when he compared his scholarship with those who had been students most of their young lives.]*

12. This I do know with full certainty, that before I was afflicted *[in capture and slavery]*, I was like a stone which lies in the deep mire; and He that is mighty came, and in His mercy lifted me up, and set me on the top of the wall.

16. Now after I came to Ireland, daily I pastured flocks, and constantly during the day I prayed. More and more there grew the

love of God and the fear of Him, and my faith increased, and my spirit was stirred up, so that in a single day I uttered as many as a hundred prayers, and nearly as many in the night so that I stayed even in the woods and the mountain. Before dawnlight I used to be roused to prayer, in snow, in frost, in rain. And I felt no harm, nor was there any slothfulness in me (as I now see), because then the spirit in me was fervent.

17. And there verily one night I heard in my sleep a voice saying to me, "You fast to good purpose, soon to go to your fatherland." And again, after a very little time, I heard the answer speaking to me, "See, your ship is ready." And it was not near, but was far off, about two hundred miles. And I had never been there, nor had I knowledge of any person there. And thereon shortly afterward, I took myself to flight and left the man with whom I had been for six years; and I came in the strength of God, who prospered my way for good, and I encountered nothing alarming until I came to that ship.

18. And on the very day I came, the ship sailed from its anchorage. And I declared that I had to sail away with them. And the shipmaster was displeased and replied harshly with anger. "On no account seek to go with us."

When I heard this, I departed from them to go to the hut where I was lodging; and on the way, I began to pray. And before I had completed my prayer, I heard one of them. He was shouting loudly after me, "Come quickly; these men are calling you."

19. And after three days, we reached land, and for twenty-eight days, we traveled through a desert; and food failed them and hunger overcame them. And one day, the shipmaster began to say to me, "How is this, you Christian? You say your God is great and almighty. Why, then, can't you pray for us? We're in danger of starvation. Hardly are we like to see a human being again."

Then I spoke plainly to them: "Turn in faith and with all your heart to the Lord my God, to whom nothing is impossible, so that He may send you food today for your journey, until you can eat no more, for everywhere He has plenty."

And by God's help, so it came to pass. Lo, a herd of swine appeared on the track before our eyes; and they killed many of them and spent two nights there, and were well refreshed, and their dogs were fed full, for many of them had fainted and were left half-dead by the way. And after this, they offered the fullest thanks to God, and I became an object of honor in their eyes, and from that day on, they had food in plenty. They even found wild honey and gave me a piece of it. But one of them said, "This is offered in sacrifice" [apparently pagan]. Thanks be to God, I tasted none of it.

23. Again . . . I was in Britain with my kin, who welcomed me as a son and in good faith besought me that now at least, after the great tribulations I had endured, I would not ever again go away from them. And there verily I saw in the night visions a man whose name was Victorious, coming as it were from Ireland with countless letters. He gave one of them to me, and I read the beginning of the letter, which was entitled, "The Voice of the Irish"; and while I was reading out the beginning of the letter, I thought that at that very moment, I heard the voice of those who lived beside the Wood of Focluth, which is near the western sea. And thus they cried out, as if from one mouth, "We beg you, holy boy, to come and walk among us yet again."

And I was deeply broken in heart, and could read no further, and so I awoke.

27. After thirty years had passed, they found [he is speaking of his elders in religion] as an occasion against me a matter which I had confessed before I became a deacon. In my anxiety, with sorrowing heart, I disclosed to my closest friend what I had done in my youth

on one day, no, in one hour, because I had not then triumphed. I cannot tell. God knows, if I was then fifteen years old, and I did not believe in the living God — nor had I believed from my infancy; I remained in death *[sin]* and unbelief until I was thoroughly chastened and humbled in truth by hunger and nakedness, and that daily.

29. Accordingly, on that day when I was rejected by the aforesaid persons whom I have described, during the night I saw in the night visions. There was a writing without honor against my face *[their accusations of him]*. And meanwhile I heard the Divine Answer speaking to me, "We have seen with wrath the face of So-and-so." (I suppress the name.) He did not say, "You have seen with wrath," but "We have seen with wrath," as if in that matter He linked Himself with me. As He said, "He that touches you is as he that touches the apple of my eye." *[And as He said: "Whatsoever you do to these, the least of my brethren, you do it to me."]*

35. A long task it is to narrate in detail the whole of my labor, or even parts of it. I shall briefly tell in what manner the most gracious God often delivered me from slavery and from the Twelve Perils by which my soul was beset, besides many plots and things which I am not able to express in words — lest I should tire out my readers. *[Bless him!]*

37. Many were the gifts proffered to me with wailing and with tears *[by those who wished him not to go back to Ireland]*. And I displeased them and also, against my wish, some of my elders. But through God's guidance, in no way did I acquiesce or surrender to them. Not my grace was it, but God, who conquered in me and resisted them all, so that I came to the Irish heathen to preach the Gospel and to endure insults from the unbelieving . . . and to meet many persecutions, even unto bonds; and so that I should give up my free condition for the profit of others.

38. Because I am greatly a debtor to God, who afforded me such great grace that through me many people should be regenerated to God and afterward confirmed, and that clergy should everywhere be ordained for them — for a people newly come to belief, whom the Lord took from the ends of the earth, as He promised of old through His prophets: ". . . I have set thee to be a light of the Gentiles, that thou should be for salvation unto the ends of the earth."

39. And there I wish to wait for the promise of Him who never disappoints.

40. For that reason, then, we ought to fish well and diligently, as the Lord forewarns and teaches, saying, "Come ye after me, and I will make you to become fishers of men . . ."

Therefore it was urgently necessary that we should spread our nets to take a great multitude and a throng for God, and that everywhere there should be clergy to baptize and exhort the poverty-stricken and needy folk, as the Lord in the Gospel warns and teaches, saying, "Go ye therefore now and teach all nations, baptizing them in the name of the Father and of the Son and of the Holy Spirit; teaching them to observe all things whatsoever I have commanded you: and lo, I am with you always, even unto the end of the world."

41. Whence Ireland, which never had the knowledge of God, but up to the present always adored idols and abominations — how has there lately been prepared a people of the Lord and the name given to them of Children of God? The sons of the Scots and the daughters of their chieftains are seen to become the monks and virgins of Christ.

42. But once especial there was one blessed lady of Scottic birth, noble of line, very lovely, and of full age, whom I myself baptized; and after a few days she came to me for a certain purpose. She disclosed to us that she had received from God a private

admonition, and it warned her to become a virgin of Christ and live closer to God.

Thanks be to God, on the sixth day after, most worthily and zealously she snatched at that vocation, as all the virgins of Christ do in like manner; not with the consent of their fathers; no, they endure persecution and lying reproaches from their kindred, and yet their numbers increase all the more and we cannot tell how many of our race are thus reborn there, besides widows and the continent. But the women who are held in slavery are in the worst toils. They constantly endure even unto terrors and threats. But the Lord gave grace to many of my handmaidens; for, although they are forbidden, they resolutely follow the example of the others. *[St. Brigid was a slave for a while.]*

43. Therefore, even if I should wish to depart from them, and thus proceeding to Britain — and gladly ready was I to do so — as to my fatherland and kindred; and not that only, but to go as far as Gaul *[France]*, to visit the brethren and behold the face of the saints of my Lord *[one of his kindred is thought to be St. Martin of Tours, and perhaps the saints he wished to see were those thought to have been his teachers, St. Honoratus of Lerins, St. Amator, and St. Germanus of Auxerre]* — God knows that I used to yearn deeply for it — yet I am bound in the Spirit, who witnesses to me that if I should do this, He would mark me as guilty; and I fear to lose the labor which I have started off — no, not I but Christ the Lord, who bade me come and be with them for the rest of my life, if the Lord so will, and if He should guard me from every evil way, so that I may not sin in His sight. *[Then he writes of how careful he has always been to be impeccably honest with these "gentiles among whom I dwell" for fear of blaspheming the name of God.]*

49. Although I be rude *[perhaps he means clumsy?]* in all things, still I have sought in some degree to keep watch over myself, both

for the Christian brethren and the virgins of Christ, and for the devout women who used to present me with little gifts, and throw on the altars various adornments, which I delivered back to them. And they were scandalized against me because I acted thus. But I did it out of my hope of immortality, that I might keep myself cautiously in all things, that the heathen, for one reason or another, might accept me or the ministry of my service, and that I should not, even in the smallest detail, give pretext to the unbelievers to defame and disparage.

50. Maybe, then, when I baptized so many thousands of men, I hoped from any one of them even as much as the half of scruple? *[A scruple is the smallest Roman unit of weight.]* Tell me and I shall restore it to you. Or when my trivial self had been the Lord's instrument for the ordaining of clergy on all sides, and I gave them my ministrations for nothing, if I required from any one of them even the price of my shoe, tell it against me, and I shall restore you the price and more.

51. I spent for you that they might receive me; and both among you and wherever I traveled for your sake, through many dangers, even to outlying regions beyond which no man, and where nobody had ever come to baptize or ordain clergy or confirm the folk, I have, by God's bounty, done everything diligently and joyfully for your salvation.

52. At times I used to give presents to the kings besides the wages I paid their sons, who went around with me; and yet they seized me once with my companions. And on that day, they most eagerly desired to slaughter me; but the time was not yet come. Everything they found upon us they plundered, and myself they bound with irons; and on the fourteenth day, the Lord freed me from their power; and whatever was our property was restored to us

for God's sake and the sake of the near friends whom we had provided beforehand.

53. You know also from your own experience how much I paid out to those who were Judges throughout all the districts which I more regularly visited; for I calculate that I distributed to them not less than the price of fifteen men, so that you might enjoy me and I might enjoy you ever in God. I do not regret it, nor consider it enough. Still I spend and will spend more. The Lord is mighty to grant me afterward to be myself spent for your souls.

55. But I see that already in this present world I am exalted beyond measure by the Lord. And I was not worthy, nor am I such that He should grant me this gift, since I know with full certainty that poverty and affliction become me better than riches and luxuries. Why, Christ the Lord was a poor man for our sakes. But I, wretched and stricken, possess no wealth even if I should wish for it; nor do I judge mine own self, for every day I expect either a violent death or to be defrauded or to be reduced into slavery, or some such disaster. But none of these things move me, on account of the promises of Heaven. I have cast myself into the hands of Almighty God, for He rules everywhere, as the prophet says: "Cast thy care upon God, and He shall sustain thee."

59. And if I ever accomplished aught in the cause of my God, whom I love, I beseech Him to grant me that I may shed my blood with those strangers and captives for His name's sake, even though I should lack burial itself, even though the dogs and the wild beasts most wretchedly should rend my corpse limb by limb or the fowls of the air should devour it. With perfect certitude, I think, if it should be my fate, I have gained a soul as profit with my body. For beyond all doubt we shall rise on that day in the crystal brightness of the sun; that is, in the Glory of Christ Jesus our Redeemer, as

sons of the living God and joint-heirs with Christ, conformed to His image which is to be. For of Him and through Him and in Him we shall reign.

62. But I pray those who believe and fear God, whosoever has deigned to scan and to take this writing which Patrick the Sinner, verily of no education, composed in Ireland, that none shall ever say it was my ignorance that achieved whatsoever tiny success was mine or whatever I showed in accordance with God's will; but make your judgment, and let it be most truly believed that it was the Gift of God.

And this is my Confession before I die.

There is nothing more sure to cut through the inadequacy of the green crepe paper, the top hats, the clay pipes, the golden harps, the potted clovers, the sugar shamrocks, the kelly-green cakes, than these fresh, beautiful, earnest words of St. Patrick himself.

*Some Gaelic Prayers*

As soon as we discovered "The Prayers of the Gael," a small volume of Irish prayers, we set about learning some. They are marvelously suited to children — and, of course, to grown-ups. Here is one to try for a change from your usual *Grace before Meals:*

BLESSING OF FOOD BEFORE MEALS
*May the blessing of five loaves and two fishes which
God divided among the five thousand men, be ours;
and may the King who made the division put luck
on our food and on our portion. Amen.*

And here is a prayer for the family to help them keep a sanctified Sunday. It is a lovely prayer to say in the car on the way to Mass:

PRAYER FOR SUNDAY

*A thousand welcomes to thee, Blessed Sunday,*
*Now coming to help us after the week:*
*My feet guide early to holy Mass,*
*Part my lips with blessed words,*
*Out of my heart banish wicked thoughts,*
*That I may look upon the Son of the Nurse.*
*Since it was the Son of God who bought us,*
*I rely for my soul's protection on Thee, O Jesus,*
*May God establish Thee within my heart,*
*Mayst Thou clear the stain and soil of sin from me*
*And fill mine eyes with tears of repentance. Amen.*

Here is another to be said by all together in the kitchen in the morning, before setting off to work or school:

PRAYER FOR THE DAY

*The grace of God and the blessing of Patrick*
*On all I see and all I undertake,*
*From the time I arise in the morning*
*Till I go to sleep at night. Amen.*

And this beautiful one for going to bed. First for the children, and later for the mothers and fathers:

PRAYER ON LYING DOWN

*May I lie down with God and may God*
   *lie down with me,*
*May I not lie with evil, nor evil lie with me.*
*Brigid's girdle around me,*
*Mary's mantle beneath me;*
*O Blessed Michael, hold my hand,*
*And make my peace with the Son of Grace.*

*If any evil thing pursue me,*
*May the Son of God protect me*
*For a year from this night,*
*And this night itself, and ever,*
*And always. Amen.*

There are many more, too many to include here. Best of all, for us, is the ancient *St. Patrick's Lorica,* or *Corslet,* or, as it is more commonly called, "The Breastplate of St. Patrick." We have used this for our family prayer on his feast day, with a grown-up reading one line and the family repeating it, then another line read and repeated. Carefully and distinctly recited, with a thought for what each line means, it is one of the most magnificent prayers in all the world. (We use it on other days, too.) The entire prayer is longer than this, but this excerpt is quite enough to tear your heart.

THE BREASTPLATE OF ST. PATRICK
*I rise up today*
*Thro' a mighty strength,*
*Thro' my invocation of the Trinity,*
*Thro' my belief in Its threeness,*
*Thro' my avowal of Its oneness*
*To the only Creator. . . .*
*I arise today,*

*God's strength guiding me,*
*God's might sustaining me,*
*God's wisdom directing me,*
*God's eye looking before me,*
*God's ear listening to me,*
*God's word speaking for me,*
*God's hand protecting me:*
*The way of God stretching out before me,*

*The shield of God as my shelter,*
*The hosts of God guarding me against the*
*    snares of the demons,*
*Against the temptings of my evil desire,*
*Against the evil inclination of my will,*
*Against everyone who plots against me,*
*Anear or afar, alone or in a multitude. . . .*
*Christ with me,*
*Christ before me,*
*Christ after me,*
*Christ within me,*
*Christ beneath me,*
*Christ above me,*
*Christ at my right hand,*
*Christ at my left hand,*
*Christ in my breadth,*
*Christ in my length,*
*Christ in my height,*
*Christ in the heart of everyone who thinks of me,*
*Christ in the mouth of everyone who speaks to me,*
*Christ in every eye that sees me,*
*Christ in every ear that hears me. . . .*

As a last treat, there is this marvelous bit from Mr. Gogarty's *I Follow St. Patrick* to be read aloud. First teach your children the Latin words *Gratias agamus*, meaning "Let us give thanks."

He was a "steadfast and unchanging man." That is the verdict of a contemporary witness — and the same a king — on him. The story arises from the fact that the Saint had set his heart on founding what was to be the headquarters of all his church organization on the Height of Macha, the present Armagh. Not far from his own dwelling at the eastern foot of the hill, King Daire granted him a little holding, on which a circular space was marked out one hundred and forty feet in diameter, and ramparted round with an earthen wall. Within were erected a Great House, a kitchen, and a little oratory, according to what seems to have been the plan of the primitive establishments of the Saint and his company. But the Saint wanted the site of what was to be his chief ecclesiastical city on the heights. At first the King refused to grant a space on the summit. He fell ill, but was restored to health by holy water which the Saint had blessed. Then the King paid a visit to the lowly settlement and presented the Saint with a bronze cauldron brought from over the sea. "*Gratias agamus,*" said the Bishop; but he said it rapidly (a man of his temperament must have spoken rapidly), in the Latin of the colonies, and it sounded in the way it has been preserved for us phonetically, "Gratzacham." This was not enough for Daire. His three-gallon cauldron acknowledged by but one word, and that unintelligible! He sent his servants to bring back that which the Bishop apparently could not appreciate. And these reported that all the Saint said as it was being taken away was "Gratzacham."

"What?" said the King, "Gratzacham?" He said that when it was being given, and he says it when it is being taken. It is a strong spell that is used for getting and losing. I will give him back his cauldron." And the King came with it and presented it in person: "Keep the cauldron, for you are a steadfast and unchanging man." And he gave him the land which was his heart's desire.

*Ah, St. Patrick, steadfast and unchanging man, pray for us!*

☙

# Chapter 9

# St. Joseph

Among the responsibilities that came crowding into St. Joseph's life after he discovered that all innocently he had taken as his betrothed the one who would be Mother of God, that which must have frightened him most, I should think, was that of being "father" to a Child who is God.

It was not that his love was wanting. Joseph had dedicated his life to God. He longed with an ardor like Mary's for the coming of the Messiah. A devout Jew felt so keenly the greatness and majesty and unspeakable mystery of God that even Christ, when He called His Apostles, let recognition of His divinity come to them slowly. To have known unmistakably at the outset would have put such a gulf between them as to make impossible the intimacy He needed with them in order to teach them as He wished. And here was Joseph, having lived a most holy life, deeply recollected, far advanced in prayer — asked to be "father" to the Messiah!

One gasps at this sort of thing. "But I'm afraid . . . I can't . . . I don't know . . . I'm not good enough . . . what will I *do?*" These must have been somewhat his sentiments. Then the angel said to him, "Do not fear. . . ." and we see that it was God's *will* that Joseph be Mary's husband. He could do what he could do; beyond that, he could do no more. Apparently it did not dawn on this humble man that *he could do what God had prepared him to do.*

Do not doubt that he had been prepared. St. Joseph did not just happen along during the preparation for the Redemption. He had been chosen, as Mary; and although he was not given her Immaculate privilege, in every way he was God's work. Strangely enough, what God needed for His divine Son was a father, and that was not a role to entrust to just anyone.

He was to be father in the everyday sense of the word. This Boy could not grow up and prepare for His mission out of some bizarre situation where there was no father. There must be nothing irregular. He must have a mother and a father, relatives, a craft, a home, a town — everything ordinary that boys have. At least they must have the appearance of the ordinary; if they were extraordinary, no one need know — now.

The only answer to the puzzle of how to raise the Child who was God was to raise Him as every Jewish boy was raised: with the help of God, *perfectly*. We assume, of course, perfectly. He was God. He was perfect. As though our Lady and St. Joseph were puppets with no will, no judgment, decisions of their own. She was full of grace; so her will in every matter was perfect. He was full of love of God and dedicated to Him; so with grace his will was perfect, too. But it is not as though they had no choices to make. Aside from the approval of his marriage, the message to go to Egypt, or the message to return, no divine revelations told Joseph how to father the Christ Child. He had what all Jewish fathers had as guide: the Law, and that was all. The pattern was given by God: parents have authority over their children; children are bound to respect and obey their parents. And St. Joseph had, as reservoir to draw on, his own rich personal life with God out of which he drew his wisdom and formed his decisions.

It was the father's role to decide where they would live, and Joseph had to make this decision a number of times. He must have learned once and for all on Christmas Eve that it would be up to him to decide. No angel appeared that night to show them a lodging.

It was his role to teach this Boy to pray the prescribed daily prayers, to conduct Him and His mother to synagogue, where He sat with His father, and on pilgrimage to the Temple in Jerusalem to offer sacrifice. He taught Him His trade and, with it, how to barter honestly, how to fix a just price for his work, how to evaluate wood, a respect for tools, the techniques of a good workman. He taught Him of crops, for almost every Jewish craftsman depended partly on the food he could grow to help support his family. If we read our Lord's parables over and see how many of them tell of the works of a man — building, planting, harvesting — we have a clue to the things Joseph must have talked about with Jesus. And although it was His Mother who formed His interior life as a Child, still there were long hours of meditation and recollection shared by Jesus and Joseph as they worked together in silence, praising God for the wood, for their hands, for the work He sent them, for the barter and monies paid them which "kept the family going."

If Joseph waited for some sign from this Boy that He could do His growing and learning without any help, it did not come. He did the things all boys did, but with a graciousness and beauty that must have made Joseph think of Adam before he destroyed the harmony of his nature.

Joseph must have wondered how He would redeem men. He must have watched Him sometimes and wondered when it would begin. He must have known, suddenly — and then as though he had always known it — that he would never see it.

Again and again, when there was something to learn, some counsel to be sought, this Boy must have come to him as quite the most ordinary boy would, and asked, "Father, do you think I should do it this way, or is it better another way?"

And Joseph, giving his best judgment and the reasons why, must have told him, as all fathers do, of some experience fetched up from his own youth, and afterward thought, "But He knew. He already knew about my boyhood. . . ."

But He gave no sign. Joseph was as fully and wholly and totally obligated to be father to this Child and husband to His Mother as any other Hebrew husband and father.

On the Cross, the Boy, grown to a man, said to St. John, "Behold thy Mother." Our present Holy Father[45] has said, "The mother of the Head is the mother of the Body." Then what of the father?

Pope Leo XIII tells of the father in his Encyclical *Quamquam Pluries*:

> [T]he Divine household, which Joseph governed as with paternal authority, contained the beginnings of the Church. The Virgin most holy is the mother of all Christians since she is the Mother of Jesus and since she gave birth to them on the mount of Calvary amid the unspeakable sufferings of the Redeemer. Jesus is, as it were, the first-born of Christians, who are His brothers by adoption and redemption. From these considerations we conclude that the blessed Patriarch [Joseph] must regard all the multitude of Christians who constitute the Church as confided to his care in a certain special manner. *This is his numberless family,* scattered throughout all lands, *over which he rules with a sort of paternal authority, because he is the husband of Mary and the father of Jesus Christ.* Thus it is conformable to reason and in every way becoming to Blessed Joseph, that as once it was his sacred trust to guard with watchful care the family of

---

[45] Pope Pius XII.

Nazareth, no matter what befell, so now, by virtue of his heavenly patronage, he is to turn to protect and to defend the Church of Christ [*italics mine*].

With Christ as our Head, we are the Church. We are St. Joseph's family.

Family life was the only life St. Joseph knew. He was not a monk or a hermit or a priest or a bishop. He was a husband and father. It is significant. *The Child was the Priest.* The father taught the Child who became High Priest, who offered Himself in sacrifice; who paid for the sins of men. For all the years He spent with His father, He showed the mark. He was formed by the father as well as by the mother; Joseph and Mary, husband and wife, father and mother, prepared this Boy for His vocation.

⌒

### St. Joseph and Vocation

Of all the claims families make on the solicitude of St. Joseph in this age and world, this seems most urgent: that together with helping us to sanctify family life, he help our children to discover their vocations. Vocation can mean only one thing to the Christian: the way to God. It is how He wants us to go to Him.

A vocation is God's secret. We see signs. We try to help our children discover their gifts and use them, but God is the only One who knows. Every day is an unfolding, and growing up is the discovering, but we can only wonder until it is revealed. And some never know, because the tragedy of our age — or one of them (there are so many) — is that men are dedicated to self-discovery, and discovering themselves, they often go no further, and never discover God. *Self* makes no sense without its relation to God. What is great about our selves is that they are made in the image and likeness of God, immortal, imperishable.

Vocation, as everyone understands, is a calling. If so, Someone must have called.

It is no longer sufficient to know that you want to be a doctor. It is necessary to know that being a doctor, if for you, is your way to God. If you are a doctor, then you must be one in Christ, and through Christ, and by Christ; and it is Christ you will see in your patients.

The same with a lawyer, and a musician, and a typist, and a telephone operator, and a teacher, and a singer, and a cop. And if you are meant to be a ditch-digger, praise God for that; in His will, if it is digging ditches, you will be happiest and best able to find your way to Him.

It is not sufficient for a parent to want his son to be a doctor, if he is called to it. He must want him to be a doctor who is a saint, or a lawyer who is a saint, or a musician saint, a typist saint, a telephone-operator saint, a teacher saint, a singer saint, a cop saint, or a ditch-digging saint.

This is it, we have said. Medicine is for me. Oh, no, it isn't. Medicine is for God. *It*, for me, is Heaven.

And what of the priests and religious?

Of all the vocations, the one to religion must be most carefully tended. Dioceses, to say nothing of missions, are hard-pressed for priests and Sisters, and this can mean only one thing: God sends the vocations, but they are lost somewhere between the first wondering and the last decision. Worldliness, mediocrity, impiety, ridicule — one could list all the things that probably contribute to lost vocations, and they would fill this page. We are not concerned with what loses vocations, but what finds them. To know that the family is made by God in order to produce saints for God; to watch and listen and pray and serve Him in it; to ask at every turn, "What is Your will?" and try to do it is all He asks.

He will make His will known, and with grace we can do it. But we must pray to know it, and we must keep hands off when we begin to see it. It is a grave thing to tamper with any kind of a vocation because it relates not only to one person and his way to Heaven, but to all in the Mystical Body. St. Paul in his letter to the Romans says:

> Each of us has one body, with many different parts, and not all these parts have the same function; just so, we, though many in number, form one body in Christ, and each acts as the counterpart of another. The spiritual gifts we have differ, according to the special grace which has been assigned to each. If a man is a prophet, let him prophesy as far as the measure of his administration, the teacher, with his work of teaching, the preacher, with his preaching. Each must perform his task well; giving alms with generosity, exercising authority with anxious care or doing works of mercy smilingly.

If there is a man who has been given the talent to be a carpenter, it is a grave wrong to make him try to be a lawyer. God has certain work for this man with the carpenter's gift, at certain places, among certain people; to these he will be another Christ. Certainly grace can compensate for the mistakes we have made in choosing, but much better to ask for the grace to choose right in the first place. And if it is wrong to misguide through clumsiness or ignorance or malice the vocations of those who work with their hands, how much more wrong to injure the budding of a vocation to serve as Christ Himself, distributing through the priesthood the works of the Spirit.

In this age of the lay apostolate, there are new vocations that take parents by surprise, vocations to family service that look like "being a maid," vocations to virginity that look like being "an old maid," vocations involving secular institutes that bind with solemn vows, as well as vocations to the cloister and the monastery.

There are vocations, among families, to poverty, and suffering, and exile. Perhaps they are not new at all but only look new, because the drums beat so loudly about "the high standard of living," "the modern way of life," comfort, pleasure, contraception, and abortion — and should they or should they not be legalized?

Not long ago, a Catholic college president told a large audience that creative talent — especially for journalism — was not less abundant than it used to be, but that the young men who possessed it were cautioned by their parents not to take the risk, "stick their necks out," when there was more and surer money to be made in law, medicine, television, engineering, and public relations. Without realizing that it was happening in them, parents have let success became synonymous with *virtue*.

So the family must pray always, and earnestly, about its vocations, especially to St. Joseph. He tended the vocation of the Son of God. This is the intention of a family novena, starting on March 10 and ending with Mass and Holy Communion (daily if possible) on March 19, the feast of St. Joseph.

⌒

### A Novena to St. Joseph

A novena may be any acceptable prayers we choose, used faithfully for nine days, with Confession and Holy Communion received at least once. We made up our own novena, including in it the prayers that Jesus heard St. Joseph say morning and evening, and which He Himself said when He was old enough. Recited from memory, these prayers (called the *Shema*) were part of *their* family prayer. Along with others, they were written on parchment called the *Mezuzah* and kept in a wooden tube fastened to the doorpost of the house at Nazareth; and also with other texts written on parchment and contained in small square boxes called *phylacteries*, which a pious Jew fastened to his forehead and arm (as many still do) when he recited the prayers. The Pharisees used to make their phylacteries very ornate and wear them in public to attract attention, and our Lord rebuked them for it: "Boldly written are the texts they carry. . . ."[46]

The first prayer taught to Jewish children is from Deuteronomy 6:4 ff.:

> Hear, O Israel, the Lord our God is one Lord.
> Thou shalt love the Lord thy God with thy whole heart,
>     and with thy whole soul, and with thy whole strength,
> And these words which I command thee this day,
>     shall be in thy heart:
> And thou shalt tell them to thy children, and thou shalt
>     meditate upon them sitting in thy house, and walking
>     on thy journey, sleeping and rising.
> And thou shalt bind them as a sign on thy hand,
>     and they shall be and shall move between thy eyes.
> And thou shalt write them in the entry,
>     and on the doors of thy house.

Loving the words of God literally, they did tell them to their children, meditate upon them sitting in their houses, walking on their journeys, binding them on their hands and between their eyes, and writing them in the entry and on the doors of their houses. This was the foundation of all their prayer. Plainly, with what follows, it lies at the heart of a Christian's vocation.

The second part of morning prayer was followed by verses from Deuteronomy 11, beginning with verse 13:

> If, then, you obey my commandments,
>     which I command you this day,

---

[46] Cf. Matt. 23:5.

*That you love the Lord your God, and serve Him*
    *with all your heart, and with all your soul:*
*He will give to your land the early rain and*
    *the latter rain, that you may gather in your*
    *corn, and your wine, and your oil, and*
    *your hay out of the fields to feed your*
    *cattle, and that you may eat and be filled.*
*Beware, lest perhaps your heart be deceived,*
    *and you depart from the Lord, and serve*
    *strange gods, and adore them:*
*And the Lord, being angry, shut up heaven,*
    *that the rain come not down, nor the earth yield*
    *her fruit, and you perish quickly from the excellent*
    *land, which the Lord will give you.*
*Lay up these my words in your hearts and minds,*
    *and hang them for a sign on your hands,*
    *and place them between your eyes,*
*Teach your children that they meditate on them when*
    *thou sittest in thy house, and when thou walkest*
    *on the way. And when thou liest down and risest up.*
*Thou shalt write them upon the posts and the doors of*
    *thy house. That thy days may be multiplied, and the*
    *days of thy children in the land which the Lord*
    *swore to heaven hangeth over the earth.*

These prayers will probably have to be explained to the children, but they are not difficult to understand. Once they begin to "see" with the poetic imagery of scriptural language (of which the Psalms are the classics), we shall have added another dimension to their spiritual perception.

The first part points out to us that to love God is the most important thing of all, and we must meditate on it often. This is possible many times a day: we have only to work to form the habit. We may turn to Him in our mind for merely a moment, frequently, and say, "I love You." Little children will do this eagerly, aloud, if their parents — particularly their mothers, who have them at their heels all day long — will help them.

The second part promises, on condition that, loving Him, we also obey Him and serve Him with all our hearts and souls, that He will "give to our land early rain and latter rain," which is like divine grace to make us faithful; that we may gather in "corn and wine and oil and hay out of the fields," like the fruits of a virtuous life; that "we may eat and be filled," which is the promise of eternal happiness to our souls, so hungry for Heaven.

But beware, lest our hearts are deceived, and we depart from the Lord and serve strange gods and adore them, and the Lord be angry and shut up Heaven. It is not hard to see what this means. There are so many strange gods to serve and adore. All the vanities and conceits since the beginning of sin are still about, camouflaged in glamors, enticing us from the pages of magazines, the screens of television sets and movie theaters, the copy in the ads, the shiny, glittery, shapely, slick media the Devil uses now to peddle his wares. We must watch and pray "lest we fall into temptation"; lest we "perish quickly from the excellent land which the Lord will give us."

What to do with my life: in every line of these prayers there is guidance. They are not prayers of petition, leaving us still in the dark, but prayers that speak to us and tell us that He will reveal and make fruitful our vocations in His good time.

Our family has added a prayer we have had tucked away in an Irish prayer book for a long time, written in handwriting Granny Newland cannot identify, but it must have belonged to one of the cousins or aunts. We think it is as beautiful as any prayer to St. Joseph that we have ever heard.

*O glorious St. Joseph, spouse of the Immaculate Virgin,*
*obtain for me a pure, humble, and charitable mind,*
*and perfect resignation to the divine will. Be my guide,*
*father, and model through life that I may merit to die*
*as thou didst, in the arms of Jesus and Mary. Amen.*

It is an Italian custom to serve very elegant cream puffs made with cottage cheese and almond flavoring on the feast of St. Joseph, but we have substituted plain cream puffs (although if you do not have cream puffs as part of your regular fare, they should hardly be called plain!). They are very easy to make for all their complicated look, and every cookbook has a recipe. Filled with whipped cream or lemon custard or chocolate pudding, they are cheered into the dining room. We make enough to send a St. Joseph's gift to the neighbors on this feast day.

At the head of the table is William Joseph, otherwise known as Father; and he is flanked by Peter Joseph, until lately known as St. Me. In his tenderer years, he could not understand that sanctity does not come automatically to those who are named after saints. Now, at the ripe age of seven, he admits the difficulties and suspects that prayer and work have something to do with it. He is "most awfully glad" of his patron. We have hopes that he will be St. Him after all.

*Patron of families, patron of fathers, patron of the Universal Church: St. Joseph, pray for us.*

Chapter 10

≈

# Ash Wednesday and Lent

It seems such a short time ago that we sought the Infant Christ at Bethlehem, adored Him, and were sure that we would never offend Him; and already on Septuagesima Sunday[47] in the Introit[48] of the Mass He cries out with the weight of our sins: "The groans of death surrounded me and the sorrows of hell encompassed me. . . ."[49]

It is but three weeks before Lent when Septuagesima arrives, and this is a warning. We have sinned, and the time is coming when we must do penance.

When we are born, we are really very like Adam right after his sin, although there is this difference: we have been redeemed, and at that time, he was not. We may do what he wished he could do. We may be born again in Baptism and start afresh, although in a fallen world, our souls now radiant with divine life burning there. Lent is the spanning of all that happened between Original Sin and Baptism. It is the summing up and the climax of what started with Christmas.

[47] The third Sunday before Lent.

[48] Used formerly in the liturgy, the Introit is a fragment of a psalm with its antiphon sung while the celebrant approaches the altar. — ED.

[49] Cf. Ps. 17:5-6 (RSV = Ps. 18:4-5).

The greatest of all mysteries is that God should love man so much. When man sinned and forfeited his right to eternal life, and there was nowhere perfect obedience or flawless love in any man to merit Heaven, He became a man in order that He might pay the debts of the family He had chosen to join. It is a kind of divine bargain They made, almost impossible to understand unless we put it in our own words. It is as though the Father had said to the Son, "How can we work it out so man may still live with us forever as we planned?" And as though the Son replied, "If there were but one perfect man, it could be done. One perfect sacrifice would pay their debt. One surrender of a man as perfect as Adam was when we created him. Alas, there is none."

Then it is as though They gazed into one another with that Love that is the Spirit of both, and They knew how it could be done. In Their gaze, a longing still burned for the creatures who had rebelled. With a look of infinite love, the Father sent the Son and He became the Man. "O happy fault, that merited so great a Redeemer."

*Sin and Sacraments*

When we teach our children about sin, and about the difference between mortal and venial sin, it is easy to leave them with the impression that as long as it is not mortal sin, they are safe: venial sin doesn't really count. This is a grave mistake. Each venial sin is a surrender of some of the soul's vitality, an impairment of its splendor, for the soul, like the body, has the faculty of forming habits. Continual venial sin unresisted prepares the way for mortal sin. Every sin is a rebellion, a choice of my will instead of God's, a repetition of Adam's fault in the garden; and it is important that children (as well as their elders!) understand this. These choices between my way and God's way are forming habits in me. It is not so easy to get my way this time; next time let God have His way. Having my way this time means that next time it will be even more difficult for me to give God His way.

This calls for constant checking of impatience on the part of parents when they are chastising and punishing, so that they may include in their correction of children a reminder of the effect on the soul of even venial sin; how important it is to be truly sorry for sin, to do penance sincerely. Correction must be gentle and earnest, even affectionate if possible, or a child will not be able to calm his rebellion, anger, fear — whatever it is — to listen or take it seriously. Then the punishment that follows seems far more just and has a salutary purpose. I admit that this is sometimes terribly difficult because parents are not without their own weaknesses, and become involved emotionally when there has been repeated rebellion; but it is easier if we keep our gaze focused on the forming of our children's souls first, and only secondly their bodies.

Happily we have renewal in the sacraments after we have sinned — sacraments Christ gave His Church as a bridegroom gives wedding jewels to his bride. These are splendid refreshment for His members, fountains gushing from the opened side of the Man who is God and our Brother.

Lent is our time to ponder these things, from the very beginning in sin to our renewal in Baptism. The Church says to us, "Look — you are dust. See what it has cost Him to love you!"

Until a few years ago, we did not know that it was proper, if the family could not get to church on Ash Wednesday, to burn the previous year's blessed palms at home, read the blessing of the ashes, sprinkle them with holy water, and use them as a sacramental. This is not the same as having a priest bless them, but it is an acceptable substitute.

The *Blessing of the Ashes* (in the daily missal) has a number of parts that are very beautiful, but one that is especially interesting to our children is the Fourth Prayer of the blessing, with reference to the Ninivites:

> *Almighty and eternal God, who didst grant the*
> *remedy of Thy pardon to the Ninivites doing penance*
> *in ashes and sackcloth, mercifully grant that we*
> *may so imitate them in our attitude that like them*
> *we may obtain forgiveness. Through our Lord. Amen.*

We have a soft spot for the Ninivites because they were Gentiles, and Jonah refused to warn them of God's anger over their sins because of his scorn for Gentiles. The purpose of God's command, which Jonah disobeyed, with dire consequences, was to teach that the Jews, even though they were the Chosen Ones, were not to despise Gentiles. The Ninivites are a *type* of ourselves, and this prayer of the blessing asks that we may be given the grace to imitate in our customs the spirit of their forty days' fast in sackcloth and ashes, which is a *type* of our Lent.

We have a special Jonah activity (explained later) for Holy Week that is fun and teaches well. The first reminder of it with this reference to Ninivites on Ash Wednesday helps the children to span with their minds the whole of Lent, rather than seeing it merely as endless day following endless day. We must try always to give them a sense of the whole, the great pattern: the Fall, the Promise, the Redemption.

After reading the *Blessing of the Ashes*, the family kneels and the father or oldest grown-up present follows the example of the priest when he signs the forehead of each with a cross of ashes, saying: "Remember, man, that you are dust and to dust you will return." And the mother may mark the forehead of the kneeling father.

It is an odd smell, the smell of burning ashes. It fills the house with a faint acrid smoke. No other day do you smell it. It seems to be particularly fitting for the first day of Lent. The Lesson for Ash Wednesday tells who is to observe these forty days:

> Blow a trumpet in Zion, sanctify a fast, call a solemn assembly, gather together the people, sanctify the Church, assemble the ancients, gather together the little ones and them that suck at the breast: let the bridegroom go forth from his bed and the bride out of her bridechamber. . . ."[50]

No one is left out, not even the babies, because the terrible price paid on Good Friday was to buy freedom from exile for all, and each one is more precious to the Son of God than all the wealth of the earth.

"Do you know, dear, that if there had been no one but you, He would have done it all the same? That is how He loves you. That is how much He wants you. You are His beloved, and He would have given His life for you alone." This is unbelievable, but it is true; so they must be told.

⤚

### The Spirit of Lent

The young and the old may not be bound by the fast, but they are bound by its spirit, each according to his capacity. If we feel that it is unnatural to ask penances of children while they are still very young — penances within their reach — we forget that self-denial must be learned very young, that it is the forming of character, that the very grace of their Baptism flows from the Cross. The end of the penitential seasons imposed by the Church is not mere performance. The Church is a wise mother, who knows that the cutting away of self-will frees our souls for a more radiant love affair with Christ. If we think of the penance without pondering its

[50] Cf. Joel 2:15-16.

effect, we misunderstand it. It is not over and done with the doing but will bear fruit, if it is done with the right spirit; not alone by the piling up of "treasure in Heaven" but by an increase in our taste for God, a change in the habits of our souls.

Our Lord tells us how to behave during Lent when He speaks to us in the Ash Wednesday Gospel (Matt. 6:16-21):

> When you fast, be not as the hypocrites, sad. For they disfigure their faces, that they may appear unto men to fast. Amen, I say to you, they have received their reward. But thou, when thou fastest, anoint thy head and wash thy face, that thou appear not to men to fast, but to thy Father who is in secret; and thy Father, who seeth in secret, will repay thee. Lay not up to yourselves treasures on earth, where the rust and moth consume, and where thieves break through and steal. But lay up to yourselves treasures in Heaven, where neither the rust nor moth doth consume, and where thieves do not break through nor steal. For where thy treasure is, there is thy heart also.

So let us remember, when we choose something to give up: no moaning and groaning! Hypocrites (our Lord was talking about the Pharisees) make much of their performances because they want attention. That being their motive, He says, they already have their reward: attention. There will be opportunities, before Lent is over, for us to attract attention; but so long as this is not our motive, we can accept and use whatever God permits to come to us.

A father will be asked by business associates why he, too, doesn't order steak for lunch. One mother will be asked by fellow club-members why she doesn't eat sandwiches and cake after their evening business meeting. Some children will be asked why they say "No, thank you," to proffered candies at school, to decline an invitation to a movie during Lent, or do not join with others to watch a television show. These are the opportunities, with many more, to give reasons "for the faith that is in you." It is as necessary to give an honest explanation if one is asked, as it is to keep quiet about it if one is not. God chooses His own time and place to teach the lesson of good example; our part is merely the good example.

"Anoint thy head; wash thy face. . . ." Be cheerful! The Pharisees wore gloomy looks and long faces to indicate the great anguish their interior purifications cost them. Not for us. Our Lord suggests that we "anoint" our heads — that is, prepare ourselves as though we were going to a banquet. Look cheery and bright even if it is Lent and we miss the between-meal snacks. Our Father in Heaven sees what it is costing us. One of the Lenten resolves in our family was to omit from all conversation the familiar groan "I'm *starving.*" Then He tells us to lay up our treasure in Heaven, because where your treasure is, there your heart is also.

⌒

### Lent at Home

It is hard to keep track of this treasure that is laid in Heaven if you are quite small and six weeks drag out like six years. We have made this part of the effort visible for the children so that they might see that they were accomplishing something. On or about Ash Wednesday, we dye lima beans purple to be used as counters in a jar. Beans, because they are seeds which, if put in the ground, appear to die only to spring forth with new life. This is what our Lord said we must do if we would have life in Him. He who seems to lose his life shall gain it. The beans remind us that daily death to self in one self-denial after another is the dying that will find for us new life in Him.

"Try to surrender your will to Him, dear, so He may have His will in you." It is excruciatingly difficult, but one must begin. And they do understand, because we have discovered that as they grow a little older, they no longer need the beans — they see in their minds what they are doing.

We dye little pieces of cloth to use as purple shrouds for our pictures and statues on Passion Sunday, as the shrouds are used in church. This is to remind us that with Passion Sunday, the last, most solemn and sorrowful week of Lent has begun. One year we dyed a square of fine soft wool to make a cope for our Infant of Prague. (Instruction: You will now throw out the dye, like a good girl. Otherwise everyone in the family will be trying to dye things in purple.)

Next, we make a candelabrum for the Stations of the Cross. For children the Stations of the Cross can conceivably mean nothing better than continual bobbings up and down with prayers. This sounds frightful, but it is true. We have somewhat the same problem teaching them to love and to know the Stations as we have with the Rosary. So we decided to make a set of candles in a candelabrum to be used after the fashion of *Tenebrae*, the dramatic service in Holy Week, to help them love the Stations and want to say them nightly during Lent (we live too far out in the country to get to church in the evenings).

Twelve candles in one long candelabrum, or two short candelabra holding six candles apiece are needed. The candelabra may be made a number of ways: a length of board with twelve holes bored for the candles; two shoe boxes with six holes apiece for the candles, or two candelabra made with plaster of paris, which is poured into two empty Kleenex boxes (one at a time!), and the candles (six of each) held in place for a few moments until the plaster hardens. The box is easily pulled away when the plaster is hard. After twenty-four hours, the candelabrum is dry enough to be carried to wherever you will use it. We keep ours on the mantel. We use white candles. The candelabrum may be painted black.

Together with these, we use a crucifix and a booklet of meditations suitable for children, although we do not always read these. Often they are used only to acquaint the family with each Station, letting some member supply a short meditation "out of his head." Whichever, the meditations must be kept short and, if possible, related to something familiar in daily life.

We light all twelve candles at the start, and put out the other lights in the room, leaving one lighted in another room so that little ones will not be frightened by complete darkness. After each Station is identified, we genuflect and say the traditional prayer:

*We adore Thee, O Christ, and we praise Thee,*
*because by Thy holy Cross Thou hast redeemed the world.*

Other prayers are optional. The Stations may be properly said in a church by going from one Station to another and merely making a meditation at each. For the sake of uniformity and in order to include what to our children is synonymous with devotional "praying," we say, after the short meditation, an Our Father, a Hail Mary, and a Glory Be. Then one of the children puts out a candle for that Station. They take turns, a different child putting out the candles every night. When we have finished the twelfth Station, *Jesus Dies on the Cross*, the last candle is snuffed, and the room is in complete darkness. If you were there, they would explain it to you this way: "It's because He was the Light of the World, and when He died, the Light was gone out of the world."

You start remembering — all the way back to Advent, when the wreath and its weekly growing light anticipated the coming of the Light of the World; back to St. Lucy, whose feast and whose name anticipated the coming of the Light of the World; back to the Christ candle, lighted at midnight on Christmas Eve to tell us that the Light had come into the world. He is our Light, our Sun, our All.

*The Practice of Silence*

The meditations for the Stations of the Cross are most fruitful if they relate to daily life some trial we are struggling with *now*. For example, our Lord's *silence* when He was condemned to death, when He was tormented by the soldiers, or when He fell under the weight of the Cross — this can be related to that commonplace of childhood: bickering. Bickering is a form of verbal cannibalism. The one who holds out longer with his pecking at another is victor, having reduced the victim to tears, goaded him to losing his temper, striking, or some other form of retaliation, which is all reported as an unprovoked injustice as follows:

"But I didn't do anything. Nothing. I just said . . ."

*"I just said"* is himself far more culpable, usually, than the poor soul he has goaded beyond endurance. There is no real remedy for this but silence on the part of victims.

Abstinence from it on the part of attackers is the perfect solution, of course, but if someone does start, silence will stop him. This, however, is awfully hard on the one who is silent, because this is how bickering goes (as if you didn't know):

"You pig. You took the biggest."

"I did not, and I'm not a pig."

"You are too."

"I am not."

"You are too. Pig!"

"I am not a pig. I'm not. I'm not a pig I'm not a pig I'm not a pig!"

"You are too. You are a pig you are a pig you are a pig."

"I'm not I'm not I'm not."

"You are you are you are."

This could go on for an hour if Mother didn't begin to froth at the mouth. Whereas the silence treatment winds up the conversation (if you can call it that) as follows:

"You pig. You took the biggest."

"I did not. And I'm not a pig."

"You are too."

*Silence.*

In other words, you *are* a Pig.

O cruel silence . . .

But children well understand that no one is really a pig; this is only a game to see who can make the other lose his temper first. It is ugly and mean; and the winner is usually the older child because he knows the extent of the younger's endurance. Out of his own store of unavenged wrongs, he chooses this way to refresh a bruised ego.

If we have taught them what our Lord said must be the very basis for our behavior, we have *the* point of departure. "Whatsoever you do to the least of my brethren, you do it to me."[51] Learning this, we know what we must know in order to put meditations on the Passion together with events out of daily life and discover how to use them. Then we can see — and children can see it — that to provoke a brother or a sister is to provoke Christ; to be silent under provocation is to be silent with Christ.

It is not good to make such accusations while saying the Stations, but rather to connect the meditations with these real problems (names of particular children omitted), and return to the principles when we are on the scene of abuses that we must correct.

"You are teasing Christ when you tease your brother. It is the same. *Whatsoever you do . . .*, He said. You torment him just for the fun of it the way the soldiers tormented our Lord. Yet you really love him, as you really love our Lord. Keep these things in the front of your mind during Lent, and try to bite your tongue when

[51] Cf. Matt. 25:40.

you are tempted to unkindness. Each time you keep from saying something unkind, it is a triumph of grace, and our Lord will strengthen you with grace for the next time. There are powerful graces coming to us during Lent, and we must try to use them to rid ourselves of our faults so that on Easter we can be free of them, like the newly baptized are free of Original Sin."

Impossible? Not really, although it will probably take a lifetime to do it. But it is the goal, and especially during Lent it is the spirit of the preparation: to be as those newborn, on Easter morning.

If we are spectators to such a moral victory, we must be sure to congratulate the hero. "Darling, I heard N. today when he called you a pig and tried to make you angry. It was wonderful, the way you didn't answer back and only walked away. You used silence the way our Lord used it, the way He wants you to use it. When you are silent in union with Him, you are growing in the likeness of Christ."

When Dominic Savio[52] was silent before an unjust accusation, he shamed the other boys into admitting their guilt. This is often the effect of heroic efforts to reach out to Christ and bear hurts with Him. Grace is the invisible ingredient in all these struggles for perfection.

For every honest effort, one may put a bean in the jar. There are beans for all kinds of things: no desserts, no jumping for the telephone (a genius in our midst suggested this to eliminate violent jostling, wrestling, racing, leaping, and tugging — an excruciating discipline); no complaining about anything; doing chores promptly; no weekly penny for candy, and many more, including that magnificent and most glorious of all: coming when called. All who do this are known as *St. Theresas*. Actually, when you scan

---

[52] St. Dominic Savio (1842-1857), student of St. John Bosco, known for doing even the smallest things out of love for God.

the long list of them, they amount to what spiritual directors call the "interior mortifications."

Our mantel is bare this season except for the two candelabra with their twelve candles and the crucifix between them. Even the bread and the bakings speak to us of Lent. Crosses of seeds decorate the bread (because when you see the seeds, you remember about "die so you may live"), and on biscuit crusts and meat pies, symbols of the Passion are cut.

⌒

*Laetare Sunday*

"Laetare Sunday," the fourth Sunday of Lent, gets its name from the Introit of its Mass:

> Rejoice [*laetare*], O Jerusalem: and come together all you that love her: rejoice with joy, you that have been in sorrow: that you may exult, and be filled from the breasts of your consolation. I rejoiced at the things that were said to me: we shall go into the house of the Lord.

It is as though, hardly able to wait, the Church (the new Jerusalem) bursts forth with a premature shout of joy. It is really not a secret, she seems to sing, what is going to happen. Because God has promised it from the beginning. Mankind is going to be redeemed. Baptism will wash away Original Sin. The flesh of the Son of God is going to be daily bread.

This day rose-colored vestments are permitted, with flowers on the altar and organ music with the choir. You will find in most missals a note about the ancient custom of blessing a rose on this Sunday. This explains the rose vestments. This custom has apparently fallen from use, but according to the *St. Andrew Missal*, "even nowadays, the Pope sometimes blesses a golden rose (or a branch or bunch of roses) and sends it to a Catholic queen: so

The Year and Our Children

Pope Pius XI, in 1923, presented one to Victoria, Queen of Spain, and in 1925, to Elizabeth, Queen of the Belgians."

So we may use flowers, too, on our previously bared mantel-piece, a rose (one is not too costly) to arrange with a bit of green beside the crucifix, recalling all these other things and also that Mary, the Mystical Rose, bore the Son of God, who wins for us our redemption.

Laetare Sunday was also called *Mothering Sunday* long ago in England. It was a custom for all those who lived away from home (such as serving maids in London) to bake a simnel cake and take it home as what we would call a Mother's Day present. Various recipes call for plums in such a cake, or for orange and lemon peel, giving considerable room to indulge personal taste. [Note: If anyone is going to bake one for me, I would like a chocolate cake with peppermint icing and bitter chocolate melted over the top.]

One other thing must be fetched and put in our house where we will see it and think: a branch of thorn. If you do not live in the country with a woods to walk to where thorn apple grows, or in the suburbs where the yards are shaded by locust trees, or on a plot of ground hemmed in with a barberry thorn hedge, you might still go to the florist or to the potted plant department in the Five-and-Ten and find a thorny cactus. They are tiny, but the thorns are sharp. Even in a small apartment they would make a thoughtful centerpiece for the table where lenten meals are eaten.

For Him to redeem us was not an easy thing. Jesus hurt.

Chapter 11

❧

# Holy Week and Easter

Once when our Lord was going about healing, they brought to Him a man who was blind and dumb and possessed by a devil, and He cured him and drove out the devil. Then the Pharisees, bitter in their hearts to see that He could do these things, accused Him of casting out devils by the power of the Devil.

Our Lord turned on them. That was ridiculous, He said, and He likened the soul of the man to a kingdom in which the King, if he held the kingdom, would not war against himself to drive himself out of his own kingdom. If the Devil possessed a soul, he would not come to the aid of a man who was trying to drive the devil out of the soul. And He warned the Pharisees in very strong language that to sin against the Holy Spirit, which is to deny the known truth when you know it is the truth, was an unforgivable sin and would not be forgiven in this world or in the world to come (which would mean Purgatory).

So the slippery, sly Pharisees asked Him, "Master, we would see a sign from Thee." As though they had not just seen a very great sign, a miracle, when He had healed the blind and dumb man and driven out his devil. This made our Lord very angry indeed, and He must have shouted at them.

He would not give them a sign, He said, because they were evil and adulterous; the only sign they would be given would be the

161

sign of Jonah the prophet. "For even as Jonah was in the belly of the fish three days and three nights, so will the Son of Man be three days and three nights in the heart of the earth."[53] (So the story of Jonah is a prophecy. We never realized that, all these years.)

This story from the Gospel of St. Matthew, chapter 12, beginning with verse 22, is the Gospel for the Mass on Ember Wednesday, the first week in Lent. It is a good Gospel to read aloud together. Then, in order to see exactly what did happen to Jonah, find the book of Jonah in the Old Testament and read it aloud (it is very short).

Once a little girl said to Monica, "I believe all the stories in the Bible but one: that silly story about Jonah and the whale. Anybody who knows anything knows a man couldn't live inside of a fish for three nights and three days."

Monica said (and she was quite small), "Oh well, I guess if God could make the world out of nothing, He could make a man live inside a fish if He wanted to." And that was that.

Jonah was commanded by God to warn the people of Ninive that their wickedness would be punished. He would destroy them and their city. But Jonah was afraid (they were that wicked, in addition to being Gentiles), so he hurried off to the seashore and boarded a ship bound in the opposite direction. Then God sent a storm on the sea to sink the ship, and the captain and crew tried throwing the cargo overboard to lighten it, but in vain. Finally the captain ran down to the hold to find Jonah and cried out in words like this: "Why are you asleep? Get up, and pray to your God to ask Him to save us, or we will perish!"

In the meantime, up on deck the sailors became suspicious that there was more to the situation than met the eye; so they decided

---

[53] Matt. 12:40.

to draw lots to see if God would indicate who was to blame. They did this, and it came to light that Jonah was to blame. Then they asked him who he was, and where he was going, and whence he came; and Jonah told them he was running away from God. So the sailors asked what they should do to him, and Jonah admitted there was nothing to do but throw him in the sea. The sailors must have been loath to do this; they even tried to row back to land, but to no avail. So finally and regretfully they threw Jonah into the sea.

"Now, the Lord prepared a great fish to swallow up Jonah, and Jonah was in the belly of the fish three nights and three days." And Jonah prayed to God, and cried out with great faith that he knew God would deliver him from the deep. So when three days were done, God made the fish vomit out Jonah upon the dry land.

After Jonah was raised up out of the sea, God again sent him to Ninive. This time Jonah obeyed. He told the Ninivites that God would destroy them for their wickedness at the end of forty days.

Now, the men of Ninive believed in God, so their king proclaimed a great fast that would include all the inhabitants of the city, even the beasts. All were to take off their garments and put on sackcloth; there were even to be sackcloth garments for the beasts. And the king wore sackcloth and sat in ashes. No one, he said, was to eat or drink, not even the beasts, and all were to turn from their evil ways and ask the Lord to deliver them. So at the end of forty days, God saw their good works and had mercy on them, and did not send the punishment He had promised.

There, as mentioned in chapter 12, is one of the types of Lent. And of course Jonah — safe and alive after the three days and three nights in the fish — is a type of the Resurrection.

But there is more, and this relates (as we said in chapter 12) to God's teaching that the Jews were not to be so proud, nor to despise the Gentiles.

When Jonah saw that the Lord refused to destroy Ninive, he became very angry. Not because he was so bloodthirsty that he wanted to see them die, but because this whole affair was going to make something of a fool out of him. People would call him a false prophet; not only that, but in the future they would ignore the warnings of God, saying He did not keep His word. More and more angry, he begged God to let him die. But God only asked him if he thought he had good reason to be angry.

Then Jonah went out a little from the city, toward the east, and built himself a hut and sat there, watching to see if anything would happen. Now, God in His goodness let a vine grow up the side of the hut to shade Jonah. And Jonah was very glad, because he was fatigued (it was a big city and that was a lot of running around). But in the night God sent a worm that gnawed the vine, so that it shriveled and died. Then He sent a hot dry wind, and a hot burning sun, and Jonah "broiled with the heat." Then he got really angry. "It is better for me to die than to live!"

Then God asked (putting it in our kind of words), "Do you think you have reason to be angry on account of the vine?"

And Jonah answered, "I am angry, with reason, even unto death."

God said, "You are grieved about the vine, for which you neither worked, nor made it grow, which in one night grew and in one night perished. Shall I not spare Ninive, that great city, in which there are more than one hundred and twenty thousand persons" — and He used a phrase that, translated into our idiom, says "who know neither their right hand from their left"?

Aren't we like Jonah? We like to have things just so. We demand to know why God does things and why He doesn't. We like to say that this is fair, and that is not. Our mercy really does not extend very far. But God's mercy does. Lent is a magnificent example of it. We adored Him at Bethlehem, and hardly finished, we betrayed Him with all our mean little secret sins and our horrid big ones. We ought to be made to pay with our lives, for even they are a gift from Him. But Christ in His Church offers us forty days to fast and pray; and at the end, He promises, His love will triumph over sin and death: at the end He will show us the sign of Jonah.

One of the symbols of this sign of Jonah — in other words, the Resurrection — is a gourd, which recalls the vine (assuming it was a gourd vine). It is interesting to know that there has been disputing over this vine ever since the beginning. Some scholars are sure it was the castor bean (a bush), some (among them St. Augustine) the gourd. If so, it is quite possible that it was a crook-necked squash. Remember this, next time you serve squash, and you will have, also, a conversation piece. At any rate, the symbol used is a gourd, and when it is used with an apple, it symbolizes the triumph of the Resurrection over Original Sin. As Easter egg decorations, these symbols tell the whole meaning of Easter.

◠

### A Jonah Project

Now for something to do. This is an activity that sums up all that Jonah teaches. The children use it during Holy Week. You need 9-by-12-inch colored construction paper, scissors, paste, and your choice of crayons, paint, or inks, and glitter. If you get glitter, don't forget a tube of glitter-glue to use with it.

Cut a fish, measuring 8 by 5½ inches, out of a folded piece of paper, with the top of the head and tail on the fold. Paste the tails together and spread apart the base so that it will stand.

Cut a ship, 6 inches high and 6½ inches long, out of a folded piece of paper, with the top of the sail on the fold. Then cut another sail from another color and paste it over the first; spread apart to stand.

Out of another folded piece of paper, cut a figure of Jonah, 3 inches high, with his hands, upraised, on the fold. Paste the heads together, and spread his legs apart.

Decorate the pieces to suit your fancy. On the sail of the ship we painted a single eye, a symbol of the watchfulness of God the Father, who saw Jonah run away and sent the storm at sea.

Pour sand or yellow cornmeal on a tray, and the figures will stand up in it. At the beginning of Holy Week, Jonah is in the ship. Standing in the prow with his arms flung up like that, he looks as though he is about to be tossed overboard. Good Friday he goes into the fish. On Easter Sunday, the first child awake runs downstairs to take him out of the fish and put him on the shore, where he stands with his arms upflung in a great and joyful *Alleluia!* On the mast of the ship the child tapes a cross, because the ship is a symbol of Christ's Church, born out of the graces of the Redemption, and the fish is an ancient symbol of Christ. *Icthus* is the Greek word meaning "fish," and each letter is the initial Greek letter of each word in the Greek phrase *Jesus Christ, Son of God, Savior.*

There is a lot of doctrine here, and it is fun to learn it this way. It works out nicely as a classroom project also.

☙

### A Word on Almsgiving

One of the points to discuss when mid-Lent is reached is whether the family has given alms. Almsgiving during Lent is as much an obligation as the fasting and penance, although somehow in modern times, the impression is current that it is optional. Perhaps if we have not denied ourselves enough in this respect, we should include in night prayers these words of St. Basil:

Is God unjust that He distributes goods unequally to us? Why do you wax rich, while he begs, except that you may gain the merits of a good distribution, and he may be crowned with the laurels of patience? It is the bread of the famished that you retain; the cloak of the naked that you keep in your cupboard; the shoes of the barefoot that rot in your keeping; the money of the needy that you keep hidden away. As much as yet remains in your power to give, by so much do you harm others.

This is a thoughtful meditation, especially when related to the purchase of Easter clothes. Originally, Lent was the final period of preparation for the catechumens before their baptism. The white linen baptismal robes they wore on Holy Saturday, when they were baptized, and all through the week after Easter, were the fore-runners of our "Easter outfits." In our times, when so many are naked and cold, hungry and sick, all over the world, our own puri-fication, "throwing off the old man"[54] in the effort to be renewed, could have a profound significance if we were to give to the poor the clothes we do not need, the money we spend for things we do not need. One of the challenges to women who are seriously Cath-olic is to use all their ingenuity to dress themselves and their fami-lies, feed themselves and their families, both well and frugally, so that there is always something left to give to the poor.

*The Paschal Candle*

Another mid-Lent consideration is the Paschal candle. The same type of candle is used as described in the first chapter for the Christ candle. The symbols used for the Paschal candle are a cross, the Greek letters *alpha* and *omega*, and the numerals of the year. These symbols may be etched on the candle and then stained or

---

[54] Cf. Col. 3:9.

painted with red oil paint. We add other symbols of the Redemption painted in the same manner as we paint the Christ candle. We have the pelican feeding her young, the cross with grapevine and wheat, the symbol above, the phoenix arising out of its funeral pyre, and the lamb triumphant on an altar with its banner of victory.

The *pelican*, according to an inaccurate legend, has the greatest love of all creatures for its offspring and will pierce its breast and feed them (this is the inaccuracy: it only appears to do this because of the way it holds its head) with its blood. This is a symbol of the Blood of Christ, by which He redeemed us and with which He feeds us in the Holy Eucharist.

The *grapes and wheat* are symbolic of the Holy Eucharist, the unbloody sacrifice that repeats daily at Holy Mass the bloody sacrifice of the Cross.

The *phoenix* is a mythical bird of great beauty that was said to die, periodically, on its own funeral pyre, only to arise more youthful and beautiful than ever to begin another life: a symbol of the Resurrection.

The *lamb* is Christ, the true Paschal Lamb on the altar of sacrifice replacing forever the sincere but insufficient sacrifices of the Jews. The banner is His symbol of victory over sin and death.

At the four points of the cross and at its center, we pierce with a hot skewer and insert at each point a clove, like the five pegs of wax and incense (they look like nails) which you see on the great Paschal candle on the altar. The incense for which we substitute the fragrant cloves is a symbol, when burned, of the zeal of the faithful; by its fragrance, of the odor of Christian virtue; by its smoke, of the ascent of the prayer of the faithful to the throne of God.

As with the Christ candle, we must plan time together in the evenings in order to prepare the candle and discuss the doctrine relating to these symbols. It is a fruitful work and truly beautiful when finished. It is saved for Easter morning when the first child downstairs, after taking Jonah out of the fish and setting him ashore, claims the privilege of lighting the Paschal candle after the others have gathered.

⌒

### Lenten Reading

It may sound a little naive to recommend reading aloud as a substitute for television, but it is an excellent substitute if it is taken seriously. A fine book for Lenten reading aloud for the family is *Jesus, Son of David*, by Mother Mary Eleanor, S.H.C.J. It is suitable for a group including children from five up (our five-year-old loved it, although now and then he had to ask questions — but questions are good), and the chapters serve as single readings for feasts, Mass preparations, and especially well (those on the Last Supper, the trial, the Passion and death, the Resurrection) for Holy Week meditations. Several times it moved them to tears, and it is good that we should weep over Christ's sufferings. We weep so easily over things of no consequence.

Evenings when our children have been too excited to pray well, when it has been a bad day with everyone at sixes and sevens, we have made night prayers one part vocal prayer (perhaps one decade of the Rosary following an examination of conscience and the *Confiteor*) and four parts reading. It calms them wonderfully and gives them a chance to return to first things first, and meditate before they fall asleep.

Passion Sunday we put the purple shrouds on the statues and religious pictures, and Palm Sunday we weave some of the palms into a mat to place under a figure of our Lady and the Christ Child. Thoroughly soaked in warm water, palms will weave easily even if they have been quite dry. A running machine-stitch all around the edge keeps the mat from coming apart. Some of the palms are saved for *Asperges* (sprinkling) when we have blessings with holy water, and some are to be nailed as small crosses to the tree by the garden after the Rogation Day procession.

⁂

### A Passover Supper on Holy Thursday

Holy Thursday we have a Paschal supper. The shopping for this must be done early in the week. As far as we are able, we serve the foods served at a Jewish *Seder* supper (their Passover meal), although ours has a different significance. These are the foods our Lord ate at the Last Supper, and this is the feast-day meal that celebrates the institution of the Holy Eucharist; so we want it to be in every way possible richly significant.

I went shopping once for the foods for such a supper, at a market where I knew I could find some Jewish clerks to help me with the recipe for *charoset* (pronounced, I believe, "haroset"). One old man brightened when I asked him. "You are having a Seder? Oh, good. It is one of the most wonderful memories of my childhood, the Seders." He told me how his mother used to make charoset, and when I was leaving, he called after me, "Happy feast day!"

I went to another counter to buy wine, and another Jewish clerk helped me eagerly, happy to think I was having a Seder.

Then I went to the fruit market and asked for the apples and raisins and nuts "needed for charoset," I said.

The smile vanished instantly from the face of the clerk. He coldly gave me my purchase and turned away. It was an odd feeling. I had never been taken for a Jew before, never felt so keenly a Christian's intolerance. It is quite different from the experience one has with people who don't like Catholics. It is much colder. Uglier.

But what is a Paschal supper?

There is much to tie together if we are to sum it up for our children — and sum it up we must, or they will make no sense of it and will miss entirely the majesty of this story of God's love.

It started with Abraham, whom God called out of a pagan land and promised to make the father of a great people. This was hundreds of years after the deluge. Abraham was a descendant of Noah's son Shem. He was a Semite. This was the beginning of the Jews; they were a chosen people. God gave Abraham the land of Canaan and sent him a son, Isaac, and it was out of this line that the Messiah would come — to save all mankind from their sins.

Isaac was the father of Jacob, and Jacob the father of that Joseph we heard St. Stephen tell about in his speech before the Sanhedrin (chapter 5, the feast of St. Stephen, December 26). When famine struck the land of Canaan, Joseph invited his father, Jacob, and his eleven brothers and their families to dwell in Egypt, and this began the four hundred years' sojourn of the Jews in the Delta in Egypt. They multiplied greatly in number and adapted to the customs of these Egyptians, becoming defiled by idolatry, acquiescing in a land of magicians and infidels, until under a Pharaoh who had no memory of Joseph or his services, they were enslaved. Multiplied as they were, to him they presented a threat if an enemy should attack Egypt and arm these foreign inhabitants; so he ordered the extermination of all their newborn male children. It was for this reason that Moses was hidden in the bulrushes, where he was found by Pharaoh's daughter and raised as her son; and in his maturity he was sent by God to be a deliverer to his people.

In this role, Moses is a *type* of Christ, and the freeing of the Jews from bondage in Egypt under his leadership is the great type of the Redemption: the freeing of mankind from bondage to sin and death by our Lord, Jesus Christ.

Through Moses, God warned Pharaoh to let His people go, but in spite of terrible plagues visited upon his land, he refused. Finally

Moses warned Pharaoh of the last, most terrible plague. God had said:

> At midnight I will enter into Egypt. And every firstborn in the land of the Egyptians shall die, from the firstborn of Pharaoh who sitteth on his throne even to the firstborn of the handmaid that is at the mill, and all the firstborn of beasts. And there shall be a great cry in all the land of Egypt, such as neither hath been before, nor shall be hereafter. But with all the children of Israel there shall not a dog make the least noise [i.e., bark at them], from man even to beast: that you may know how wonderful a difference the Lord maketh between the Egyptians and Israel.

But Pharaoh would not hear.

Then God gave Moses the instructions for the first Pasch (pronounced "pask"), the meal which was to be eaten that night and as a memorial every year thereafter to commemorate the night God would *pass over* Egypt to slay the Egyptian firstborn and free the Jews.

This month in which would begin their freedom, He said, would be the beginning month of the year, and every family was to obtain on the tenth day of the month a yearling lamb without blemish. If they were not a large enough family to consume it themselves, they must find a neighbor whose family could consume it with them. They would keep the lamb until the fourteenth day and on that evening sacrifice it, dipping branches of hyssop in its blood to smear the transoms and lintels of their doors so that God would pass over their houses when he slew the firstborn of Egypt.

They were to roast the lamb and eat it all, head, feet, and entrails, and break not a bone; eat it with unleavened bread and wild herbs, and whatever was left of the lamb was to be burned in the fire. They were to eat it in haste, wearing their shoes, their cloaks girded about them, and with their staves in their hands, ready for the journey.

It is almost impossible to put into words all the mind sees here. The sacrifice of the lamb becomes the signal. The blood of the lamb the sign. They are to be ready, for when this is done, they will be on their way to freedom. We have only to recall that St. John the Baptist pointed to Him and said, "Behold the Lamb of God,"[55] to see what it means.

The Gospels of our Lenten reading (if it has been on the life of Christ) show us that He timed His appearance in public carefully — before the raising of Lazarus, after the triumphant entry on Palm Sunday — so that He would be there to celebrate the Pasch with His Apostles. It is at this meal, where He ate the Paschal lamb with them, that He broke with tradition (and He loved the Law), blessing bread and wine, instituting an entirely new act at the Paschal meal: the Holy Eucharist. Only His divine hand could have consecrated that first bread and wine for the sacrifice — for all He had the power to give to priests — because the bloody sacrifice of the Lamb had not been completed.

It was when He left the supper, and went to meet the Cross, that all men were on their way to freedom.

This is a beautiful night. We want to celebrate it tenderly and lovingly, but it takes years to manage it perfectly, I think, because children will be children and break the spell. But we can keep the spell in our hearts as we teach them the meaning of it, and someday they will be as thrilled as we. The seed we are planting this night is the seed of their own hungering after Holy Communion.

For our Paschal meal we try to have lamb, although not always roast lamb. The reason they were to roast the lamb was because of

---

[55] John 1:29.

the need for haste: it was the quickest way to cook it. At a Seder, a roasted bone, the *z'roah*, is placed on the Seder tray to recall the roasted lamb.

We have a salad of "bitter herb," including as many of the original herbs as we can find in the market. Botanists and scholars now believe that these were probably endive, chicory, lettuce, watercress, sorrel, and dandelion, although in Europe in later ages, horseradish was substituted and is now used. (If you say that sorrel is not available, look around your potted plants and see if you have oxalis; that is sorrel — taste it and see.) The custom of eating meat with herbs and bread was acquired from the Egyptians.

We have unleavened bread, matzoh, which was commanded by God because there was no time for them to set a yeast dough; and we make charoset by combining equal parts of peeled and chopped raw apple, raisins, and nuts, a shake of cinnamon and, if you wish, a few drops of wine, although the apple makes it moist enough. Apparently one combines these ingredients to taste or by instinct. It makes a delicious relish, rather like a raw conserve, and at a Seder, the bitter herb is dipped in this before it is eaten. Charoset is to recall the mortar used in brick-making — the work of the enslaved Jews in Egypt; and the bitter herb, *maror*, recalls the bitterness of their sufferings.

There are two other interesting objects on a Seder tray, although we do not duplicate these: the *beitzah*, a roasted egg symbolizing the required offering brought on all festivals in the Temple. "The egg, while not itself sacrificed, is used in the Seder as it is the Jewish symbol of mourning (in this case, for the loss of the Temple, where the sacrifices were brought)"; and the second is the *karpas*, a piece of parsley or lettuce symbolizing the meager diet of the Jews in bondage. "It is dipped into salt water in remembrance of the tears they shed in their misery. The *karpas* also signifies Springtime, the season of Passover."

Wine for the grown-ups, grape juice for the children, together with the unleavened bread, recalls what for Christians is the most poignant part of this repast: the institution of the Holy Eucharist. At the Seder, an extra goblet of wine, the "cup of Elijah," is kept on the table in the hope that the prophet Elijah may appear as a messenger of the Almighty and announce the coming of the Messiah. As Christians we might keep the extra goblet filled to remind us of our beloved brothers, the Jews, out of whose faith and tradition our Faith has come, to whom the Messiah *has* come, and with longing awaits them. They are His blood brothers, and He longs for them. We must pray for their conversion in our daily prayers.

For our dessert we bake a lamb cake. There are molds to be bought for these, or you might do as we have and, using a homemade pattern, cut a large flat oblong cake in the shape of a lamb. We ice it with coconut frosting and use it as the centerpiece for our table with candles on either side.

One thing more before we begin: the hyssop. It is generally conceded now that the common hyssop was not the plant the Israelites used, since it is not native anywhere but in southern Europe. Most likely the hyssop used throughout the Old Testament for "sprinkling" and for this night of the Exodus was a Syrian or Egyptian marjoram, while it is thought that the hyssop used at the Crucifixion (sometimes called a reed) was a sorghum. We must remember that since every Jewish family was to use the hyssop, it had to be a weed they could reach out and pick practically from their front doors. So if you have a potted marjoram, or marjoram in your garden (even though it may not be the very same kind), you might pick a spray to put on your table this night as one more fragrant aid in the telling of this story. For processions in the summertime, a cluster of it would serve nicely for the *Asperges*.

The program of our meal — the prayers, the story — changes a bit each year to suit the size of our family and the endurance of the little ones. Recently we have found it best to read the story in preparation for it on Wednesday, relating dinner-table conversation to its symbols in the meal on Thursday. The "Hallel" Psalms (112 through 117[56]), all beginning with *Alleluia*, were recited traditionally at the Paschal meal, and so also at the Last Supper; you might follow your Grace before Meals with the shortest of these: Psalm 116,[57] a hymn of praise and thanksgiving. "Alleluia! O praise the Lord, all you nations, give Him glory, all you peoples; all powerful His mercy toward us; the Lord is true to His promise forever."

The father of the family reads the *Blessing of Bread* (chapter 4); and in our family we use the *Blessing for All Things* when he blesses the wine. We repeat that this is not the same as when a priest blesses, but a layperson makes use of that dignity bestowed on him in Baptism, when, sharing the Christ-life, he also may claim a share in His Priesthood, and as a lay priest gives these domestic blessings.

> *Let us pray. O God, by whose word all things are made holy,*
> *pour out Thy blessings on this creature, wine, and grant that*
> *whosoever uses it in accordance with Thy will and Thy law,*
> *and with a spirit of thanksgiving, may experience by Thy*
> *power health in body and protection in soul as he invokes*
> *Thy most holy name. Through Christ our Lord.*
> *R. Amen. (Wine is sprinkled with holy water.)*

Not only do we want a benediction over our wine for this meal, but we also want to use the opportunity — and every opportunity that arises — to teach the children that wine is one of the fruits of the earth, to be savored and enjoyed and used with Christian

---

[56] RSV = Ps. 113-118.
[57] RSV = Ps. 117.

reverence, especially since it was the substance our Lord chose to sanctify by His sacramental use of it in the Holy Eucharist.

In the Gospel for Holy Thursday, in which our Lord washes the feet of the Apostles, He indicates in it the kind of service He expects of us. To be a Christian demands an immolation of our entire self, pride included: "If, then, I being your Lord and Master, have washed your feet, you also ought to wash one another's feet. For I have given you an example, that as I have done to you, so you do also."[58]

After the smallest are in bed, we can include in our final night prayers the other Hallel Psalms. The celebration of the Paschal meal, its meaning, will have helped them especially to love Psalm 113.[59]

There is a legend from a *Midrash* (an ancient Jewish commentary on Scripture) which tells that on the night of the Exodus, the angels desired to chant song before God, and "the Holy One, blessed be He, prevented them, saying: 'The work of my hands is in distress, are drowning in the sea, and you wish to utter song before me?' "

This is a legend, but a divine sentiment. Just as God had mercy on the Ninivites when they were sorry for their sins and did penance, so He sorrowed that His Egyptian children would not. They were souls who were drowned in the Red Sea, not just bodies. The desire in our hearts must be to lead all men to Christ. This feast celebrates the sacrament which, when we receive it together, binds us together in one Flesh, one Body. "As the loaf is one, we, though many, are one body, for we all share one loaf."[60] We must pray that all the world will join us.

---

[58] John 13:14-15.
[59] RSV = Ps. 114.
[60] Cf. 1 Cor. 10:17.

⌒

*Good Friday Activities*

For the hours spent at home by those who cannot get to the rites of Good Friday, it is good to plan special activities in order to help all keep a spirit of recollection. With many little children, silence is almost impossible, but as they grow older, they begin to cooperate.

Friends of ours have had their children make the garden of Joseph of Arimathea outdoors, separately, on Good Friday. They used whatever they could find at hand — stones, mosses, sticks, acorns. A drawing project will keep Peter occupied. Having said the Stations of the Cross during Lent, he applies himself seriously to illustrating them. Rereading the passages about the Passion will keep another child busy, read out of Scripture or from a favorite life of Christ.

For a boy who is fidgety and must be active, a solitary chore that is a penance is better: perhaps cleaning the goat stalls or spreading hay and manure from the goose's pen on the garden. I know many mothers who, because they must be at home with their babies during this time, save a task that especially tries them. Each has his or her way of best spending the hours of Good Friday, but it will work out most successfully if the program for the day is well planned.

Perhaps one of the tasks for several of the children can be copying Psalm 21[61] to be used at night prayers this evening. Our Lord quoted the first line of it from the Cross. It prophesied Christ's Passion and death and our salvation: "My God, my God, why have You forsaken me. . . ."

This was the great prayer of our Lord on the Cross. The family may divide itself and read the lines alternately.

[61] RSV = Ps. 22.

⌒

*Holy Saturday and Poppy-Seed Cake*

Holy Saturday has always been the busiest day of all — a day of rushing and waiting at the same time. And with the Easter Vigil for all, great will be the joy of preparing for Easter morning at the beginning of the day, so that we may await its coming at the end.

Easter breads must be set the first thing (unless you bake them early in Lent, freeze them, and leave nothing for this day but the thawing). We have a recipe, also, for a special poppy-seed cake that is traditional with the Ukrainians at both Easter and Christmastime. It always reminds us of Maud and Miska Petersham's *Poppy Seed Cakes*, which my sisters and I read to rags when we were little girls.

UKRAINIAN POPPY-SEED CAKE

¾ cup poppy seeds
¾ cup milk
¾ cup shortening
1¼ cups sugar
3 eggs
¼ teaspoon salt
2 cups sifted flour
2 teaspoons baking powder
1 teaspoon vanilla

Soak the poppy seeds in milk for five to six hours. Cream shortening and sugar. Add 1 egg yolk at a time, and beat well after each addition. Add vanilla, milk with poppy seeds, then flour sifted together with baking powder and salt. Mix well. Add egg whites, beaten stiffly. Bake at 375 degrees for about 30 to 40 minutes in 9-inch tube pan.

You may sift powdered sugar over it, or ice it with a thin confectioner's-sugar icing, or serve it plain. It is nice plain, rather like a pound cake.

We like to bake the *Poppy-Seed Cake* for Easter because it reminds us of the whole lesson of Lent: the seed thrust into the ground to die, that it might live. The circle of the cake, baked in the tube pan, is like the circle of eternity — and that is the point of death to self: to live forever.

⁂

*Easter Eggs*

Easter eggs are next. With a big family, it is only smart to dye and start to decorate Easter eggs early in the week; but sometimes we aren't so smart in this family. Anyway, we decorate them with symbols. Heaven help those who don't know the symbols of the Redemption or of their patron saints: they'll never be able to tell which eggs are theirs. No one decorates his own eggs, you understand. We decorate many with the Easter symbols, then plot to see who will decorate whose.

You draw the design lightly on the egg with a pencil, then paint them with poster paints and outline them with black paint or india ink. All except the very smallest children decorate Easter eggs, and even though some turn out somewhat dubiously, they qualify. If it is absolutely impossible to identify a design, it is permissible to ask the artist what it is. After reading about Msgr. Hellriegel's mother's golden Alleluia egg, we quickly added one to our collection; so now in our house, too, the finding of the Alleluia egg is the high point of the egg hunt of Easter morning. The winner receives a prize of something good to eat — which he must share with the rest.

Once someone asked me what our children did on Easter. I told them, describing the Easter eggs. "What? You don't let them put Easter bunnies on their eggs? Oh! You take the fun out of everything!"

I could have told them about last Easter, when visiting children came. After viewing Jonah and the whale, the Paschal candle, the Easter eggs, the baskets, the gifts, the hunt prize, hearing the Newlands sing an Alleluia after their *Grace at Table*, the guests said, "Boy, you have an awful lot of fun on Easter. I wish we did all this stuff." But it would have sounded as though I were making it up.

I have nothing against Easter bunnies, but they have no religious significance whatever, and they appear in this springtime feast only because it was a pagan custom to use them as symbols of fertility at this time of the year. With our Christian tradition so rich in symbols that do have meaning, it would seem that the children are cheated if we do not use them.

Easter *is* fun — and deeply religious at the same time. There is a true spiritual joy in it which is more than the children's greedy delight in being permitted to eat a lot of candy at last. The purple beans they have saved during Lent are divided, and after the children are in bed on Easter Eve, these are put into little bags (the kind you buy chocolate coins in) as symbols of the treasure stored in Heaven. Each child receives a gift to which the bag of treasure is tied, as a little sample of his reward in Heaven.

☙

### Keeping the Vigil at Home

Not all will be able to attend the Easter Vigil. Babysitters will be needed. So perhaps those at home can prepare for the return of those who go to keep the Vigil. These in turn might bring back with them some of the drama and joy of the Vigil, in a lantern lighted with the newly blessed Easter fire, and a bottle of some of the newly blessed Easter water. These radiances of joy and blessedness can touch the house itself.

Those at home may make the last beautiful preparations before the joy of the Risen Lord. They may be the ones to put the Paschal candle in its place, to remove the shrouds from the statues, to return the planters to the mantel, where they decorate it once more with thick green, reminding us all year of the True Vine. The Infant of Prague must have on His Easter cope, and the table must be prepared for the festive Easter breakfast.

Reading the prayers of the Vigil at home, the babysitting ones will be ready for the return of the others. Perhaps if they have small fry to see to bed, theirs will be the privilege of telling the story that is, for me, the most beautiful of all the Easter stories. It should be the very last thing at night, after prayers, for the staying-at-home little ones. Ours have heard it as they lay in their beds.

It is about Mary Magdalene and how she found Him in the garden on Easter morning. She did not really understand. After all He had said about rising on the third day, still she wept and wrung her hands and looked for Him. Even when she saw the angels, it did not dawn on her. Then — she saw Jesus. Thinking He was a gardener, she heard Him say, "Woman, why art thou weeping? For whom art thou searching?"

And she said, "If it is thou, Sir, that hast carried Him off, tell me where thou hast put Him, and I will take Him away."

Then that lovely moment. He said simply, "Mary."

And she knew.

How tender, the love that inspired them to record this scene. We know that He appeared to His Mother first. It is an ancient tradition in the Church, and St. Teresa of Avila[62] and many others confirm it. But for us who are sinners, the scene described so carefully is this meeting with the one who was such a great sinner.

---

[62] St. Teresa of Avila (1515-1582), Spanish Carmelite nun, mystic, and Doctor who reformed her order.

It should be a part of every child's Easter Eve, and often it will make them weep. But these are fine, good tears, that come because they understand that He loves them.

If the parish Vigil is early, perhaps some children will attend, or at least be permitted to stay up until their parents return; in this case, those at home could read the prayers of *Blessing for the New Fire* and the *Blessing of the Paschal Candle* (unless someone has successfully returned with the already blessed new fire). A new fire can be kindled at home, with a flint, by using a lighter. (I would never have known, if someone hadn't pointed it out.) Each time it is lighted, it is a new fire. The *Blessing for the New Fire* is a beautiful prayer.

### BLESSING FOR THE NEW FIRE

V:    The Lord be with you.

R:    And with thy spirit.

*Let us pray.* O God, who, through Thy Son, the corner-stone, hast bestowed on the faithful the fire of Thy glory, sanctify this new fire produced from a flint for our use; and grant that by this paschal festival we may be so inflamed with heavenly desires, that with pure minds we may come to the feast of perpetual light. Through the same Christ our Lord. R. Amen. (*Sprinkle with holy water.*)

We make a hole for each of the five cloves to go in the Paschal candle, by piercing the candle with a hot skewer; then we insert the cloves, light the candle with the new fire, and read the prayer for the *Blessing of the Paschal Candle*.

### BLESSING OF THE PASCHAL CANDLE

V:    The Lord be with you.

R:    And with thy spirit.

*Let us pray*. May the abundant infusion of Thy blessing descend upon this lighted candle, we beseech Thee, almighty God: and do Thou, O invisible Regenerator, look down on it, shining in the night; that not only the sacrifice that is offered this night may shine by the secret mixture of Thy light: but also into whatsoever place anything of this mystically blessed object shall be brought, there the power of Thy majesty may be present, and all the malice of satanic deceit may be driven out. Through Christ our Lord. R. Amen. *(Sprinkle the candle with holy water.)*

These blessings are out of context. Their place is in the Easter Vigil. We use them here, as we said, to inspire those at home and reflect some of the joy of the rites at the church. Used as prayers, simple petitions made by lay priests asking God's blessing on their domestic sacramentals, they should still bring down His blessing.

The prophecy from the book of Jonah (3:1-10) is no longer used in the shorter form of the Easter Vigil, but it is an excellent reading for children left at home, especially if they have used the Jonah project described as part of their Lenten activity. The Litany of the Saints is another prayer used in the Vigil which is especially appropriate for those at home. Our children are more than ever enthusiastic about the Litany since we learned to sing it — or at least to sing the invocations to saints, followed by "Pray for us." How did we learn to sing it? A priest friend sang a few lines of it. It was that easy. Why it didn't occur to us to ask someone to sing it long ago, no one knows. If only the Trapp Family lived next door, we keep saying. But they don't, so we plod along.

If it is still early enough in the evening for the little ones to be up, the renewal of baptismal vows is a perfect ending to their vigil at home. If this is not possible, perhaps the babysitter would like to make this the climax of his, or her, evening, when the family returns from church, having just renewed theirs. If possible, provide blessed candles to be lighted and held by those renewing their vows.

*Leader:* Do you reject Satan?
*All:* I do.
*Leader:* And all his works?
*All:* I do.
*Leader:* And all his empty promises?
*All:* I do.
*Leader:* Do you believe in God, the Father Almighty, creator of Heaven and earth?
*All:* I do.
*Leader:* Do you believe in Jesus Christ, His only Son, our Lord, who was born of the Virgin Mary was crucified, died, and was buried, rose from the dead, and is now seated at the right hand of the Father?
*All:* I do.
*Leader:* Do you believe in the Holy Spirit, the holy Catholic Church, the Communion of Saints, the forgiveness of sins, the resurrection of the body, and life everlasting?
*All:* I do.
*Leader:* God, the all-powerful Father of our Lord Jesus Christ has given us a new birth by water and the Holy Spirit, and forgiven all our sins. May He also keep us faithful to our Lord Jesus Christ forever and ever.
*All:* Amen.

This form of renewal of baptismal vows may also be used when children renew their baptismal vows at a family feast celebrating their Baptism or a patron saint's feast day, or the feast of Pentecost. A renewal at home at least once a year is a beautiful family rite, and the ideal way to teach children an awe and love for their Baptism.

⌒

*Alleluia at Last*

Easter morning. Alleluia! *The Hallel*, greatest of Hebrew expressions of praise, together with *Jah*, the shortened form *of Jahve*, God's name, combine to make this lovely word. Dom Winzen writes:

> On the eve of Septuagesima Sunday, the *Alleluia* was buried. Now it rises out of the tomb. . . . [T]he *Alleluia* is the heart of the Opus Dei; the song which the Moses of the New Testament sings together with His People after He has passed through the Red Sea of His Death into the glory of His Resurrection.

The first child awake races downstairs to take Jonah out of the fish, set him on the beach, and with him sing *Alleluia!* Quickly they all gather and at last the door to the living room is opened. There are the marvelous baskets, resplendent with decorations, with gifts, with goodies. Walk carefully. The eggs are hidden everywhere. All together sing another *Alleluia!* as the early one lights the Paschal candle.

Then to Mass, to the great joy of Easter Communion. He is in each of us; therefore we are one in Him. At every Mass, He will be our Paschal Lamb, the perfect sacrifice, the perfect victim, offered everywhere for us, always, until the world comes to an end.

Home to the beautiful breakfast table, the delicious Easter bread, the excitement of the egg hunt, and the opening of gifts. It has been so long since we have sung *Alleluia* after Grace. What a glorious morning! The Paschal candle is lighted. While we rejoice, it burns with a steady flame. It says, *"I am risen, and am still with thee, Alleluia!"*

Chapter 12

⁀

# Rogation Days before Ascension

In the first Canto of Dante's *Inferno*, there is a description of a morning and a leopard.

> The time was at the beginning of the morning; and the sun was mounting up with those stars which were with Him when Divine Love first moved these fair things; so that the hour of time and the sweet season caused me to have good hope of that animal with the gay skin.

This is the feeling of Rogation days, which come in a sweet season and cause us to have good hope. They come in the after-season of Easter, when morning recalls the Resurrection, and, looking about, we cannot escape the beauty in a world of spring with Divine Love showing again in all its fairest things. Even in the city there is beauty. There is a freshness in the air, a newness in the sunlight, a waking of beauty in places one would never seek it. There is an excitement peculiar to spring, as though, watching long enough and quietly enough, we might spy God's hand moving or glimpse His face.

It is His personality that is sensible to us in the spring, sensed in the beauty and color and design and weight and sound of the things of the universe, all of them tasting of what we will find in Heaven. There is gladness and joy in God; we know, because He has created daffodils and leopards.

Rogation days are a time to see God again in things visible, such as the new leaves on the trees and the new green of the grass, and in the promise of what is invisible, such as the seed buried in the brown earth or the bulb in the flowerpot's drab little womb. And Rogation days are an especially happy occasion for a family celebration.

*Rogation* comes from the Latin verb *rogare:* "to ask." There are four Rogation days each year. The first, April 25 (feast of St. Mark), was an effort to offset the ancient Roman Robigalio, a celebration with processions and prayers beseeching the god of the harvest. The three Rogation days preceding the feast of the Ascension were established by St. Mamettus, Bishop of Vienne, in Gaul (modern France) about the year 450; these were days of prayer and penance to appease God's wrath, and ask protection from the great calamities, and a blessing on the harvest — both the harvest of the gardens and the harvest of souls, for in either case, unless the seed fall on fertile ground, it will not yield good fruit.

Today Rogation days are associated mostly with prayer for blessing on the harvest — something about which all must have a vital concern, since there is no one who does not depend on it to sustain the life that is in him. Whether our food comes from our garden or the freezer at the supermarket, someone had to grow it; and before that, God had to plant the mystery of life in the seed, or even the most skillful farmer could not make it yield.

The Gospel for the Rogation day Masses is all about parents and children:

Which of you, if he ask his father bread, will he give him a stone? Or a fish, will he for a fish give him a serpent? Or if he ask an egg, will he reach him a scorpion? If you, then, being evil, know how to give good gifts to your children, how much more will your Father from Heaven give the good Spirit to them that ask?[63]

On the Sunday before, Our Lord said emphatically, "If you ask the Father anything in my name, He will give it to you." We are supposed to ask. We are told to ask. We must not think it unseemly to ask. The Church has gone so far as to prepare special days for asking. It would be nice if one of the parish priests could join the family for the procession, giving the blessing and leading the prayers, but no one will deny the valid claims on his time. So once again the Church exhorts the faithful to give these blessings themselves if their priests cannot be there to give them.

For families who live gardenless in towns or cities, or for those who do not live at home but in rooms or apartments, hospitals, hotels, or rest homes, it is fitting that they join the others with their prayers, even blessing the plants in their flowerpots or window boxes, if they have them. On these days, the voice of the whole Mystical Body prays, asking for a fruitful harvest: Christ and clergy and people together as one. The needs of *all* men must be provided.

In French Canada, it is a custom to have grains blessed on this morning; after Mass, the farmers go up to the sanctuary to get some, so that they may throw a handful in each of their fields. In city churches attached to monasteries, and in the convents and monasteries elsewhere, the religious may have Rogation-Day processions before Mass. It is nice to pray with them if you live nearby.

⁀

*A Procession and the Litany of the Saints*

In terms of our own daily life, these days relate to the very sandwiches we put in the lunch boxes, the tea in Granny's cup, the

63 Luke 11:11-13.

boiled egg for Daddy's breakfast. So we have a procession, too. Our children rate processions very high on the list of best things to do, and although our form is not orthodox, what we lack in style we compensate for with enthusiasm. Three or four children prepare large crosses to be carried at the head of the column, and rather than eliminate these, we abound in them, thus simplifying the problem of a shortage of musical instruments. One member is appointed to read blessings. Another member is appointed to lead the Litany of the Saints. Another carries a vessel of holy water and a sprinkler; this made with a cluster of Palm Sunday palms. Small fry play triangles, beat drums and cymbals. The anthems for matching are hymns and *Alleluias;* then we sing the Litany when we arrive at the garden. If there are neighbor children around, they are invited to come along — and off we go singing.

The Litany of the Saints is a magnificent prayer. There isn't a child who wouldn't love it if he heard it often enough. It is long but full of friendly names; and if the lives of the saints are familiar, the invocations are greeted by beams, whispers, and pokes. It is highly improper, but — we have added to the list St. Monica and St. Christopher, to smooth these two ruffled Newlands who feel the composition of this prayer to have been in the hands of a highly partial board of Fathers.

Preparation is important, however, or halfway through, the pleasure gives way to "Will this never end?" and "How long does this last?" It is a long prayer, but to explore its meaning is more fun than you would think.

"What do you suppose this means: *From the snares of the Devil, O Lord, deliver us*"? We had taken a long walk with the neighbor children and said part of the Litany going through the woods. Back home in front of the fire, we were finishing. Jamie thought a minute. Then, "Well, it means — you know — from the way he plays tricks on you and makes you be bad."

"But how? I mean, how does he play tricks on you and make you be bad? For instance, how does he get you to tell a lie when you weren't even thinking of telling a lie?"

"Oh. You know. Say, let's see. . . . Oh, pretend you were playing ball by a window and the ball went through your hands and broke the window and your brother was right there. He'd do it then. Not real fast, understand, but little and little and little. Like he says, 'Hey, your brother was right there. Hmmmmm. That's an idea. Maybe you could say he did it. Then you could see him get heck 'stead of you.' " John (his brother) nodded vigorously, "Yeah. And all the time chuckling." He demonstrated a brief devil-chuckle.

This sounded very grim indeed; so we repeated with feeling: "From the snares of the Devil, O Lord, deliver us!"

We stopped to talk about other meanings now and then: *Through the mystery of Thy Holy Incarnation, O Lord, deliver us.*

"Who remembers what Incarnation means? No? It means God-and-Man, both in Jesus, Son of Mary, and Second Person in the Blessed Trinity."

"Oh yes. That's right."

*Through Thine admirable Ascension* we understand. We are preparing for Rogation days, which come three days before Ascension; so who could forget the meaning of this?

*Through the coming of the Holy Spirit, the Paraclete.* That's about Pentecost, another feast. Ten days after the Ascension. This is a season of great feasts!

*That Thou wouldst vouchsafe to humble the enemies of Holy Church, we beseech Thee, hear us.* "Can anyone think of something to explain this one?"

No one can. But the grown-ups do. On the wall is a little picture of Bishop Ford, who died in prison in China, and a snapshot of Sister Jean Marie and Sister Rita Marie, who were also in prison, for no reason except they loved God and had given their lives to Him. They were locked away so that they could no longer teach the people of China about the dear God who loves them, who died to save them. Many more were in prison with them. Many still are.

The *enemies of Holy Church* are those who try to prevent the teaching that our Lord commanded when He said to His Apostles: "Go ye forth, teaching all nations."[64] He left them this command just before He ascended into Heaven. To pray that His enemies be humbled means that we ask they see the error and sin in their deeds, see the truth, be sorry for their sins against Christ and His Mystical Body.

One of the neighbor children was wide-eyed. "But you said we were supposed to love everyone. How can you love people like that?"

We talked more, about the Passion and death of our Lord, and how He said to His Father at the end, "Forgive them Father, they don't know what they are doing."[65] It is because they do not know Christ that they do these things — in China, in Siberia, in Russia, in South Africa, in South America, in our own land also, in Europe, wherever men work to destroy the Church because they know that she is a source of holiness. We must hate what is sinful, but love the ones who sin, for Jesus' sake, pray for them, sacrifice for them, hope for their conversion.

We covered much doctrine in this conversation. It is one thing to talk about all this in the words of the catechism. It is another to talk about it while you walk through the woods, scramble over stone walls, watch His frogs jump into His brook, or sit at home snug up to a grown-up who loves you, and gaze into the fire. It is so much easier to see the beauty in all these truths if you learn about them while you are enjoying yourself.

[64] Cf. Matt. 28:19.
[65] Luke 23:34.

But this was to be about Rogation days. . . .

⸒

*The Blessings*

After the Litany (in our procession), we read the *Blessing of the Sprouting Seed* — or, I should say, Grandma Reed reads it. She is the Grandma with the green thumbs.

BLESSING OF THE SPROUTING SEED

*Leader:* Our help is in the name of the Lord.
  *All:* Who made Heaven and earth.
*Leader:* The Lord be with you.
  *All:* And with your spirit.

*Let us pray.* To Thee, O Lord, we cry and pray: Bless this sprouting seed, strengthen it in the gentle movement of soft winds, refresh it with the dew of heaven, and let it grow to full maturity for the good of body and soul.[66]

How many times might not the damping off of seedlings be avoided by the "Blessing of the Sprouting Seed"! Man must look so funny, knee-deep in dusts, powder, sprays, and techniques to ward off pests and diseases, and all the while neglecting to ask God's help first.

*Strengthen it in the gentle movement of soft winds, refresh it with the dew of heaven.* This is like feeling His breath in your face, catching the drops of water that fall from His hand. For children it is a magnificent lesson in detachment. It hems all the world in springtime in the arms of the Father and makes every leaf and sprout a miracle.

---

[66] From *With the Blessing of the Church*, National Catholic Rural Life Conference, Des Moines.

We send our blessing from crop to crop. Over the potatoes, the corn, the beans, and the peas Monica sprinkles holy water generously. Grandma reads the blessing again over a side garden where small children are hauled out of carrots and beets; and someone points out where one lad sowed lettuce in a fit of temper.

"As you sow, so shall you reap" — apropos here, where lettuce is coming up every which way, plainly scattered to the four winds by an angry fist. Gracious! This *is* telltale evidence of misdeeds, and humiliating too, now that he can no longer remember why he was angry. It will serve for a long time as a reminder that every angry word and thrust sent into the world makes a difference, increases its disorder. The rows that were planted with love are neat and straight. It is a good contrast between love and anger.

We progress to Grandma's fruit trees and vines. She reads with feeling the *Blessing of Young Crops and Vineyards*.

BLESSING OF YOUNG CROPS AND VINEYARDS
*Leader:* Our help is in the name of the Lord.
*All:* Who made Heaven and earth.
*Leader:* The Lord be with you.
*All:* And with your spirit.

*Let us pray.* We appeal to Thy graciousness, O Almighty God, that Thou wouldst shower Thy blessing upon these first-fruits of creation, which Thou hast nurtured with favorable weather, and mayest bring them to a fine harvest. Grant also to Thy people a sense of constant gratitude for Thy gifts, so that the hungry may find rich nourishment in the fruits of the earth, and the needy and the poor may praise Thy wondrous name. Through Christ our Lord. Amen. (*Sprinkle with holy water.*)

At each little group of fruit trees and grapevines, new berry bushes, transplants, she reads — and we are startled to hear the quiet passion as she improvises before the pear tree: ". . . we ask Thee in Thy fatherly love to pour down the rain of Thy blessing on this poor little pear tree which that wicked goat has tried so many times to eat!"

Ah — Helen. Indeed she has, and many's the time Grandma has hinted we might better read the *Prayer against Harmful Animals* over Helen each spring before it is too late for the *Blessing of Young Crops*. What Helen strips off in five minutes of truancy it takes God a full year to grow back again. We sigh and recall that it is a fallen world, and that is why we need prayers about rain, please, and sun, please, and if You please, not so many cutworms this year?

We finish, and the boys drive the crosses in place at points of vantage, while Monica makes her palm brush into a cross and nails it on the big sugar maple that overlooks the garden. There is a *Blessing of Crosses to Be Placed in Fields and Vineyards* to be given on May 3, the feast of the Finding of the Holy Cross.

BLESSING OF CROSSES TO BE
PLACED IN FIELDS AND VINEYARDS

*Leader:* Our help is in the name of the Lord.
*All:* Who made Heaven and earth.
*Leader:* The Lord be with you.
*All:* And with your spirit.

*Let us pray.* Almighty, everlasting God, Father of goodness and consolation, in virtue of the bitter suffering of Thy Sole-Begotten Son, our Lord, Jesus Christ, endured for us sinners on the wood of the Cross, bless these crosses which Thy faithful will erect in their vineyards, fields, and gardens. Protect the land where they are placed from hail, tornado, storm, and every assault of the enemy, so that their fruits ripened to the harvest may be gathered to Thy honor by those who place their hope in the holy Cross of Thy Son, our Lord, Jesus Christ, who liveth and reigneth with Thee eternally. Amen. (*Sprinkle crosses with holy water.*)

If only we had known! This is the answer to the fence-jumping cows. And ought not the blessing be part of every year now that we have had our experiences with New England floods!

Processions are satisfying. There are days during the long summer out of school when there is nothing quite like a procession to suit the mood. Sometimes they celebrate the feast of a patron saint, and sometimes they are just manifestations of a restless spirit that wants to praise (I should say, a number of restless spirits).

The *Canticle of the Three Youths* is a pattern of praise found in the book of Daniel.[67]

With a motley array of musical instruments, the children will swing along the pastures, around old trees, or down by the brook, shouting and banging on oatmeal boxes, pot lids, tissue paper on combs, blowing through the tubes from the paper toweling. Very good children get to use the triangle, the *real* cymbals, the harmonicas — if they can find them.

> *All ye puffballs, praise the Lord.*
> *All ye tadpoles, praise the Lord.*
> *All ye minnows and frogs, birds and bugs,*
>     *praise the Lord.*
> *All ye bushes and trees, flowers and weeds,*
>     *praise the Lord. . . .*

The echo praises the Lord, the children praise the Lord, the everlasting hills praise the Lord. It is easy to understand at times

[67] Dan. 3:57 ff.

like these the "desire of the everlasting hills," and the fields and the sky and the trees, and what St. Paul meant when he wrote that they groaned and travailed until the day when they, too, would be restored to harmony.

Chapter 13

～

# The Ascension

Forty days before the Ascension, and we have lessons to learn.

When I was a child (I am now, as Peter says, almost a hundred — sixty years to go), I learned all that I knew about the Faith from the catechism. I honestly think there was no other source. Catechism lessons were taught by generous laywomen who donated their time and willingness, and knew no more about the Faith than the children they were teaching. Grace was taught, of course, but I am speaking here of formal teaching.

Once I was a member of a parish sodality, and I remember asking our spiritual director about grace. He had said that one of our group had spent part of a summer at a course of some kind, and had studied grace. I said, "Grace. But I don't know anything about grace. Tell us about it."

He looked at us kindly, seemed about to say something, then changed his mind and said, "Oh, it's a pretty complicated subject." So we didn't learn anything about grace. We were learning by grace, of course, but oh, the years that we spent — my generation (when you are as old as I, you talk about "my generation") — trying to find what the Faith was all about.

It's different for our children. It turned out, after all, that although we were the great untaught (this applies even to many who had parochial education; they learned doctrine but somehow they didn't connect it with what went on in the world outside), we were born at the right time, because ours is the time of the awakening of laymen, the waking up and calling to the banquet table of starving laymen who want to learn about their Faith more than they want to learn about anything else. Not all feel like this, but many do; and for those who do, we not only have books to read now that really take us seriously, by writers who believe we are worth being taught, but we begin at last to get *the sense of the Faith*, which makes us finally at home and capable of teaching it. Now parents can teach it to their children out of their hearts and minds instead of out of the catechism alone — that is, if they really want to do it. To *read* about it, and *pray* about it, and *think* about it is all that is necessary. This is the way to learn, and what we learn we will be able to teach.

A good example of what and how we can teach our children is to be found in the lessons of the after-season of Easter. There are three outstanding lessons to learn from Christ during these forty days. He taught them to His Apostles, and we are meant to learn them, too. I rake back through my childhood and try to remember how I learned them in catechism class.

I think I learned about the Ascension when we studied the Creed, about penance when we studied the sacrament of Penance, and about the primacy of the Pope when we studied "The Church," and how he was the "Vicar of Christ on earth." None of these three things had any connection in my mind with the *life* of Christ, even though they were things He taught. As a child, I stored them away in black and white print in my mind as things "the Church teaches."

Do not misunderstand. I love the catechism: marvelous, concise, economical statement of doctrine. But all alone and dry, right off the printed page, it just doesn't do the job. Especially when the world uses every imaginable appeal to teach *its* lessons.

*Supplementing the Catechism*

I speak the truth when I say that our children (Newlands, that is) never groan about going to catechism class or about learning catechism lessons. It presents no such difficulties — or even such distaste — for them as it did for me. Their only difficulties flow from their inheritance from their Father Adam, and they are not always as well behaved as we would like; doctrine-wise there is little trouble. They are at least familiar, more often well-acquainted, with everything it teaches, and only the formulae are strange. These they learn more easily and without rebellion because the sense of the thing is already growing in them.

How to give children all this knowledge, and when? If anyone were to ask me, I would risk my all on the combination of the daily struggle of the family to follow Christ, plus one hour every evening for being together, for examination of conscience, prayers, reading aloud, and conversation.

"Good grief!" someone will moan. "Where do you find an hour a day?"

I think I said the same thing myself before I looked to see where I wasted it. More compelling than this, however, is to look to see what is the first and most important job of parents: *to form their children in Christ.*

Because this is the most important of all the things we do, we ought to be the most lavish with our time. We take an hour for ever so many other things, but for prayers? How did our timing get so topsy-turvy? Here we find ourselves spending most of our time duly rendering to Caesar the things that are Caesar's — and we have no time left to render to God.

Because it is the most important of all the things we do, we ought to be the most lavish with our love. One of the great dangers of hectic family life is that prayer time, coming at the end of the day and the end of everyone's frayed nerves, instead of being one of the most delicious of all the day's experiences, will be the most strained. We will fondle our children, hold them on our laps, let them cuddle beside us, stroke their hair, smile deep into their eyes, at every other time, and at prayer time, for some strange reason, we are quite capable of being very sober and stern. We can seem to be most of all looking for something to disapprove, looking to see how they are not saying their prayers right, or how surely they are saying their prayers wrong.

This is how we would make a lovely thing of their relationship with God?

The last hour before bedtime is psychologically one of the most important of the day. Very little children get hugged and kissed and put to bed, of course, but from five years on, they can share this family experience — and if your family hasn't tried it, I promise: the best is yet to come. When you have done it, you'll see.

Not all family situations lend themselves to this schedule, certainly. But plan a schedule, somehow. It can be done. Even in families where husbands and wives do not share the same faith, even where there are serious trials and difficulties, it is not hopeless. Ask our Lady. She will find a way. Somewhere in your daily life, she will help find an island of time for enjoying with your children this joy that is "talking about God."

Wherever it comes, if it is quite regular, it becomes a returning to first things first. It is calming, and peaceful, and enriching. It opens horizons for all of you, you come to know Christ together, and the Faith begins to take on flesh for you.

⁀

*Lessons from the Liturgy*

This season following Easter, preparing for the Ascension and Pentecost, is a time for this kind of learning. We are full of the active joys of Easter. Now we can sit together while the Paschal candle burns in our midst, to remind us of Christ risen, and read and listen to Him teaching us before He ascends to His Father.

The Masses for the season contain these lessons in their Gospels; using them as our key, we can open the four Gospels and discover exactly what He said and how it was written down. It is important for families to own good commentaries on both the Old and New Testaments, and also a good Catholic dictionary. If the price of these books seems high, figure out for a moment how much we spend on things we do not absolutely need. Good books are as important for our souls as good food is for our bodies. It is imperative, if we would really learn the meaning of the Faith, that we *read*.

The Monday after Easter, the Gospel is about our Lord walking with the two disciples on the road to Emmaus. In it, He is teaching us in preparation for His Ascension. They did not know who He was, their eyes being "held," and they mourned aloud to Him over the death of their Master. He said to them, "O foolish . . . and slow of heart to believe in all the things which the prophets have spoken! Ought not Christ to have suffered these things and so to enter into His glory?" Then, beginning with Moses and the prophets, "He expounded to them in all the Scriptures the things that were concerning Him."[68]

We are exactly like those two disciples. We have to be shaken by the shoulders to be made to see. We have to be told to use our heads, to read, to think; then we shall see. We can recognize our own need to think and learn, that we may understand, when we see the need in our children. When we were reading about the arrest and trial of our Lord during Holy Week, Stephen interrupted to ask (with real tears running down his face), "Will He get away?" How real, and present, it always is for children.

---

[68] Luke 24:25-27.

No. He wouldn't get away. He could, but He wouldn't, because this thing had to happen. He loved us, and it was something He had to do in order to have us with Him forever. It meant Heaven for us, and the sacraments, all the gifts that poured into the Church from His sacrifice there on the Cross.

Then Stephen said, "Oh yes, I see."

Now, to rejoice in the Ascension, we must look up and see even more. We must see how great God's plan really was. We have been caught up in the pondering of the Resurrection; wait until we discover what there is to be found in the Ascension! That is what our Lord was saying to the disciples on the road to Emmaus when He said, "Ought not Christ to have suffered these things and so to enter into His glory?"

Once they understand it, children explain it like this: "God is smarter than the Devil."

We must help our children to see that the Ascension is Christ's and their own joyful victory, because they are the brothers of God-who-is-smarter-than-the-Devil.

The Devil had thought we were doomed! Man, so much less glorious than the angels, had fallen easily into his trap there in the Garden; so he took his eyes off God to gloat over poor fallen man. That was his big mistake. All the while he watched men wallowing in their sins, he failed to see that God became a man; that God joined the human family and made Himself a blood brother to all men from the beginning to the end of the world; that God took on Himself the Headship of the family, and chose to let the price of men's crimes fall on Himself so that He could be their ransom, buying back their gift of supernatural life.

The Devil must rage on the feast of the Ascension. Because it celebrates the day the God-man rose in glory to enter Heaven and sit at the right hand of His Father — and human nature, created lower than the angels, was lifted higher. It was exalted by the

Incarnation and established in Heaven at the Ascension. The sacred Body as well as the Spirit of the Son of God ascended to Heaven, and there He prepares a place for us.

Our Lord is reminding us of something else. All that He has done, He has done that we may follow Him. If this glory He has won with the price of His suffering is for us to share in Heaven, we must expect to suffer, too, so that we may enter it. *I am the Way*, He said. He entered His glory by way of suffering and death. It is good to be reminded. Suffering is necessary and sanctifying if we use it in imitation of Him; and the way to Him finally is through death. We must teach this to our children, else they, too, like so much of the world, may fail to see that suffering is a divine invitation, and death the doorway to Heaven.

The same day, Jesus appeared to the Eleven in Jerusalem. St. Luke tells about it in the Gospel used Easter Tuesday, and St. John in the Gospel for the Sunday after Easter.

At first they were alone, and then suddenly He was there. It frightened them! "Peace be to you," He said. "It is I. Do not be afraid."[69]

But they *were* afraid. They thought it must be His Spirit. So He tried to calm them. He showed them His hands and His feet. "It is I myself — touch me and see."[70]

Still they weren't sure. Then He thought of something. (He must have smiled.) "Have you anything to eat?" And He ate a piece of broiled fish and a honeycomb.[71] A ghost does not eat!

Then, as He told the disciples on the road to Emmaus, He told the Apostles: "These are the words which I spoke to you while I was yet with you, that all things must needs be fulfilled that are

---

[69] Cf. Luke 24:36.
[70] Cf. Luke 24:39.
[71] Luke 24:41-42.

written in the law of Moses, and in the prophets, and in the Psalms, concerning me."[72]

⌒

*How the Sacrament of Penance Began*

Twice He has said how important it is to see that He is the Messiah of the prophets and the Scriptures. Quite plainly He tells us to read Holy Scripture.

Then (in St. John's Gospel) He said, "As the Father hath sent me, I also send you." And breathing on them, He said, "Receive ye the Holy Spirit: Whose sins you shall forgive, they are forgiven them: and whose sins you shall retain, they are retained."[73]

Here is the sacrament of Penance. It is as important for our children to know this scene by heart as it is for them to know the words of our Lord concerning Baptism and the Eucharist. These are sacraments He instituted Himself, leaving no room for doubt concerning their meaning. He, not some subsequent council or pope, gave His priests the power to forgive sins in His name in the confessional.

For years I did not know the words said over me in absolution in the confessional. They are marvelously beautiful, and comforting:

*May almighty God have mercy on thee, forgive thee
thy sins, and bring thee to life everlasting. Amen.*

*May the almighty and merciful Lord grant thee
pardon, absolution, and remission of thy sins. Amen.*

*May our Lord Jesus Christ absolve thee, and I by His
authority do absolve thee from every bond of excommunication
and interdict, as far as I can and thou needest it.*

[72] Luke 24:44.
[73] Cf. John 20:21-22.

*And so I absolve thee from thy sins, in the name of the
Father and of the Son and of the Holy Spirit. Amen.*

*May the Passion of our Lord Jesus Christ, the merits
of the Blessed Mary ever Virgin and of all the saints,
whatever good thou hast done and whatever evil thou
hast borne, be to thee unto the remission of sins, the
increase of grace, and the reward of everlasting life. Amen.*

What a difference it makes to learn about this sacrament from our Lord Himself! He anticipates it with such gentleness, calming the fears of the Apostles, reassuring them in their doubt. *Peace be with you. It is I. Do not be afraid.* Might not the family, reading this story, retelling it often, especially in this season following Easter, impress the young minds with its great tenderness in a way that will inspire in them a special love and longing for this sacrament of forgiveness? It is a sacrament that flows from His longing for us.

Then St. John goes on to tell of Thomas the Doubter, the twin saint, who was not there at this meeting and, on coming later, was told of the appearance of the Lord.

"But he said to them, 'Unless I shall see in His hand the print of the nails, and put my finger into the place of the nails, and put my hand into His side, I will not believe.' "[74]

So our Lord came again (but He let Thomas doubt a whole week before He did), and then St. Thomas made the most powerful declaration of faith in Christ's divinity in the entire Gospel: "My Lord and my God."[75]

When they know this story of St. Thomas well, they can say these words with love and understanding at the elevation at the Mass.

[74] John 20:25.
[75] John 20:28.

⌒

*A Picnic Breakfast*

There is a special treat for the family in the Gospel for Wednesday of Easter week. All this time, you recall, our Lord appeared and disappeared, having no need for doors. This is a glorified Christ: no longer dwelling intimately with the Apostles night and day, but appearing to teach and comfort, then disappearing. This "glory" is one of the mysteries we will have to wait for Heaven to understand.

Now, on this occasion, Peter and Thomas and Nathaniel and James and John and two others had gone fishing. They had fished all night and caught nothing. When morning came, Jesus stood on the shore (but they did not recognize Him), and He called out to them, "Young men, have you any fish?"

They answered Him, "No."

Then: "Cast the net to the right of the boat, and you will find them."

How marvelous! Especially for boys who fish. We have two such who are just learning the trick of dropping a fly into the brook to tease the trout out from under the banks. Oh, to have a Friend who could look right through the shadows behind the rocks and say, "Drop your line here, and you will find them."

"They cast, therefore, and now they were unable to draw it up for the great number of fishes. The disciple whom Jesus loved said therefore to Peter, 'It is the Lord.' "

John would know, instinctively. He was so quick to see things. But Peter would immediately *go* — that was his way. And girding his tunic about him, he threw himself into the sea and began to lunge through the water toward the shore. The rest came behind with the boat, dragging the net full of fishes.

Now comes the best part of all. "When, therefore, they had landed, they saw a fire ready, and a fish laid upon it, and bread.

Jesus said to them, 'Bring here some of the fishes that you caught just now.' "

So Peter went aboard and hauled the net to land, and it was full with 153 large fishes. But it was not torn. And Jesus said to them, "Come and breakfast."[76]

A picnic!

This is the season of the year — why not? A picnic for us, too! In the morning — a picnic breakfast! If you live in the country, choosing the site is the problem. Under the sugar maple in front, or under the sugar maple in back? Down by the brook? There are beautiful dewy things early in the morning down by the brook, gone as soon as the sun gets high The water sounds are beautiful, and the birds — new ones coming back every day — are there, and the first skunk cabbage, the first cowslips, the first violets. After-Easter comes in so many different parts! This season has so many little seasons!

Or, if you live in the town, breakfast on the back porch or the backyard or the breezeway? Or, if you live in the city, breakfast on the roof? Or do you have a little areaway in back (supposing you are on the ground floor) or a park nearby? It could be breakfast in the park early in the morning right after Mass, with hot coffee and cocoa in thermoses, and maybe fat bacon rolls in the lunch-box. Just for the fun of sharing an outdoor breakfast once a year with Him.

If you have no place, only a room, or an apartment, still have a picnic with Him in your heart. Have something very good to eat — special bread, maybe, or rolls — and bring some of the spring in with you, perhaps flowers off a pushcart; and bring Him home in your hearts from Mass and have a place at the table set for Him. He will really be there among you.

[76] Cf. John 21:1-12.

It happened on the shore of the sea of Tiberius, on an April or May morning.

After they had finished their breakfast, He said to Peter, "Simon, son of John, dost thou love me more than these do?"

"Yes, Lord, Thou knowest that I love Thee."

And He said to Peter, "Feed my lambs."

Then He asked him a second time, "Simon, son of John, dost thou love me?"

Then Peter said, "Yes, Lord, Thou knowest that I love Thee."

"Feed my lambs." Then he asked Peter a third time, "Simon, son of John, dost thou love me?"

Then Peter was truly grieved. He did not have to ask the reason for the question *three times*. Our Lord was letting him say, "I love You" thrice to make up for his three denials. "Lord, Thou knowest all things. Thou knowest that I love Thee."[77]

Our Lord was also here asserting the primacy of Peter. To solemnly repeat three times in the presence of witnesses such a charge as this gave the act a legal seal of validity. "Before memory and the spoken word were replaced by documents and signatures, that was the recognized way of making a good juridical disposition."[78] Thus, before witnesses, Peter was made head of the Church and the faithful were in his care, as they would be in the care of all the Peters who would follow him. This occasion, and the time He called Peter a rock and said, "On this Rock I will build my Church,"[79] are our Lord defining the Papacy. We must teach our children this.

On the fortieth day on a hillside near Bethany, Christ gave them their final instruction: "All authority in Heaven and on

---

[77] John 21:15-17.

[78] *Catholic Commentary on Holy Scripture.*

[79] Matt. 16:18.

earth has been given to me; you, therefore, must go out, making disciples of all nations, and baptizing them in the name of the Father and of the Son and of the Holy Spirit, teaching them to observe all the commandments which I have given you. And behold I am with you all days, even until the consummation of the world."[80]

He said that they were to be His witnesses even to the ends of the earth.[81] (St. Patrick, in his Confession, said that was the reason he braved the far, wild lonely places in Ireland, where he went in search of pagans in order to baptize them.) He told them to go back to Jerusalem and wait for their baptism of fire, which they would receive not many days hence, "the fulfillment of the Father's promise"; and He was promising them Pentecost.[82]

Then they saw Him lifted up and carried out of sight in a cloud, and as they gazed heavenward, two men in white garments were suddenly standing at their side. "Men of Galilee, why do you stand here looking heavenward? He who has been taken from you into Heaven, this same Jesus, will come back in the same fashion, just as you have watched Him going into Heaven."[83] This is the scene of the Second Glorious Mystery of the Rosary. Then they returned to Jerusalem, to the Upper Room, and there, with Mary, the Mother of Jesus, and the other holy women, gave themselves up to prayer.

We are apostles, too, like these first Apostles. Each of us is sent in the frame of his own life and work to do the work of Christ. If we are to do it well, however, we must know Him, and how He taught, and the things He taught. We will find Him in the Gospels. If we are a family, we should find Him in the Gospels together.

---

[80] Cf. Matt. 28:18-20.
[81] Cf. Acts 1:8.
[82] Cf. Acts 1:4-5.
[83] Acts 1:10-11.

# The Year and Our Children

⌒

*Eating Alfresco, and Evening Mass*

Last year we started an entirely new custom in our family for the feast of the Ascension. We planned to go to Mass at seven in the evening. But that posed a problem. School was out at 2:30, and the children were home by three. From then till after seven — fasting? Not Newlands, who wear their appetites on their sleeves. We could hear the moans and groans — and we wanted this to be a joyful feast.

So we planned a mid-afternoon cook-out under the sugar maple (in the back) for 3:30, to fill everybody up so that they could last until after seven. Hot dogs, green salad, potato chips, pickles, ginger ale, cake — all-American food. And it was a joy. Then off to Mass with two other families in their cars. For an extra treat, we bought ice cream on the way home and shouted to the others, "Come on home and have ice cream with us. It's the feast of the Ascension!" We can tell you something else we will never forget either. We don't remember dates very well in this house, but we remember feasts. We had twin kids born to our goat Helen last year, too, named Schwani and Barli. When? We couldn't tell you the date, but we'll never forget the season.

"The day before the feast of the Ascension!"

Chapter 14

# Pentecost

I wish I had learned long ago about the fruits of the Holy Spirit.
We did learn the names of them, that is true, but we never went
further than that; and because, all strung out in a row, they merely
sounded like the virtues of nice people, we took it for granted that
they came automatically with being "good." Like patience, for example. Anyone could consider the quality of patience and see that
there was a great gap between patience and being patient; but
most of the time, we were convinced that those who were patient
were born that way. We had no real conviction that you could get
that way. It was all very vague. After a while, even the names of
them got mixed up with the names of other things. We couldn't
remember if they were fruits, or gifts, or virtues, or what. It was safe
to say that they were nouns.

Now we discover that the whole struggle between the flesh and
the spirit could be changed if we understood about the fruits of the
Holy Spirit — and acted on that understanding. It is the most encouraging thing yet to realize that the fruits are the effects of using
the gifts, not just something you grit your teeth and vow to acquire
or bust.

It is hard to explain why we never put the same practical sense
to work applying the Gospels as we did applying other things. Like
seeing a sign that said "Turn right," and we turned right. Our Lord

talked about the fruits enough, in the Gospels, but for some reason, we never took Him literally, the way we did the traffic signs — for all we believed it was important to get to Heaven, and these were apparently the directions for getting there. Just as we never dreamed that what He said about abiding in us applied literally to His indwelling, so we also missed what He said about the trees and vines bearing or failing to bear fruit. We had ears to hear, but we did not hear. We listened to His parables year after year from the altar and supposed He was saying over and over again that good Catholics go to Heaven and bad Catholics don't — never realizing that, instead, He was giving the directions for *being* a good Catholic.

It would take too long and more space than we have here to discover why — but that isn't necessary. What we can do at once is explain to our children that He means what He says *literally*, most of the time. (There are a few exceptions, such as cutting off your hand or plucking out your eye.) He means literally that the fruits of the Holy Spirit are fruits that grow in the soul that strives to use the gifts, and — joy of joys — that the gifts are that, *gifts*, freely given when the Holy Spirit comes to dwell in us at Baptism.

Living in Christ, reborn after Baptism, we could do great things with these gifts — if we would use them. Great things — such as being saints. At Pentecost, the Holy Spirit comes down upon us in an abundance of grace. Could we not beg Him, in our preparation for His feast, to enable us to understand and use the gifts, that we may bear fruits?

We prepare first in prayer, imitating our Lady and the Apostles, who spend the nine days between Ascension and Pentecost in prayer. A family novena to the Holy Spirit invites Him to prepare our souls to receive best the great graces to come. Novenas to the Holy Spirit are available in booklet form, or the family may prefer to put together favorite prayers to the Holy Spirit, Psalms, hymns, and readings, and use these for the nine days.

Then there must be the story of Pentecost found in the second chapter of the Acts of the Apostles. It is full of excitement and intriguing details that children love, and is both good reading and good telling. Acquaintance with it ensures a thoughtful meditation each time the Glorious Mysteries of the Rosary come around.

And then, after prayers and a retelling of the story, it is easy to direct conversation to the gifts and fruits of the Spirit, so that we may consider in a practical way how they apply to our lives and our duties.

Lastly, in order to extend this lesson through all the year, we prepare a gift for each member of the family and decorations for our feast day that will enable all of us to remember that we must use the gifts if we would bear the fruits.

First, the story. There were Jews from all over that part of the world in the city at that time because it was the Jewish feast of Pentecost and they had come to celebrate the harvest. *Pentecost* is a Greek word meaning "fifty" — the fiftieth day. On the seventh week following the Passover (and one of its ceremonies had been the waving of a sheaf of grain before the Lord as a communal offering), the Law said that male Jews were to reassemble in Jerusalem and present to the Lord at the Temple two loaves of bread made from the fine white flour of the newly harvested wheat. This feast was also to commemorate the promulgation of the Law.

As always, the time for the event that was about to take place in the Church seemed to have been chosen for the significance of the season, for it was to herald the coming of Love Himself to dwell, a living Law, within the new Church, and its outcome that very first day was to mark the beginning of the harvest of souls. Some spiritual writers have called it the birthday of the Church. Others, like Leo XIII, describe it as an Epiphany:

The Church, which, already conceived, came forth from the side of the second Adam in His sleep on the Cross, first showed herself before the eyes of men on the great day of Pentecost.

And always, our Lady was at the heart of it. If we are to prepare for and celebrate the feasts of our Redemption well, we must unite ourselves to her first, the chosen one of the Holy Spirit, His bride and His beloved. She was at the heart of all these comings forth, from the first one to the last. In her, the Word was uttered and became Flesh. She brought Him forth in Bethlehem. She held Him in her arms at the first Epiphany so that the Gentiles might see this Jewish God who would graft them to Himself. At her word, He proceeded at Cana to His first act in creating a Church that He would build by teaching and miracles for three years, then leave in the hands of men. To her He entrusted His Church from His travail on the Cross: "Behold thy Mother."[84] She alone understood His promise of birth in glory out of the tomb. And now there gathered about her the ones He had chosen to sanctify in the life-giving fire of the Holy Spirit, that they might go forth and preach to all men the need and the way to be born again.

There came the sound of a great wind, so loud that the Jews outside in the city were attracted to the scene; and the zeal kindled by the tongues of fire in the souls of those men was so great you might say they were exploded out of the Upper Room. The gift of tongues, the quality of their enthusiasm, was so far beyond the comprehension of the crowds that the scoffers assured themselves they were drunk.

But it was only nine o'clock in the morning! St. Peter said to them that men do not get drunk so early in the day. This was not

[84] John 19:27.

drunkenness, but the fulfillment of a prophecy from the prophet Joel: ". . . and I will pour out my spirit in those days, upon my servants and handmaids, so they will prophesy."[85]

He preached to the Jews about David, who prophesied that one of his sons would God set upon his throne, that he would not be left in death, but be resurrected, and His body would not see corruption. They were the witnesses themselves. They had seen that God raised this Jesus from the dead; and He had this day poured out His Holy Spirit, "as you can see and hear for yourselves."

Indeed they could, in their own tongues — Parthians, Medes, Elamites; those from Mesopotamia, Judaea, Cappadocia, Pontus or Asia, Phrygia or Pamphylia, Egypt or the parts of Libya around Cyrene, some from Rome, some Cretans, Arabians. . . . "When they heard this, their consciences were stung; and they asked Peter and His fellow apostles, 'What must we do?'

" 'Repent and be baptized, in the name of Jesus Christ, to have your sins forgiven; then you will receive the gift of the Holy Spirit.' "

And there was a harvest that day of three thousand souls. Three thousand to whom the Holy Spirit came — and with Him His gifts.

*The Pentecost Gifts*

How explain to children the gifts of the Holy Spirit — *habits*, as they are called, that make it possible for the soul to do certain things? We use the word *habit* so differently. It is hard to understand its use here.

A comparison on the natural level helps. Men have the habit of eating. God has given them this ability so that they may eat and stay alive. It is a wonderfully complicated thing: He designed our

[85] Joel 2:28.

bodies so that they can use the food we eat to make flesh and bone and blood. This is an ability, a habit, He has given to us freely, with which we had nothing to do (as we have with forming the habit of taking cream in our coffee). God made it a part of our nature, and the whole process is a natural gift.

In the same way, but on a supernatural level, He has given us habits of soul. These enable us to follow the inspirations of the Holy Spirit. The man with the natural habit of eating will, if he is in his right mind, follow the prompting of his body and eat to keep strong and do his work. In the same way, the man with the supernatural habit, or gift, in his soul must follow the Holy Spirit's promptings to keep His soul in the state of grace, and to increase in sanctity.

Now, it is quite possible that the first man may refuse to heed the promptings of hunger, for some perverse reason refuse to eat — and he will die of starvation. Foolish he. In the same way, it is possible that the second man may refuse to heed the promptings of the Holy Spirit, refuse to use the gifts given his soul, and he will die eternally. More than foolish, this man. He is lost.

This sounds very drastic, until we hear what our Lord says about the necessity of our bearing fruit:

> I am the true vine, and my Father is the husbandman; and every branch in me that beareth not fruit He taketh away, and every branch that beareth fruit He purgeth that it may bring forth more fruit. Abide in me, and I in you; except the branch abide in the vine, it cannot bring forth fruit; without me you can do nothing.[86]

He is talking about us, the baptized Catholics who are the branches in Him. Every branch abiding in Him that does not bear fruit will be taken away.

[86] Cf. John 15:1-5.

He says it another way, equally drastic:

Already the axe has been put to the root of the trees, so that every tree which does not show good fruit will be hewn down and cast into the fire.[87]

He says it a third way:

And this was a parable he told them: There was a man that had a fig tree planted in his vineyard, but when he came and looked for fruit on it, he could find none; whereupon he said to his vinedresser, "See now, I have been coming to look for fruit on this fig tree for three years, and cannot find any. Cut it down; why should it be a useless charge upon the land?"[88]

He said something else, quite frightening. He said that it is impossible to be safe and stay in the middle. "Every tree is known by its fruits; either make the tree good and the fruits good, or make the tree corrupt and the fruits corrupt." You cannot halt between. "The axe is laid to the root of the tree. Every tree therefore that doth not yield good fruit is cut down and cast into the fire."[89]

It is important, therefore, that we see whether or not we are bearing fruit, and if we are not, in what way we are wanting in our use of the gifts of the Holy Spirit. Having arrived at applications that are dear enough for our (Newland) children to understand, and which are by now quite familiar to them, we return to them again and again, trying to find fresh examples each week or month or Pentecost, to see if we are using the gifts, bearing the fruits.

[87] Matt. 3:10.
[88] Cf. Luke 13:6-7.
[89] Cf. Matt. 7:16-19.

# The Year and Our Children

*The Gifts and Their Fruits*

The gifts are *fear of the Lord, piety, knowledge, fortitude, counsel, understanding,* and *wisdom.* If they are used, they bear the fruits: *charity, joy, peace, patience, kindness, goodness, long-suffering, faith, mildness, modesty, continence,* and *chastity.*

*Fear of the Lord:* the example we use is the phrase from the Act of Contrition: ". . . I dread the loss of Heaven and the pains of Hell, but most of all because I have offended Thee, my God, who art all good and deserving of all my love." One of the signs of the faithful use of this gift would be a love for frequent Confession. A child who has made his First Communion should know that unless he is in the state of mortal sin, he may — and should — receive Holy Communion, after a devout Act of Contrition or *Confiteor* indicating his sincere sorrow for sin and his sincere intention to try to sin no more. But it is good to see that he is growing in love for the sacrament of Penance, because it is a sacrament and will give his soul precious grace, because it is an indication of Christ's love for Him, and because he has a desire to be vigilant about even venial sin. These could be signs of a salutary *fear of the Lord,* which has nothing servile in it, but rather much of awe and reverence.

*Piety* is described by Cardinal Manning as a gift that, among other things, helps us to have loyal devotion to God and all His creatures, because they are His creatures.

St. Gregory says that *piety* manifests itself in tenderness and mercy toward our neighbor. We might examine ourselves with a literal application on this score. Do we reserve judgment with a tender mercy, remember that often our neighbor has not had the same moral instruction, has not been taught to practice the love of God, to see Christ in all men?

*Knowledge* relates not merely to a knowledge of things, but to a knowledge of God's will and, in this light, the ability to see how things are to be used in relation to it. We relate this for our boys to the use of guns and the popular pastime, gun-play. Guns are intricate mechanisms invented by man and called lethal because they are able to kill. They are used in our environment for hunting game in season, for the purpose of eating the game. They are used in self-defense in time of war, or when attacked by a bear, a tiger, an elephant, or the like, or — as they recently read in a newspaper story — by a poor crazed man who went about shooting bystanders so that an officer had to fire at him. Some people believe that even these uses are not permitted; so the use or non-use of them is a question to read, think, and pray about, and decide for oneself one day.

God has given a commandment: *Thou shalt not kill,* which demands of us reverence for life — our own as well as others'. It is not in keeping with this reverence for life that anyone make a game of killing. To kill is never a game, and to play at it is a poor substitute for a game. As training for a Christian who will one day share the responsibility for keeping the peace of the world, it is a poor point of departure. Children can see all this quite readily, if it is explained to them. At times they will be sufficiently enthralled by the excitement in a neighborhood game of good guys and bad guys to indulge, but when they do, we return to the principle, explain all over again, and, best of all, keep our weather eye out for other games to substitute. They are willing to substitute, if there is something good to substitute.

The last time this happened, two little lads from down the lane arrived with brand-new double-holster belts with twin pistols in each. They crept carefully past the back porch, but Eagle-Eye-Indian-Mother saw them all the same. "You fellows, packing those guns," she said cheerfully, "park your hardware here. No gun games in our yard, please. Pretend-killing is a very poor game. We've talked about it before. Play something else."

"Gee — like what?"

"Like zoo. I have peanuts in their shells, very fine for play-ing zoo."

"Boy! I'm an ape." And they ran off and played zoo. (Always keep a big bag of peanuts in their shells for any apes you may know who like to play zoo.)

*The Gifts Help Each Other*

The gifts of the Holy Spirit support and perfect one another. *Fortitude*, for example, supports *knowledge* with its strength. It gives the soul confidence to persevere in trials for the love of God. Boys who have been helped to consider gun-play, play at killing, in the light of God's will for guns and men are nevertheless tempted because everybody plays it and it is exciting. Sometimes they give in and run with the pack. But *fortitude* will be the reason they sometimes hold fast to the principle.

"Shooting isn't such a hot game. I've got a baseball. Come on, let's play that." This supposes that parents have carefully explained the principles of Christian behavior to their children, helped them aspire to them by means of daily prayer, by thinking, reading, talk-ing about these principles. One holds to them out of love of God; so their love of God must be carefully tended by their parents.

*Piety* moves us to defend others; *fortitude* gives us the courage to do it openly. Without *fortitude*, one "feels bad" about injustice but takes no stand, lacks the courage to correct wrongs, to stand firm and give good example.

The gift of *counsel* "enables us not only to see what is right and what is wrong, to see what is obedience, but also . . . to know that which, between two things both good and right, is better, higher, and more pleasing in the sight of God." It points out the way to perfection.

The use of *counsel* can begin in early childhood, but it is with such seemingly insignificant things that only those in the heart of the family would see them or know their great importance. Little ones use, or respond to, the gift of *counsel* when they "give in," for the love of God, in such matters as sitting by the window in the car, sitting next to Granny at table, having the first piece, the best, the end piece (of meat loaves, frosted cakes, and homemade bread) even though it is their "turn." *Counsel* gently persuades us that self-love is the impediment to union with God, and helps us see the ways to overcome it. In older children, it is used in such actions as letting others get ahead of you in line, accepting the worn books in school, letting someone else who wants to pass the papers, give out the pencils, erase the blackboards — unless the teacher *tells* you to do it. In that case, you must be obedient. These things and many others, done for the love of God, work great effects in the soul with the help of the Holy Spirit. The Little Flower's permissive acceptance and love for the chipped jug, the leftovers from the kitchen, the old nun's abusiveness; Dominic Savio's acceptance in union with Christ, of blame when he was blameless — all for love of God, show them using this gift of *counsel*, to draw step by step nearer to God.

These five gifts are called the moral gifts, enabling the soul to live a perfect moral life if it will use them. The gifts of *understanding* and *wisdom* are said to be the gifts that enable us to contemplate God.

*Understanding* is a supernatural gift that is better understood if we use a natural example. When a boy reads a page of a book, his eyes read the letters on the page, but his natural understanding reads the meaning of the letters and penetrates the sense of the message written on the page. In the supernatural order, *understanding* is the gift that enables us to see, to comprehend, truths and aspects of God in which we already have faith. "The Word was made flesh" is an example. Understanding enables us to see in these words the entire doctrine of the Incarnation: God made man.

The family uses this gift when it endeavors to live the year in union with the Church, using all its natural and supernatural resources to teach in many varied ways the great lessons of the Faith. Probably it is more accurate to say that this effort is *aimed* at the gift of *understanding,* at offering the members of the family opportunities to use the gift and see the unutterable beauty of divine Truth. Examples would be the use of the Christ candle, which, when lighted, speaks to the mind and soul of Christ, the Light of the World; and the pelican, carved on the altar front, which speaks of the Blood of the Lamb which was the price of our Redemption. The gift of *understanding* enables us to see these things and progress from the visible image or idea to the contemplation of its meaning in God.

"Fear of the Lord is the beginning of *wisdom.*" Although *wisdom* is a gift and accompanies the other gifts of the Holy Spirit into the soul, it has the capacity to expand or contract as the soul cooperates with the Holy Spirit — or refuses to. "The gift of wisdom gives to the soul a special love for those things that God loves, and a special hatred for that which is hateful in His sight. It is intuitive and instinctive before all reasoning, and of a supernatural sense."[90]

It is the final blossom, he says, growing from a root which is *fear of the Lord*. It is *wisdom* that makes us want to be friends with God. He says that some souls have greater facility at acquiring it than others, among them children fresh from the waters of Baptism, whose souls are not yet stained with sin; whose hearts are not yet darkened.

Here, *wisdom* touches our effort, indicating what should be our caution and zeal to implant truth and love of God in the souls of

---

[90] Cardinal Manning, *The Internal Mission of the Holy Ghost.*

our children early (and it is never too early). We shall need love and patience, tenderness, gentleness, sweetness, joy — many qualities, if we are to teach well. These qualities are the fruits the Holy Spirit will bear in us if we will use His gifts well.

*Charity*, *joy*, *peace*, *patience*, *kindness*, *goodness*, *long-suffering*, *faithfulness*, *mildness*, *modesty*, *continence*, and *chastity*, the fruits that the gifts will bear in us, will form in the most positive way our relation with our children and our ability to communicate teaching to them, as well as their receptiveness to our teaching.

*Charity*, *joy*, and *peace* are the fruits that touch our soul's relation to God Himself. *Charity* is our love for God, the fruit of His love in us. *Joy* is our spirit of thankfulness, our joyous awareness of His goodness. *Peace* lets us rest in God, and be at rest with ourselves, with the members of our family, with all men. It will do us little good to know doctrine perfectly and be able to communicate it, if our teaching is not warm and glowing with these qualities.

*Patience*, *kindness*, *goodness*, *long-suffering*, *faithfulness*, and *mildness* are qualities that have to do with our relations with our children, our families, and our neighbors. *Patience* "bears with" infinite numbers of trials, as every parent knows. *Kindness* is not irritable or resentful, is lacking in malice. *Goodness* pours out goodness, warming the hearts of all around it with goodness. *Long-suffering* "puts up with," waits for the answer to prayer, waits before judging or losing patience before discouragement, perseveres and does not throw up its hands and vow it "can do no more for such a one." *Faithfulness* means that we are impeccably truthful, our word is as good as our oath; we are punctual, not given to exaggeration, to flattery. *Mildness* means that we are gentle and forbearing, overlooking wrong, slights, and harboring no ill will or resentment.

*Modesty*, *continence*, and *chastity* have relation to ourselves.

That *modesty* is a fruit of the Holy Spirit sheds much light on the overwhelming immodesty of our times. We had thought it was a decision one made for oneself. Now we discover that it comes of following the inspiration of the Holy Spirit — or else one is not modest. This rings true. Immodesty of bearing, conduct, dress, demeanor, or regard for others is like a flood unimpeded by any channels of convention. The immodest scoff at the modest as though they themselves had weighed both sides of the matter carefully and made an enlightened and uninhibited choice. One is not free to choose. *Modesty* is a fruit, not a choice. It is a state of mind, an attitude, which grows in the soul that follows the prompting of the Love of God. This clarifies the whole question, and should spur parents to a more careful, more zealous tending of their children's souls, encouraging them to explain the gifts, to pray together for the grace to use the gifts.

*Modesty* also relates to the moderate use of things, even those things that are lawful. Here it seems especially to be one of the fruits of *counsel*.

*Continency* means repression of the passions: the passion of anger, the passion for pleasure, for honor, for wealth; the sexual passions. Indeed, to understand that *continency* is a fruit, and not a choice, does explain a lot.

*Chastity* relates to the chaste custody of the senses because they are the avenues to the soul by which sin enters. One easily sees that *chastity* is a fruit of all the gifts: of *knowledge*, which teaches how and why we are to use our senses; of *fear of the Lord*, which wishes not to offend Him in the use of them; of *piety*, which teaches us a respect for our neighbor's soul and body as well as our own, and so forth.

To state that these are fruits, not choices, does not imply that we are not free to choose to be chaste or modest or continent. But there is a difference between blithely choosing, and then failing to be. The will is tempered and made strong and pure only by its cooperation with the Holy Spirit. Here is where our choice lies.

We choose to work with Him or against Him, and whatever our choice is here foretells our fruits.

All of this is simplified, in an effort to relate the use of our gifts in a practical way to our daily life. We have learned so much about our bodies — and so little about our souls. To study the liturgy for Pentecost, the feast of the Holy Spirit, will profit us only in the most meager way if we do not make continual effort to *know* the Holy Spirit. How can we praise with the rest of the Church, in the prayers and Masses of the season, when we barely know what it is we praise? We know the work of God the Father as our Creator, and the work of God the Son as our Redeemer. Let us strive to know the Holy Spirit and His work, for He is our Sanctifier. Then on Pentecost we will understand what it means that He pours forth His grace upon us. We will know how to go about using His grace, and we will be able to thank Him with full hearts.

*Celebrating Pentecost*

Now to prepare a gift for each member of the family that will remind us all year to use the gifts so that we may bear the fruits. We first heard of this idea through a friend of a friend of a group of Sisters. As Pentecost favors, they make bookmarks in the form of white doves cut from parchment and threaded with red satin ribbons for markers. On one wing, or on one page of a tiny folder held in the dove's beak, is lettered a gift of the Holy Spirit; on the other, a fruit. They are placed all together in a basket, and each Sister chooses one. The gift written on her dove is the gift the Holy Spirit wishes her to work on for the year. Sometimes it is the same gift year after year. In such a case, one can hardly fail to get the point!

We varied this custom by cutting two-piece doves and stapling the wings on so that they are three-dimensional, then hanging them in a flock by red ribbons of varying length. Pentecost morning we each chose a dove, blindfolded. A gift and a fruit were lettered on the wings of each. They were a brilliant display of "Holy Spirits," and we let them hang there through the Octave. Lots of people who came into the house asked questions.

Red, or an orange-flame, is the color for table decorations on Pentecost, the color of divine love. Red cut-outs of candles, or red paper cut-outs of doves for place cards or Grace-before-Meals cards, are easy to make with construction paper. Doves pasted to tongue depressors or lollipop sticks, or mounted on wire or drinking straws, can be anchored in individual clay bases or all together in a larger one to make a fine Pentecost centerpiece. Little children can make place favors with red Lifesavers stuck with frosting on cookies and a tiny red birthday-cake candle. Lighted when Grace is said, they burn for a few minutes to remind us of the "tongues of fire."

During the preparation for the feast, children can learn the gifts and fruits by making their own mobiles with wire clothes hangers. Tie a wire clothes hanger to a string, use it as is or bend it into an interesting shape, or suspend additional hangers from it. Let the children cut doves, candles, flames, circles, or other shapes from heavy paper and letter on them the gifts and the fruits. Suspend them at varying heights with black threads, sometimes with small objects to weight them so they will swing slowly in space.

Jamie made a beautiful mobile of the Holy Spirit and His work in us. An odd piece of wire bent to an interesting shape had suspended from it an orange cut-out of a dove; the sheet of orange paper from which the dove was cut (thus giving also a space dove surrounded by paper); a piece of transparent plastic that changed the color of the dove when it swung in front of them; a shell — because He comes to us first in Baptism; a small candle to symbolize the light He brings us as well as the tongues of fire on the first

Pentecost; and a silver button that the children thought looked like a strawberry recalled to them the fruit of the Holy Spirit effected in us if we bid Him welcome and use His light. This took him only about an hour to dream up and assemble, and it is an eloquent meditation as well as a work of art.

We have also a mixture called, quite inelegantly, *Gook*. It is sometimes called *Muck*. This is not much of an improvement over *Gook*. If this is to be used in preparation for the feast, plan the work session with it a week ahead of time in order that the objects you make will have time to be thoroughly dry. Most mothers will recall using it at one time or another in their childhood, at arts or crafts class, in the Girl Scouts or Campfire Girls. It is a mixture of salt, cornstarch, and water cooked, which dries as hard as a rock — most of the time. We have concluded that the few times it didn't were due to insufficient cooking. If you are an adventurous family and like inexpensive media for creating, do try it. Work with it in a place where the mess can be easily cleaned up afterward.

GOOK

1 cup table salt
½ cup cornstarch (laundry starch also works)
½ cup boiling water

Mix salt and cornstarch in saucepan. Add boiling water, and stir until well mixed. Hold over burner, and stir rapidly until mixture is thick and of a consistency for modeling. Let cool a few minutes after removing from pan. Avoid modeling anything too delicate, or rolling too thin for the cookie-cutting. Individual batches of it may be colored with vegetable coloring. This mixture takes about five minutes to prepare.

We have modeled doves, inserting a candle in each dove for the "tongue of fire." We have cut doves out of it with a cookie cutter, affixing a candle. We have used it as well to cut Christmas-tree ornaments with cookie cutters, for making beads, Indian "wampum," for modeling simple little figures, for homemade beads for rosaries on which little children may "learn" by counting out the beads and stringing them properly in decades. Round balls stuck full of toothpicks are porcupines. Round balls stuck half-full of toothpicks are turkeys. We have used it for homemade jewelry, for little fruits to go in boutonnieres, and on rainy days for just plain old something-to-do. It takes poster paints admirably and, if necessary, shellac. Pieces that are to become beads or ornaments must have the appropriate holders, holes, threads, or wires, punched in or affixed before they are dry. These may be decorated with glitter or gilt paint.

It will take more than one Pentecost celebration, even when we are well prepared, for us to learn what it means to be filled with the Holy Spirit. But even one observance will teach us what our Lord meant when He told His Apostles of the mission of the Holy Spirit: "the Advocate, the Holy Spirit, whom the Father will send in my name. He will teach you all things and bring to your mind whatever I have said to you."[91]

This Holy Spirit is His love. His love for His Father, returned to Him by His Father. It is their gaze of love, their delight in each other, out of which came their desire for us. Let us say together, often:

*Come, Holy Spirit, fill the hearts of Thy faithful:*
*and kindle in them the fire of Thy love.*
*Send forth Thy Spirit, and they shall be created,*
*and Thou shalt renew the face of the earth.*

[91] John 14:26.

Chapter 15

~

# Mary Shrines and the *Angelus*

May is Mary's month, and during the May in Mary's Year, we decided to do something twice as special in her honor. The very best thing of all seemed to be shrines.

Right here is the place for me to make a confession of sorts. I have never been terribly enthusiastic about transforming my house into a shrine. Not that I have anything against shrines nor, I think, that I lack a right devotion to our Lady; but sometimes shrines seemed to end up more shrine than living room and the effect on callers as well as the family has been slightly dampening. People glance around uneasily in the presence of too many vigil lights, and an ordinary family fracas about playing allies on the living-room floor, with small boys to be hauled apart and given a word or two about wrestling in the house, seems far more sacrilegious than the occasion merits when performed in front of an altar. That, it seemed to me, was not the purpose of shrines: to make everyone uncomfortable.

Then, too, much of the shrine material available left something wanting, and I was forever telling myself someday we would get to work and make the kind of shrines we would like for our house. Apparently our Lady decided that her year was the time, and it didn't take much ingenuity after all. We made shrines from things we had around the house, and they are quite lovely.

# The Year and Our Children

There is *Our Lady of the Kitchen*. She stands in a square glass dish about 4 by 4 inches on a windowsill above the kitchen sink. In front of her is a tiny donkey, resting after all the trips to Bethlehem, Egypt, the hill country in Judea, Jerusalem, and back to Nazareth again. Around them is a bit of green moss from the woods and some delicate fernlike trees that happen to be carrot tops Grandma Reed sprouted. Everyone knows about sprouting carrot tops. You cut them off about a half-inch above the green stalk from which the leafy tops have been removed, set them in water for a week or ten days, and they will sprout. Sweet potatoes will sprout the same way, although they take longer. Both have a beautiful lacy foliage that is very Mary-like.

Jamie made a shrine for *Our Lady of the Dining Room*. He took his idea from a little Mexican wall shrine of *Our Lady of Soledad*, which means "our Lady of Solitude" — and everyone laughs about that in a house with two parents, two grandparents, and seven children. It is a dear little glass and tin shrine, like a tiny showcase with ornamental tin around it, the way the Mexicans do. Inside is a Mexican madonna in black and gold with gaudy foil flowers decorating the background.

First he carved a little Mary out of soap (with some help, but each time they need less help; and the result need not be perfect in any case). He made her simple and block-like, somewhat as Jean Chariot makes Mary. He painted her very bright colors: royal-blue skirt, fuchsia blouse, tangerine veil with a yellow cross on it; like all Latin-American color schemes that sound wild on paper, it is perfectly lovely to see. Her face is not modeled at all but a flat oval on which we painted her features with a small brush. Then we took a little wooden box that used to hold dried codfish (a cigar box without the cover would do), covered and lined it with aluminum foil, and tucked in a little scalloped cuff at the top. Inside the shrine above her head at the back is a garland of tiny artificial flowers and bells, tied with a small black velvet bow (part of an old boutonniere). And there she stands, very cheerful on the dining-room wall, bidding everyone enjoy their meal and hoping that, because of her presence, the children will eat nicely.

Monica made a shrine for her bedside table with a print of a Hans Memling *Annunciation*, postcard size, and a small wooden box with a hinged lid and stood on end to open like a diptych. Cardboard boxes with hinged lids would do as well, but these should be painted first. The Annunciation she used had the figures far enough apart so that it could be cut in two with our Lady pasted in one cover of the box, Gabriel in the other. She mounted the two pictures on gold paper first to provide a narrow rim of gold around each. Finally, she treated the whole box, pictures and all, with white shellac.

Another bedroom shrine was once an empty cornmeal box. It is made the same way as a doll's cradle from a cornmeal or oatmeal box, but this time it stands up on one end. We removed the top lid and cut a piece out of the front of the box, a little less than half the circumference, leaving the bottom rim intact. Then we lined the box with yellow construction paper, replaced the top lid and taped the seam. Next, in a wallpaper-sample book, we found a lovely blue-green paper with a small medallion that seemed Mary-like, and this we pasted over the entire outside surface of the box. Inside stands a slim little figure of our Lady. The shrine is very nice on a wall bracket over a child's bed.

For our living room, we have a shadow-box shrine. An empty baby cereal box was cut to fit the back of an old gilt frame, lined with a soft deep-blue paper and taped to the back of the frame. This we hung with a gold ribbon against a drape of sapphire-blue velveteen. We change the arrangement every month or six weeks. Sometimes we hang a miniature of the Immaculate Heart in it, sometimes a woodcarving of our Lady with a small blue ceramic turtle who loves to look up at her; sometimes we install the soap carvings of Mary and the Infant — part of our crèche group but so beloved we like to bring them out more often than once a year. This is where the family says the Rosary. With a pot of ivy on the shelf below, and a candle that moves her shadow so softly that sometimes she seems to be really moving, the effect of this shrine is just right. It dampens no spirits but keeps her present in a tender, warm, comforting way.

The more we worked, the more ideas came to us. For example, our Lady isn't just our Mother in our house, but the Mother of all men, and we ought to have a shrine to remind us to pray to *Our Lady, Mother of the Russians*. We mounted a reproduction of an icon with a Russian Mary and Child (if you can't find one, a print of *Our Lady of Perpetual Help* does beautifully) on top of a shallow cardboard box cover that had been covered with gold paper. A plain box cover would do, painted one of the colors in the icon — perhaps the lovely brick red, or a shiny black, or varnished with dark varnish. With poster paints we did a decorative band on either side of the print and on the sides of the box and then covered the whole with white shellac. It is so light that it will hang on a thumbtack. If Stephen is around, he will remind everyone who passes by to "Please ask our Lady to help the Russians find God."

For Christmas that year, Monica received a beautiful oblong basket with a hinged lid that was made in Indochina; so we made a shrine to *Our Lady of the Orient* with that, to remind us to pray for her help with the missions there. Standing on one end with the lid open like a door, it is a small tabernacle, and its character is so oriental no one could possibly mistake its meaning. We found in the wallpaper book a handsome sample of an oriental paper: elephant-gray background with a design of a willow tree and a little oriental gate. With it cut to fit as a background, our Lady stands against it, very oriental indeed. We fitted this shrine in between books in a bookcase in still another room.

Last of all, we decided to have a shrine for *Our Lady of Africa*, and she is the one I love the most. She is fine and slender, white china — not very expensive when she was bought long ago. And when my father lay dying of cancer, wrestling with the Faith, thinking one day he had the right desire, wondering the next, she stood on the bureau facing his bed, "watching over him." When the men came to remodel the little house from which we would soon have to move, and started to blow insulation into the walls, someone took her down for fear the vibrations might shake her too violently and she would fall and break. Suddenly he was calling in a poor sick voice, "Where is our Lady? Who took her away? Put her back — she is there to watch over me."

So we put her back, and she never did fall down. And after a long struggle with terrible pain and terrible doubts, together with her Infant Son, she called my father back from the doorway to death and he asked to be received into the Church. It was a glorious Mass, his requiem, and a real joy in the midst of sorrowing. Long afterward, she did fall down, but my mother glued her back together. And now we have her in a shadow-box shrine. We painted just her face and her hands black, and as a black madonna she is so beautiful.

We lined her macaroni-box shrine with straw matching made from placemats bought from the Five-and-Ten, but woven in the Orient. We cut one strip of the mat to curve in back of her like a niche, fitting against the sides of a natural wood frame. Small pieces were cut to fit as floor and ceiling to the box, and other pieces were glued to the outside, taped firmly in place overnight while the glue dried, with the tape removed the next day. At her feet are three tiny carved elephants — treasures Granny Newland has saved for many years. Two are trumpeting in praise, one is resting quietly, and all three are dwarfed by the grandeur and power and beauty of the Queen of angels and of men.

I cannot describe the effect of this black madonna in her African niche with the usually enormous beasts now so small and creature-like at her feet. It is the whole conversion of Africa. It is Africa's hope. It is by the love and Motherhood of Mary that these and all men will finally come to Christ.

With so many well-loved shrines, we should certainly pray very well. A prayer that always goes with shrines in a special way is the *Angelus*, the prayer recited morning, noon, and night at the sound of the *Angelus* bell. No one seems to know exactly how the Angelus began, but it is supposed that in conquered countries where a bell was rung for curfew as a signal for lights-out (a precaution against meetings and conspiracies), it became quite naturally also a signal for night prayers. A similar custom developed in the monasteries from the recitation on certain days of the Little Office of the Blessed Virgin, which includes the salutation of the Archangel to Mary and the versicles now incorporated in the *Angelus*. "The people began to use these as ejaculatory prayers, and recited them as a part of their evening devotions at the sound of a bell."

A custom in the fourteenth century ordered the recitation of three Our Fathers and three Hail Marys at the sound of a bell early in the morning; and at noon a bell called the faithful to the ancient practice of meditating on the Passion of Christ at first only on Fridays, and eventually every day.

Possibly all these customs and more wove themselves together around devotion to our Lady so that today we have the *Angelus*.

THE ANGELUS
*The Angel of the Lord declared unto Mary,*
*And she conceived of the Holy Spirit.*
  Hail Mary . . .

*Behold the handmaid of the Lord;*
*Be it done unto me according to thy word.*
  Hail Mary . . .

*And the Word was made Flesh,*
*And dwelt among us.*
  Hail Mary . . .

*Pray for us, O holy Mother of God.*
*That we may become worthy of the promises of Christ.*

*Let us pray.* Pour forth, we beseech Thee, O Lord, Thy grace into our hearts, that we to whom the Incarnation of Christ, Thy Son, was made known by the message of an angel, may, by His Passion and Cross, be brought to the glory of His Resurrection. Through the same Christ, our Lord. Amen.

From Easter until Trinity Sunday, the Church substitutes the recitation of the *Regina Coeli:*

THE REGINA COELI
*Queen of heaven, rejoice, Alleluia.*
*For He whom thou didst deserve to bear. Alleluia.*
*Hath risen as He said. Alleluia.*
*Pray for us to God, Alleluia.*

*V. Rejoice and be glad O Virgin Mary! Alleluia.*
*R. For the Lord hath risen indeed. Alleluia.*

*Let us pray.* God, who through the Resurrection of Thy Son, our Lord Jesus Christ, hast vouchsafed to make glad the whole world, grant us, we beseech Thee, that, through the intercession of the Virgin Mary, His Mother, we may attain the joys of eternal life. Through the same Christ our Lord. Amen.

# The Year and Our Children

If someone had told me, touchy as I am on the subject of shrines, that one day there would be shrines all over my house, I'd have very politely objected. I should explain that it's a very big house; so they aren't all crowded together in one room. At that, there are many — but not too many, and each one reminds us of a different thing and brings Mary very close. One shouldn't be so surprised that old antagonisms in regard to shrines could be overcome like this, for with all her other titles she is, in addition, *Mother Irresistible*.

Chapter 16

⌒

# Summer Saints and Some Are Not

Because all the people in this chapter are saints, the pun in the title of this chapter should be explained. How else can St. _____, whose feast is in February, be fitted into the summer part of this book? Yet our family had such a lot of fun celebrating his feast that it would be a shame to leave him out.

All those who know which apostle took Judas's place, please stand up.

Now you two sit down.

No need for the rest to be fussed. Hardly anyone ever knows. It was St. Matthias, whose feast is on February 24. We decided we should get acquainted with him and celebrate his feast.

⌒

### Number 13: St. Matthias

Actually, little is known about him. After our Lord had ascended into Heaven, the Apostles returned to the Upper Room where our Lady, the holy women, and the remaining disciples gathered to wait for the coming of the Holy Spirit. This is narrated in the Acts of the Apostles. While they waited, St. Peter said that something should be done to replace Judas. He quoted a passage from the Psalms where it was prophesied that one would be a traitor and another should "take over his office." Two men, Justus and

Matthias, were suggested. All prayed to our Lord, asking, with His help, to choose the right one; they drew lots and Matthias was chosen. One of the two traditions about him holds that he evangelized Palestine and was martyred there; the other says it was Ethiopia. Whichever, he was one of the Apostles, and he is in the Canon of the Mass.

*To us, also, Thy sinful servants,*
*who hope in the multitude of Thy mercies,*
*vouchsafe to grant some place and fellowship*
*with Thy holy apostles and martyrs:*
*with John, Stephen, Matthias . . .*

Knowing so little about his life, we decided not to separate him from the rest of the Apostles but celebrate a feast in his honor that would include the others — and remind us, incidentally, that the superstition about unlucky thirteen is nonsense. It wasn't unlucky for St. Matthias; he died a saint. The story of his election is told in the letter for his Mass, and his Collect is a beautiful addition to *Grace at Table* this day:

*O God, who didst associate blessed Matthias*
*to the company of Thine Apostles, grant, we beseech*
*Thee, that by his intercession we may ever experience*
*Thy tender mercy toward us. Through our Lord,*
*Jesus Christ, Thy Son, who is God, and liveth*
*and reigneth with Thee in the unity of the*
*Holy Spirit, world without end. Amen.*

Feast-day dinners in our family are begun by singing "Happy Feast Day to you" to the tune of the birthday song. While not liturgical, it is a custom of long standing and comes from the heart. The big feature of this dinner celebration is the dessert: twelve gingerbread Apostles.

⌒

*Apostle Cookies*

Any good gingerbread cookie dough will do, and any good gingerbread-boy cookie cutter will make a gingerbread Apostle (or you may cut them freehand with a knife). The twist is in the decoration. We decorated each one with his own symbols, tied a ribbon through a hole pierced (before baking) in the top of each cookie, served them on a tray, covered, with only the ribbons showing; you got your dessert by choosing a ribbon, finding the cookie, and identifying it. This is an excellent way to learn all the Apostles. The combination of head and stomach is hard to beat.

The frosting is a confectioner's sugar recipe tinted with vegetable colors. The symbols may be made with stiff frosting squirted through a decorator tube, if you have one, or may be cut from foil, paper, or made of any materials that suggest themselves. Here is how we decorated the cookies.

• *St. Peter (June 29)*. Red frosting because he was a martyr. Symbols: two keys, a cock crowing, an upside-down cross, a fish, a sword. The keys remind us that Jesus gave him the keys of the Kingdom; the cock recalls his denial of our Lord; the cross tells that he is supposed to have been martyred head down; the fish — he was a fisher of men; the sword tells of his temper on the night he cut off Malchus's ear. Our Peter cut a silver-foil fish for this cookie and stuck it in the frosting. You could do the keys and sword of foil also, with the cross of melted chocolate. The cock can be drawn or cut from a picture and stuck on. St. Peter is the patron of locksmiths and cobblers.

• *St. Andrew (November 30)*. He is next because he is Peter's brother. Red frosting for martyrdom. Symbols: a fish hook, a fisherman's net, two fishes, a cross saltire (X) because he is supposed to have died on such a cross, preaching joyously until death came. This shows the inspired origin of "X marks the spot." When we put Xs on exam papers, licenses, and ballots, we might remember St. Andrew and ask him to help us choose well. The fishing symbols recall that he was, like his brother, a fisher of men as well as of fishes. He is said to have evangelized Scotland, and so is a patron of the Scots, as well as of fishermen and fish dealers; he is invoked by women who wish to become mothers.

• *St. James the Great (July 25)*. He is called great because he was the tall James. He was the son of Zebedee and the brother of St. John the Evangelist. Our Lord called these two the Sons of Thunder: partly, we are told, for their vehement defense of Christ and His teaching, and partly because they wanted Him to burn up the Samaritans inside their houses with fire from Heaven, like the three little pigs, because they wouldn't welcome them into their village. Our Lord rebuked them for it. He said that He came to give life, not destroy it — which teaches a good lesson in resisting the temptation to "get even." This was certainly the opposite of the meekness He said would "inherit the earth."[92] This James was the first Apostle to die for Christ, beheaded in Jerusalem by Herod Agrippa. His symbols — the pilgrim's cloak, staff, hat, purse, and scallop shell (always the symbol of pilgrims) — signify that he went on long missionary journeys. A tiny shell stuck to the frosting on this cookie was the clue we used.

• *St. John the Evangelist (December 27)*. He is the brother to the tall James, and is best known as the "disciple Jesus

---

[92] Cf. Matt. 5:4.

loved."[93] It was Salome, the mother of these two, who asked our Lord for the best seats in Heaven for them. He was the only apostle who lived to a very old age and died a natural death; so the frosting on his cookie is white. His symbols are awfully complicated for cookies: a cauldron with an eagle rising (escape from boiling oil); a chalice with serpent emerging (escape from poisoned wine); an eagle, symbol of the fearless evangelist. We made up one, to tell how he loved our Lord: a heart.

• *St. Philip (May 11)*. He was one of the first to follow our Lord and was present at the miracle of the loaves and fishes. At the Last Supper, he asked Jesus, "Lord, show us the Father." And Jesus' answer is one we should remember when people question the divinity of Christ: *"Whoever has seen me has seen the Father."*[94] His symbols are a basket and loaves; a cross, a spear, stones to describe his martyrdom. We put a snip of bread on his cookie.

• *St. Bartholomew (August 24)*. The mystery man. His name, Bar-Tolmai, indicates that he is the son of Tolmai. He is an old friend of St. Philip and is often mentioned with him. It is supposed that he is the Nathanael to whom Philip made his announcement under the fig tree. Nathanael was skeptical that this Man was really the Messiah, and our Lord commended his skepticism because Israel was often thick with self-appointed messiahs. "Behold a true Israelite, in whom there is no guile," said our Lord, as Nathanael came toward Him down the road. Then to Nathanael: "Before Philip called thee, when thou wast under the fig tree, I saw

[93] Cf. John 13:23.
[94] Cf. John 14:9.

thee!" Then didn't Nathaniel believe! He lost his heart that moment. "Rabbi thou art the Son of God! Thou art King of Israel!"[95] St. Bartholomew's symbols are about as grisly as you'll find: flaying knives, a cross, an axe, and such, because his was a wild and bloody death; and then there is our pet symbol for him — a branch of the fig tree. Make this with melted chocolate and green candy leaves meant for cake-decorating.

• *St. Thomas (December 21)*. The twin, best remembered because he doubted our Lord's Resurrection. When our Lord finally came and showed Thomas, He made reference to us: "Blessed are those who have not seen, and yet have believed."[96] St. Thomas was allegedly a missionary to India, where he preached and built a church with his own hands; hence, he is one of the patrons of builders and has carpenter's tools among his symbols. He was stoned but did not quite die; so he was shot down with arrows next (according to tradition); then, still alive, he was run through with a spear by a pagan priest. None of these symbols suited us; so we made up another: five red cinnamon candies to remind us of the Blessed Wounds he was told to inspect. Remember to make the intention to gain the indulgence for the Souls in Purgatory when you say his prayer at the Elevation of the Mass: "My Lord and my God!" He is also the patron of masons.

• *St. Matthew (September 21)*. He was the publican, the tax collector, and since so few of these were honest, they were despised by all (there is nothing new under the sun). Our

[95] John 2:49.
[96] Cf. John 20:29.

Lord was going along His way after curing a paralytic when He saw Matthew sitting in the countinghouse at his table. "Follow me," was all He said, and up jumped Matthew without even saying goodbye or giving two weeks' notice. That is how we are supposed to obey Him — *right away*. Matthew is supposed to have been martyred in Ethiopia on a T-shaped cross (called a Tau cross), with his head chopped off with a battle-axe. There's a better symbol than that to help children learn about him: a bright new penny. Whoever draws this cookie gets to keep the penny.

• *St. James the Less (May 11)*. This is the short James, sometimes called St. James the Small. It is said he spent so much time on his knees that the skin became as tough as a camel's. His mother was a close relative to our Lady, which would probably make our Lady Aunt Mary to this James (only, since they were Jewish, she would be Aunt Miriam). He said in his letter that although our tongues are small, they are mighty, and capable of great evil. "How small the flame, yet how mighty the forest fire it kindles."[97] He was about ninety-five when they threw him off the temple parapet, probably AD 62, in Jerusalem, where he was Bishop. But he was a tough old saint and didn't die then; so they stoned him, then finished him off with a blow from a weaver's bat. One of his symbols is a windmill, but we could never decide why. Perhaps because they pushed him off into mid-air; or could it have something to do with what he said about tongues and talking? An easier symbol is three stones, which we could find in the driveway or fish bowl or Mother's bowl of narcissus. Wash them well and stick to red

[97] Cf. James 3:5.

frosting, and warn all present that they must be removed before biting. No broken front teeth at this feast, if you please.

• *St. Jude (October 28)*. Called Thaddeus, the "saint of the impossible." He was brother to James the Less, so he is also a cousin to Jesus. He asked our Lord at the Last Supper to tell them why He revealed Himself to only these few and not to the whole world. Jesus seemed not to hear, but said, "If a man has love for me, he will be true to my word, and then he will win my Father's love and we will both come to him, and make our continual abode with him."[98] It hardly seems an answer at first glance. He speaks of the indwelling of Himself and His Father in our souls. But if you read it again: "If a man has love for me . . ." Only a few — compared with the many who had seen Him day after day — loved Him. He said at other times that men have eyes to see, and do not see. It really was an answer. St. Jude is almost always in the company of St. Simon, and together with him is said to have been sent to preach Christ in Persia, where they both were martyred. The nicest of his symbols is a boat with a crossed mast. We cut a tiny boat of colored paper and stuck it on his cookie.

• *St. Simon (October 28)*. He is called the Zealot for his great zeal and, some say, because he may have been a member of a sect called the Zealots. This is debated. He is supposed to have been martyred by idolatrous priests who either crucified him or sawed him in two, like Isaiah. Among his symbols we find a ship with a fish, so we put the same kind of little boat on his cookie as we put on St. Jude's, and added a

---

[98] Cf. John 14:23.

silver-foil fish because he was a fisher of men. He is the patron of curriers and pit sawyers (men who saw wood over a
pit — one standing above wood, one below).

• *St. Matthias (February 24)*. His symbols refer to his martyrdom: a number of dreadful things such as a sword, a scim-
itar, stones, and a spear. Best of all, we thought, was to
choose a broomstraw for him. After all, he had been chosen
by lot. We washed one well and stuck it to him so that we'd
never forget how they voted him in. He is the patron of carpenters, tailors, and repentant drunkards and is invoked
against smallpox. It's a funny thing about St. Matthias. He
would never have been an Apostle if Judas hadn't done
what he did to our Lord. He would have remained a disciple, but not one of the Twelve. I suppose when he considered how he got to be one, he thought, "I've *got* to be a
saint."

*The Story of St. John Baptist*

St. John the Baptist has a birthday on June 24; one of the oldest
feasts in the liturgy and, aside from the birthdays of our Lord and
His Mother — and Pentecost, if you will — the only saint's birthday to be celebrated. All the others were born with Original Sin
on their souls, so the day of their death, or their particular hero-
ism, or the founding of their Order, is celebrated. How St. John
came to be born without Original Sin on his soul is a story almost
everyone knows, but fewer realize that there is mention of him
seven centuries before in the prophecy of Isaiah.

Isaiah, the children must be reminded, is the prophet whose
words are so prominent in the Advent liturgy, foretelling the coming of Christ. For example, he says something that they recognize

immediately: "Behold, a virgin shall conceive and bear a Son, and His name shall be called Emmanuel."[99] His words are also used in all four Gospels to describe St. John the Baptist; in fact, St. John says them about himself, "The voice of one crying in the wilderness: make ready the way of the Lord."[100]

Learning all these things one at a time in our family, we finally came to Isaiah, and in addition to discovering how and what he prophesied, we looked for some autobiographical facts about him. He came to a violent end, we discovered, sawed in half by his son-in-law, Manasses. "Sawed in half," said one. "Heavens! Which way?"

This is a minor detail alongside his prophecies, I agree, but the children consider it one of the more interesting facts they have picked up about saints and martyrs.

The story of St. John the Baptist begins, "In the days of Herod, king of Judea."[101] So that sets the scene. The time was before the birth of Jesus, but the king was the same. Up in the hill country, in a town of Judea, there lived an old man and his wife, Zachariah and Elizabeth, holy and good but with neither chick nor child, and this was their great sorrow. Zachariah was a priest, and twice a year for a week at a time he went down to Jerusalem to serve in the temple. At the time the story begins, Zachariah had been chosen by lot to offer incense on the altar of incense during the morning and evening sacrifices. One day when he went to the holy place alone, he saw an angel standing by the altar and was troubled and much afraid. But the angel told him not to be afraid. He had come to tell Zachariah of a son God would send him, in whom he would have "joy and gladness . . . for he shall be great before the Lord . . .

---

[99] Isa. 7:14.
[100] Cf. Isa. 40:3.
[101] Luke 1:5.

and shall be filled with the Holy Spirit even from his mother's womb."[102] (It was here foretold that the son would be born without Original Sin.)

But Zachariah was old and his wife was old, and it was uncommon for folks as old as they to start having babies; so he asked, "How shall I know this? For I am an old man and my wife is advanced in years."

Then the angel said, "I am Gabriel, who stand in the presence of God — and behold, thou shalt be dumb and unable to speak until the day when these things come to pass, because thou hast not believed my words which will be fulfilled in their proper time."[103] And when Zachariah came out of the temple and faced the wondering crowd outside, he made signs to them as best he could, and they saw that he was dumb. (This is a marvelous episode for a charade. The first time we did it was one night in the middle of the kitchen when even the oldest was very small. I had been telling the story as we washed and wiped the dishes together. A charade suggested itself. By now they have acted it out so often that they automatically respond to any mention of Zachariah by putting a finger to their lips.)

So Zachariah went home and Elizabeth discovered soon that she was to have a child. She retired from public view, the Gospel says: to be quiet and prepared, and ponder her precious secret.

Six months went by, and the same angel appeared to Mary in a town of Galilee called Nazareth, and greeted her with words that will never be forgotten: "Hail, full of grace, the Lord is with thee. Blessed art thou among women." Then, as he said to Zachariah, he said to Mary: "Do not be afraid." He told her that she would bring forth a son and call His name Jesus, and that "He shall be great and

[102] Luke 1:14-15.
[103] Cf. Luke 1:18-20.

be called the Son of the Most High." Then, after he had told her the child would be conceived of the Holy Spirit, he told her Elizabeth's secret and explained, as he did to Zachariah, that although Elizabeth was very old, it would come to pass — "for nothing shall be impossible with God."[104]

Then Mary, in words so simple it is hard to grasp that they were to change the history of the world — not merely change it, but stop it still, and startle time and space and fill eternity — said, "Be it done unto me according to thy word."[105]

*The Visitation*

And she "rose up and went with haste" to visit her cousin in the hill country. She probably rode a donkey there in the company of a caravan.

I wish St. Luke had not been so sparing with words, especially when he tells of her arrival. All he says is that she entered the house of Zachariah and saluted Elizabeth. If we only knew what she said. It was probably some Hebrew custom, some form of asking a blessing on the house and its occupants; but try as I might, the only thing I can ever imagine is that she called out, "Elizabeth dear, are you home?"

And it came to pass, when Elizabeth heard the greeting of Mary, that the babe in her womb leapt. And Elizabeth was filled with the Holy Spirit and cried out with a loud voice, saying, "Blessed art thou among women and blessed is the fruit of thy womb! And how have I deserved that the mother of my Lord should come to me? For behold, the moment the

[104] Cf. Luke 1:28-37.
[105] Luke 1:38.

sound of thy greeting came to my ears, the babe in my womb leapt for joy. . . ."[106]

Father Bruckberger tells in his *Mary Magdalene* of a little church in southern France where there is a painting of the Visitation, and in it the painter has fashioned a little window in the garments of Elizabeth through which we may see the tiny unborn John, "sitting as though in an armchair, full of enthusiasm and playing a violin." John's first greeting to Jesus. . . . Our smaller children will explain, when it is their turn to do the Second Joyful Mystery, "St. John jumped for joy inside his mother." It was the moment of his sanctification, being cleansed of Original Sin by the Holy Spirit; and right after it came Mary's *Magnificat*.[107] No wonder he leaped for joy. The world should have leaped for joy.

"And Mary remained with her about three months and returned to her own house."[108] No one is sure, they say, if she stayed for the birth of St. John. I am amazed. So is every mother I know. Let the scholars haggle over it if they will; of course she stayed. Elizabeth was old, she had never carried a child before. What else but Mary's concern would have moved her to rush to her side like that? Elizabeth would be urged to rest while Mary cooked the meals, fed the chickens (if there were chickens), and tended to the little labors of that quiet household. And in the evenings after prayer, two such women would sit and ponder the promise God had made to save the world.

And there is this to remember (then you know she stayed): this child who was expected was to go before the path of her own Son, and prepare His ways. With all her heart Mary would have wanted to see and assist at his birth.

[106] Cf. Luke 1:39-44.
[107] Luke 1:46-55.
[108] Cf. Luke 1:56.

Elizabeth brought forth her son, St. Luke says, to the delight of her family and neighbors, and announced on the day of his circumcision that he would be called John. "What?" protested her friends and relatives. "John!" No one in the family was named John. Far better to name him for his father, Zachariah. Quite sure Zachariah would want precisely that, they made signs to him to make his wishes known. Zachariah asked for a writing tablet. On it he wrote the words, "John is his name" — and immediately was able to speak. Such a fear came on the neighbors that they whispered about all the hill country: "What, then, will this child be?"[109]

Well they might ask. Those who stayed to hear Zachariah's canticle should have guessed, for in it he said: "And thou, child, shall be called the prophet of the Most High, for thou shalt go before the face of the Lord to prepare His ways, to give His people knowledge of salvation through forgiveness of their sins. . . ."[110]

*John and Jesus*

St. Luke used almost the same words to describe the child John that he used to describe the child Jesus: "And the child grew and became strong in spirit and was in the desert until the day of his manifestation to Israel."[111]

The desert where St. John lived and fasted and prayed was actually a grazing land, unfit for growing crops but able to sustain the life of hermits and herds; nor was it rare in those days for hermits to seek a life of solitude in the desert. That he ate locusts (grasshoppers, if you prefer) invariably draws a shudder, but this was not uncommon, and is not today, when Arab and African people still

---

[109] Cf. Luke 1:66.
[110] Luke 1:76-77.
[111] Luke 1:80.

dry and save them as protection against famine. Or they may have been carob beans, a common "fruit" used for thousands of years in Mediterranean lands and called by the name of *locust*. Wild honey, on the other hand, sounds quite delicious.

His garment, like the tents of Saul of Tarsus, was cloth woven of camel's hair, and he wore a leather girdle about his loins. This is the extent of his physical description. It is only when we meet him in public life that we discover what he was like; and when we hear him addressing the Pharisees and Sadducees in almost the same words our Lord used later, we realize the divine cunning in naming John the Voice that would announce the Word.

"Brood of vipers! Who has shown you how to flee from the wrath to come?" he cried out to their faces.[112]

"Serpents, brood of vipers, how are you to escape the judgment of Hell?" Jesus would cry, perhaps to the same faces.[113]

But John was tender; and when earnest seekers asked him what to do, he gave them straight answers that they could understand.

"Let him who has two coats share with him who has none, and let him who has food do likewise."

When the soldiers asked what they should do, he said, "Do not plunder, nor accuse the innocent falsely, and be content with your pay." He told the tax collectors to take no more than was due from the people they taxed.[114]

When the followers who loved him began to wonder if he was the Messiah, he finally spoke the words for which he is most famous: "I, indeed, baptize you with water. But one mightier than I is coming, the strap of whose shoes I am not worthy to loose."[115]

[112] Cf. Matt. 3:7.
[113] Cf. Matt. 23:33.
[114] Luke 3:11-14.
[115] Luke 3:16.

# The Year and Our Children

Never, among all the excuses and delays responding to the familiar refrain: "Jamie, John, Monica, someone! Please tie the baby's shoe!" has anyone offered, "I am not worthy." Most sinners, even pint-size, are certain that their business is far too important to be interrupted for the tying of shoes. But when St. John says he is unworthy to tie our Lord's shoe, it makes one think. St. Peter said, Holy Thursday night, that he was not worthy to have our Lord wash his feet, but Jesus said He must, all the same. Put like that, it's hard to understand. It can be sorted out, however, and this is what it means:

If we are to see Christ in our brothers and sisters, then, like St. John, we are not even worthy to tie their shoes. But Jesus did the work of a servant before us and told us to imitate Him. It is being another Christ and seeing Christ in one another, at one and the same time. To *be* like Him, we must do as He did. To see Him in one another, we must feel as St. John did.

John was an amazing man. Imagine the faith of him, doggedly preaching the advent of Christ, whom he would not recognize if he saw Him. That day Jesus approached to be baptized, he guessed, but not until it was done did he know. It had been so many years since their childhood and they had both changed so much.

Ironically enough, after all those years of self-denial and hardship, his death became an entertainment at a king's birthday party. Another Herod was king, a son (one of the lucky ones) of the Herod who was king when John was born; and beside him on the throne sat the impure wife of his brother. She hated John because he had shouted at the sinfulness of their trumped-up marriage. Not content to have him thrown into prison, she was determined to have his life. Slyly she watched Herod admire the dancing of her daughter. Greedily she waited for Herod to offer the girl a gift. When he did, the mother whispered what it should be, and the child ran back to the king and said, "I want thee right away to give me on a dish the head of John the Baptist." The strange thing is that Herod didn't want to, as Pilate didn't want the death of Jesus. But high men in high places cannot bear to lose face. St. Mark tells that because of his promise, and "because of his oath and because of his guests," he sent an executioner and commanded that his head be brought on a dish.[116]

John's death, like Christ's, was a spectacle, and St. Mark concludes his account of it with words that could refer to the death of our Lord: "And his disciples, hearing it, came and took away his body, and laid it in a tomb."[117]

*A Bonfire for St. John*

Since his birthday comes in the middle of summer, it is an ancient custom to celebrate it that night with a great bonfire. Granny Newland remembers such bonfires in Ireland, from which coals were always taken to lay in each of a man's fields. The significance of the bonfire was taken from Zachariah's canticle, where he sang out in praise of John that he would "enlighten them that sat in darkness."

A cook-out is inevitable with a bonfire; and although it's hard to think of any use for grasshoppers on the menu (which is too bad when they are so plentiful), a comb of honey would be fitting. There is an interesting connection between the bonfire and St. John as the last of the prophets of the Old Law. To celebrate the end of the Old Law, people used to burn in the bonfires all the things they had been trying to get rid of (carted off to the dump) all year. This is an idea for people who are short of fuel for bonfires.

[116] Mark 6:27.
[117] Mark 6:29.

Another beautiful tradition was to decorate the door of one's home with "birch leaves, St. John's wort, and white lilies" on the eve of this feast. If you are not acquainted with St. John's wort by name, you must be by sight — having ignored it as a weed (with small yellow blossoms) all these years. The wildflower books in your local library will tell you which weed it is you are to pick.

Another tradition was to hang out, along with the flowers, a lighted lantern (in our century, the porch light) on the night before the feast. How nice this would be if all the neighbors left their porch lights on this eve to salute this saint who enlightened those who sat in darkness.

After Mass and Holy Communion in his honor, the next best tribute is to have the father or an older member of the family read the *Blessing of a Bonfire*, sprinkle it with holy water, and before the picnic, lead the group in the reading of Zachariah's canticle. It would be ideal if a priest could read the blessing and lead the prayers.

BLESSING OF A BONFIRE

*Leader:* Our help is in the name of the Lord.
*All:* Who hath made Heaven and earth.

*Let us pray.* O Lord God, Father almighty, unfailing Ray and Source of all light, sanctify this new fire, and grant that after the darkness of this life, we may come unsullied to Thee, who are Light eternal. Through Christ our Lord. Amen.

Then the group divides and reads alternate lines of the Canticle of Zachariah (to be found in Luke 1:68-79).

John is the patron of bird dealers, of cutters and tailors, and is invoked against spasms, convulsions, epilepsy, hail, and prayed to for protection of lambs.

He is one of the patrons of French Canada, and they celebrate his feast with great devotion, reckoning it by the calendar as we do, and another way as well. It falls on the day of the year when, in their part of the world, day begins to last longer than night. Like St. John, they say, as he said: *"He must increase, but I must decrease."*[118]

⁀

*Paraphrasing the Letters*

Once in a while, I wish I could have lived during those first years of the Faith. I'm grateful, of course, to be one of those our Lord told St. Thomas would believe without seeing, but sometimes there is a terrible longing to have been there at the beginning. For example, I should like to have been the receiver of a letter, or to be mentioned in one — like Phoebe, Archippus, "my dear Epenetus," and "dear Persis," and Rufus and his mother, and Nereus and his sister Olympias.[119] Maybe all the lay apostles whose mothers don't understand what their children are doing ought to pray to Rufus's mother. She sounds as though she understood, and as though she'd be a great help.

I think about the new-made Christians at Thessalonica listening to the last lines of Paul's second letter to them, and wonder if they didn't elbow and push in a Christian sort of way to see the letter that finished with, "Here is Paul's greeting in his own hand; the signature which is to be found in all my letters; this is my handwriting. The grace of our Lord Jesus Christ be with you all."[120]

St. Peter's letters were the first encyclicals. Like our present Holy Father, he sent out letters encouraging the faithful to crown their faith "with virtue, and virtue with enlightenment, and enlightenment with continence, and continence with endurance,

---

[118] John 3:30.
[119] Cf. Rom. 16:1; Philemon 1:2; Rom. 16:5, 12, 13, 15.
[120] Cf. 2 Thess. 3:17-18.

and endurance with holiness, and holiness with brotherly love, and brotherly love with charity."

Sorting out passages in the letters that I thought would appeal to the children, I used to think: If only there were some way to communicate to them the excitement of the *letter-writing* and the *letter-receiving*. They still think that these letters come out of books — which is all wrong. They are *letters*. If only it could be as full of promise to read a letter as it is running up the lane to see what Mr. Bradway has delivered in the morning mail.

All of a sudden, I knew what to do. Why couldn't the children get letters from St. Peter? Not whole letters, but parts of a letter especially suited to them, mailed so that they would be delivered on June 29, the feast of the apostles Peter and Paul.

The letter for the Mass of June 29, from the Acts of the Apostles, tells of St. Peter's deliverance from prison by an angel, and, in the Gospel, our Lord declares him the Rock. These are grand stories to tell in preparation the night before, for the children must have a broad hint that something apropos will come in the mail so that anticipation will lead to enthusiasm.

Now to choose passages the children will like and be able to understand. It is true that loose paraphrasing of Holy Scripture can sometimes stray far from accuracy, but it is also true that children must have Scripture recast in their kind of words or they won't even listen to it. The first thing to do is ask the Holy Spirit to help you find the right words, without changing any of the meaning. The next thing to do is search for passages relating to some concrete problem each of the children is struggling with; or, if it is a child who needs to be told again and again how much he is loved, find a passage that does that.

The beginning of St. Peter's first letter gives us a lovely salutation: "Peter, an apostle of Jesus Christ, to the elect who dwell at Glen Echo, on South Hampden Road in Monson, Massachusetts."

Or perhaps it will be "who dwell at 147 Prairie Avenue, Wilmette," or "50 Danforth Road, Portland" — or Green River or Brooklyn or Chicopee Falls.

Starting with the fourth verse, this letter has something for a child with a seemingly heavy cross. This is how we wrote it:

> We are to share a reward that will never decay, or be spoiled, or fade. It is stored up for you in Heaven, and meanwhile, because of your faith, the power of God will keep you safe till you reach it, this salvation which is waiting to be shown to you at the end of time. Then you will be triumphant. What if you have many kinds of hard things to sadden your hearts in this short time between? That must happen, so you may prove your faith, a much more precious thing (faith) than the gold that is tested by fire; and your faith proved will bring you praise and glory and honor, when at last you see Jesus Christ. You never saw Him, but you learned to love Him; you may not see Him even now, but you believe in Him, and if you keep on believing in Him, how you will triumph!

Children from seven on should understand this. Ours did. If they read their letter aloud with a parent, talking it over together, it can be related to problems without straining. It could help one who had difficulty holding his tongue when he is teased; one who might be too chubby to be pretty and must restrain a ravenous appetite (and guard against gluttony); one who is frail and can't keep up with the rest in games; one who is the butt of some grown-up's constant irritation; one who has a struggle in school, and so on.

⁀

## On Childhood Trials
Someone who does not know children might object that these are hardly the "trials of many sorts" St. Peter was referring to when

he wrote to the early Christians. But the trials of children are very heavy, even when they are small, and these are Christians trying to learn how to be Christian in a world beset with challenges for Christians. There is no need to wait for the terrible scourges to come before helping them bear trials. They have trials on and off all day long; maybe they last for only five minutes at a time, but something — a thoughtless remark, a humiliation in front of friends, a clash of personalities with an adult — which seems as nothing to us, can be to them an intolerable suffering, impossible to bear. We cannot eliminate their trials, nor should we want to if merely for the sake of saving their feelings, for part of the pain is in themselves in the form of self-love. This is always painful to root out. It is far better to try to help them understand trials and learn to bear them.

In this letter, St. Peter confirms what we have tried to teach: that trials will make them strong and prove them in their faith. If we are going to use the daily life of the Church to help them grow in love for what she teaches, we must use the lives of the saints she honors, for by their teaching they guide us. This is a day to honor St. Peter. Let us learn of St. Peter.

What of the little ones, who will also want a letter? In the fourth chapter there is something for them:

Above everything else, always have love among yourselves; love covers over much of your naughtiness. Give each other the things you have, unselfishly, sharing with everyone whatever gift you receive, as is right for children who receive so many graces from God.

A free translation, but it certainly hits at the heart of the problems that plague them:

"This truck is mine."

"It is not, it's mine."

"It is not, it's mine!" And on and on and on and on.

Explaining that St. Peter says we must share nicely and will help us if we ask him is a new way of rephrasing the old refrain they have heard over and over.

There must be no confusion about the actual authorship of the words. They must understand that they were copied out of Holy Scripture by a mother or a father or possibly an older sister or brother because their parents thought it would be fun and helpful for them to pretend that they were really getting a letter from St. Peter.

As we said, this should be explained ahead of time because lack of preparation would spoil it. Unprepared for, it might seem only to be a novelty, something new and different in the mail to startle you for a moment, then off to go swimming. We prepared our day so the arrival of the mail found us with the time to read the letters carefully, talk about them, sit and think about letters and what it was like to get one.

*Letters to Fathers and Mothers*

A passage addressed to presbyters in the fifth chapter of this letter applies so well to fathers that the father in this house received that excerpt in the mail:

> Bow down, then, before the strong hand of God; He will raise you up, when His time comes to deliver you. Throw back on Him the burden of all your anxiety; He is concerned for you. Be sober, and watch well; the Devil, who is your enemy, goes about roaring like a lion, to find his prey, but you, grounded in the faith, must face him boldly; you know well enough that the brotherhood you belong to pays, all the world over, the same tribute of suffering. And God,

the giver of all grace, who has called us to enjoy after a little suffering, His eternal glory in Christ Jesus, will Himself give you mastery and steadiness and strength.

The mother got a letter, too — from the beginning of the third chapter:

> You, too, who are wives must be submissive to your husbands. Some of these still refuse credence to the word [he means they had not yet become Christians]; it is for their wives to win them over, not by word but by example; by the modesty and reverence they observe in your demeanor. Your beauty must lie, not in braided hair, not in gold trinkets, not in the dress you wear, but in the hidden features of your hearts, in a possession you can never lose, that of a calm and tranquil spirit; to God's eyes, beyond price. It was thus the holy women of old time adorned themselves, those women who had such trust in God, and paid their husbands such respect. Think how obedient Sara was to Abraham, how she called him her lord; if you would prove yourselves her children, live honestly and let no anxious thoughts disturb you.

The letters really are for us. They were written at the time for a small group of Christians who believed what we believe and had to struggle as we have to struggle. In the first chapter of his second letter, St. Peter tells of his having soon to "fold my tent." He knew his death was near. But he promised, "I will see to it that, when I am gone, you shall always be able to remember what I have been saying." We have his letters to remind us, his love, his prayers for us in Heaven, and his powers handed down to all the Peters who follow him. These are the many ways St. Peter, when questioned by our Lord — "Dost thou love me?" — answers to the command *"Feed my lambs."*

When the recipients did go off to the brook, we gave them feast-day surprises: big yellow fish cut out of cardboard and tied on strings to willow wands skinned of their bark. Monica wasn't too much intrigued, but the boys thought this was great stuff. Art supply stores have beautiful colors of poster paper, and it pays to buy a sheet or two for such surprises as this.

P. Stewart Craig in *A Candle Is Lighted* writes that in Yorkshire, St. Peter's day was a feast of fishermen, who decorated their boats and celebrated among their families and friends. We like the author's suggestion of using a prayer from the Mass for those at sea in family prayer this day, perhaps following *Grace at Table*, since a large part of New England's economy depends upon the fisherfolk:

*O God, who didst bring our forefathers through the
Red Sea and guide them in safety through the overflowing
waters, singing praises to Thy holy name, we humbly
beseech Thee that Thou wouldst ever keep from all danger
Thy servants who are on board ship, granting them a
calm voyage and the haven which they desire.*

### The Mass Is Best of All

We have the whole year, and all its feasts, to celebrate: so many mysteries, so many saints. Plainly, a busy family cannot spend every day elaborately celebrating feasts. But as members of the Mystical Body, we may unite ourselves to Christ, as He celebrates each day, offering Himself on the altar by the hands of His priests. To be there daily, to meet Him in Communion, is the ideal, but it is not possible for everyone. When we cannot be there, we can give Him our minds and hearts each morning, placing our day, our life, our prayer, our joy and sorrow, everything — together with His. A liturgical calendar tells us what day it is, whose feast, something about it. If it is a saint or feast that relates in a special way to our family, we can dream up something delicious or delightful to emphasize it.

The Mass is the highest act of the Church at worship day by day through the year; after it comes the Divine Office. Perhaps in a little while the family will get to know it, and how to say its evening prayer, *Compline*, and will add that to their prayer in union with the whole Body. We are still clumsy with Compline in our family, and we do not say it regularly; but now that the children are older and more of them can read, prospects are better. They have already learned the Compline hymn, "Now with the fast departing light . . ." and like to sing it often. This hymn is adapted with simpler words in *The Story of the Redemption for Children*.

The Rosary is nonliturgical prayer (that is, not part of the daily official worship of the Church), but prayer of high purpose nevertheless. We pray this nightly in our family; children understand it from the time they are very small (if we take the pains to help them enjoy it); it teaches them much doctrine, the lives of our Lord and our Lady; it follows the liturgical cycle for the year. From time to time, we add to it or substitute the prayers for the great vigils and feasts.

☞

## Some Favorite Saints

Now follows a list of our favorite saints and feasts, chosen because they are related to things that interest us in a particular way. If we do not have special prayers to say in their honor, we may use some or all of the prayers from their Masses. The object of these customs is not simply to have customs. The popular women's magazines are full of pretty customs that relate to not very much at all. What we want our customs to do is to perfect us in the love and knowledge of God, assist us through the days and months and years of preparing for Heaven. We want to pray to the best effect. Praying with the Church day after day, we add our voices to all those in the Mystical Body who are praying with Christ, our Head, thus ensuring that we give honor and glory to our Father in Heaven.

• *St. Balthasar (January 6)*. Although Omer Engelbert's *Lives of the Saints* lists this saint on this date, there is no special Mass for him in any of our missals, and he is usually included in the Epiphany feast. The prayers for the Epiphany are appropriate for him, plus a prayer or two from the Mass for the Sick, since he is the patron of those with epilepsy. There is a state hospital for epileptics in our town; so we ask him to take care of the patients there. He is also patron of the manufacturers of playing cards, and of sawmen.

• *St. Francis de Sales (January 24)*. Patron of writers. Enough said!

• *St. Brigit of Kildare and St. Severus (February 1)*. Brigit is one of the patronesses of the Irish. An old Irish tale recounted in Lady Gregory's *The Book of Saints and Wonders* tells how Brigit helped the Mother of God and in reward asked that her feast day precede the Purification.

> "Put my day before your own day," said Brigit. So she did that, and Saint Brigit's day is kept before her own day ever since. . . . And from that time to this the housekeepers have a rhyme to say on Saint Brigit's day, bidding them to bring out a firkin of butter and to divide it among the working boys. For she was good always, and it was her desire to feed the poor, to do away with every hardship, to be gentle to every misery. And it is on her day the first of the birds begin

to make their nests, and the blessed Crosses are made with straw and are put up in the thatch; for the death of the year is done with and the birthday of the year is come. And it is what the Gael of Scotland say in verse:

> "Brigit put her finger in the river on the feast day of Brigit, and away went the hatching-mother of the cold.
>
> "She washed the palms of her hands in the river on the day of the feast of Patrick, and away went the birth-mother of the cold."

St. Severus is a patron of wool manufacturers and weavers, as well as of drapers and silk makers. Since one of the principal industries of our town is a woolen mill, we have prayed many times with our friends through the trying periods of layoff for New England woolen workers. May he prosper our mill and our mill workers.

• *St. Appolonia (February 9)*. Patroness of dentists and those with toothaches, she had all her teeth pulled out. Being informed that she was to be burned alive, she is said to have been inspired by the Holy Spirit to leap into the flames ahead of time, welcoming death. There is a place for St. Appolonia in every household along with the toothache remedies, the appointment cards from the dentist, and the love of God.

• *St. Florian (May 4)*. Patron of firemen. Very interesting to small boys and also to firemen and their families. He is invoked against fire, and we have lettered on our fire extinguishers, placed advantageously here and there, "St. Florian, pray for us, protect us from fire."

• *St. Dymphna (May 15)*. Another Irish saint, she is the patroness of the mentally ill. She was martyred by her father when she refused to marry him after the death of her mother. Pursuing her to the little town of Gheel in Belgium, he beheaded her with his own dagger. We like especially the prayer for the ninth day of a novena to her, with its relation to chastity.

> O God, Lover of innocent souls, who gave to St.
> Dymphna the virtue of angelic purity which rendered
> her reserved in all her actions, so modest in her dress,
> so attentive in her conversation, so circumspect in her
> bearing that she shed her blood to preserve this precious
> virtue, we beseech Thee that Thou bestow upon us the
> virtue of chastity so that we may enjoy peace of con-
> science in this life and the pure eternal joys of Heaven
> hereafter through Jesus Christ, our Lord. Amen.

• *St. John Nepomucene (May 16)*. Invoked for help with a good confession, he was tortured and imprisoned by the Bohemian emperor Wenceslaus the Idle (not *our* Wenceslaus) in an attempt to discover the contents of the empress's confessions, but without success. Set free, he again raised the emperor's wrath over the election of an abbot and was forthwith tied and bound and tossed into the Moldau. Remember him when you hear Smetana's "The Moldau." He is invoked for the protection of bridges (we wish we had known this at the time the flood was battering down our little bridge on the lane) and against indiscretions and calumnies.

• *St. Erasmus or Elmo (June 2)*. He is one of the Fourteen Holy Helpers and is shown carrying a windlass, around which are wound his entrails. He was martyred by having his stomach torn open and his interior thus disturbed, and although we have made the acquaintance of all the "mothers' saints," this is the only one we know of who is to be invoked while enduring the pains of childbirth. I am sure he had an idea of what they are like. He is also the patron of navigators, is invoked against storms, colic, and the intestinal diseases of children.

• *St. Anthony of Padua (June 13)*. There is a beautiful *Blessing of Horses or Other Animals* that can be used any time but is especially fitting on this feast of St. Anthony (although the legend of the donkey kneeling in the presence of the Eucharist is highly questionable). Since the blessing mentions him, however, it is apparently the connection with this story that inspires its use for such animals. Here is the translation by Father Weller:

> *Let us pray. O God, our refuge and our strength, give ear to the entreaties of Thy Church, Thou source of mercy, and grant that what we seek with faith, we may receive in fact. Through Christ our Lord. Amen.*

> *Let us pray. Almighty and everlasting God, who didst assist Saint Anthony to emerge unscathed from the many temptations of this world, grant Thy servants to progress in virtue by his illustrious example; and by his merits and intercession, free us from the ever-present dangers of life. Through Christ our Lord. Amen.*

> *Let us pray. Let these animals receive Thy blessing, O Lord, to the benefit of their being and, by the intercession of Saint Anthony, deliver them from all harm. Through Christ our Lord. Amen.*

St. Anthony is thus invoked for the protection of asses and horses; it was St. Francis de Sales who said he had the power of finding lost objects.

• *St. Felicitas of Rome (July 10[121])*. Since she was supposed to have been the mother of seven sons, and is invoked for the bearing of male children, it is a good thing for us that my birthday is July 11 instead of July 10, or no doubt we should not have even our one daughter. You can see the powerful influence of her octave, even so.

• *St. Christopher (July 25)*. Being such a big saint, he has a lot of responsibility on his shoulders. He is the patron of archers, market carriers, fruit dealers, motorists, and Christopher David Newland, and is invoked against sudden death, storms, hail, toothache, impenitence at death, and, last of all, he is the patron of fullers, who are weavers — and, as I said, our town is full of weavers.

• *St. Anne (July 26)*. St. Anne is very special with us because she found our present house and land when we were being evicted elsewhere. She is the patroness of old-clothes dealers, seamstresses, laceworkers, housekeepers, carpenters, turners, cabinetmakers, stablemen, and broommakers, and she is invoked against poverty and to find lost objects. Although the martyrology doesn't say so, she must be the patroness of Grandmothers, and we love her for that because we could never get along without our grandmothers — and both have Ann in their names. The children love to recall that if she was still there when the Christ Child learned to talk, He called her *Grandmother*. The nicest of

---

[121] The memorial of St. Felicitas of Rome is now celebrated on November 23.

her symbols, we think, is a cradle with the infant Virgin Mary in it. It is only tradition that her name is Anne and her husband's Joachim; and now and then a non-Catholic will challenge the source of the "St. Anne" who we say is the Virgin's mother. But our Lady had a mother and father, and they must have had names, and it is as suitable to call them the traditional names of Anne and Joachim as it is to call them anything else. It is only the name that is open to challenge. The role is not. Unless, of course, they wish to propose that the Blessed Virgin was miraculously produced without the conventional parents. Even Catholics think that's going too far. They stubbornly insist that she must have had parents; and they love her parents because they brought her into the world.

We think the best way to celebrate in honor of St. Anne is to do something lovely for the grandmothers. Little girls might dress their best dolls as the tiny Mary this day and lay them in flower-bedecked cradles. We borrow words in her praise from the Greek liturgy this day, to add to our night prayers:

> Hail, spiritual bird, announcing the
>    spring time of grace!
> Hail, sheep, mother of the ewe lamb, who by
>    a word, conceived the Word, the Lamb that
>    taketh away the sins of the world!
> Hail, blessed earth, whence sprang the branch
>    that bore the divine Fruit!
> O Anne, most blessed in God, grandmother of Christ
>    our Lord, who didst give to the world a shining lamp,
>    the mother of God; together with her intercede that
>    great may be the mercy granted to our souls.

*Let us cry to holy Anne with cymbals and psaltery.*
*She brought forth the mountain of God and*
*was borne up to the spiritual mountains,*
*the tabernacles of Paradise.*

• *St. Lawrence (August 10)*. Now you remember him: he was roasted on a gridiron. Guess whom he is patron of? Cooks. Let no one say that the Fathers who wrote the martyrology or assigned the patrons didn't have a grand and grisly sense of humor. He is also invoked against lumbago and fire (you'd better put his name on the fire extinguisher along with St. Florian's) and for the protection of vineyards. He is also the patron of restaurateurs.

• *St. Raymond Nonnatus (August 31)*. He is called "non-natus" because he was not "born," but delivered by Caesarian section. Since so many of our friends have their babies this way, we feel it is important to have his friendship. His mother died at his birth but he ended up a cardinal and a saint; so you see, God does take care of His little ones. He is the patron of midwives and is invoked for women at child-birth, and for little children.

• *St. Giles, or Egidius (September 1)*. He is invoked against cancer, sterility in women, the terrors of the night (anyone have nightmares at your house?), and madness, and is the patron of cripples and spur makers. (Incidentally, the Com-pline hymn is a beautiful going-to-bed song for children who have nightmares: ". . . far off let idle visions fly, no phantom of the night molest.") There is a famous legend of St. Giles and a doe that was his friend and lived in a cave with him by the banks of the Rhone in France. One day, while running through the woods, the doe was pursued by a

271

pack of hounds and hunters. She raced back to the cave and disappeared inside, and the hunter leading the pack shot an arrow after her. A moment later, Giles appeared with the arrow in his knee and the blood flowing freely. The hunter was filled with remorse, introduced himself as the king, Flavius, and offered to bring the royal physicians to treat the poor knee. "No," said St. Giles, "it is quite all right with me if God has permitted me to be crippled like this. He probably has some reason." As indeed He had, for Giles, bearing his infirmity with sweet patience for the love of God, became the patron and friend of all who share such infirmities with him.

• *SS. Cosmos and Damian (September 27)*. These twin saints are the patrons of medicine and pharmacy, Philip Damian Newland, and Grandmother Reed, M.D. They administered to the sick and the poor without remuneration and were dispatched into forever by that famous martyr-maker Diocletian. They are also the patrons of doctors, surgeons, druggists, and midwives. Cosmas was the M.D., Damian the pharmacist.

• *St. Michael the Archangel (September 29)*. Pope Pius XII made St. Michael the patron of policemen in 1950. He is also the patron of coopers, hatmakers, swordsmen, haberdashers, and grocers, and is invoked for a happy death. That magnificent edifice, Mont-Saint-Michel, was built "at the cost of great hardship" after he had appeared in a vision to St. Aubert, Bishop of Avranches, during the eighth century. He pointed to the rock rising out of the sea, said that it was under his special protection, and requested that a church be built in his honor there. This is the only reasonable explanation for why anyone would ever try to build a church there. That it is of such enduring beauty is due to him also, without doubt. A mobile with St. Michael hanging high and Lucifer at his feet with the flames of Hell around him would be a stirring decoration for this feast, with, of course, Michaelmas daisies on the table. These are common weeds to most people, but if you look them up at the same time you look up St. John's wort, you will know which are to be picked for this day. We should be sure to know the prayer to St. Michael recited at the end of each Mass, and recite it on his feast.

• *The Guardian Angels (October 2)*. It is generally agreed that all Christian communities, countries, families, dioceses, churches, and religious houses have each their Guardian Angel, and St. Francis de Sales wrote that bishops have another angel as such, in addition to their Guardian Angel. We can add more angels to the mobile on this day, one for each in the family (make them very simple shapes, recognizable by a sweep of wings), and write the name of each person on an angel. "Dear Angel, Ever at My Side" is a simple hymn for children to be found in the *Pius X Hymnal*, and a few days' practice ahead of time would prepare us to greet our angels with this at the feast-day dinner in their honor. An Angel Pie is a luscious dessert we could make as a climax. A recipe for meringue, a half-pint (or more if you are a big family and need two pies) of whipping cream, and fresh or canned fruit, drained, are the ingredients. You bake the meringue in a pie tin instead of in individual portions, whip the cream very stiff, fold in the fruit, pile it in the shell and serve.

• *St. Gomer (October 11)*. He is the patron of the unhappily married, and since everyone who ever gets married thinks sooner or later that he is unhappily married, it is high time we stirred up devotion to this saint. He is probably an expert at showing up for what they are all hurt feelings, self-pity, piggishness, and all the other things we suffer or perpetrate but don't admit. For those truly unhappily married, I am sure that he will show them that eternal happiness is bought with such sufferings as theirs. Omer Engelbert writes of him: "Courageous soldier and relative of Pepin the Short, who thought to reward him by making him marry Gwin Marie; he suffered terribly from the frightful disposition of this incorrigible woman. He ended by leaving her and withdrawing to a solitary place which became after his death a place of pilgrimage and the site of the town of Lierre (Belgium)." So this saint knows what an unhappy marriage is all about. He is also the patron of woodcutters, turners, glovemakers, and cowherds, and is invoked against hernia.

• *St. Martin of Tours* and *Armistice Day*[122] *(November 11)*. It is odd that Armistice Day falls on the feast of a soldier who was brave enough, but refused to go out to kill. The emperor gave orders that he was to be forced into battle at sword's point, and Martin prayed all night in his cell. Before battle the next morning, the enemy surrendered and there was no need for a fight. (This seems to mean only one thing: if we prayed enough, we could end the wars. Our Lady said so at Fatima.) He is the St. Martin who divided his cloak with the beggar and saw our Lord that night in a dream, wearing the half-cloak and saying, "Martin has given me half his cloak, and he is not even baptized." He is the patron of tailors (naturally!) and also horsemen (he was on horseback

[122] Now known as Veterans Day.

when he met the beggar), and is especially invoked for the protection of geese because, according to one of the Martin tales, he had no wish to become Bishop of Tours and so hid himself from the people who had come to acclaim him, and his hiding place was betrayed by the honking of a goose. We tolerate the honking of our goose Michael with slightly more patience than before we had read this. John Michael Newland is invoking St. Martin for protection of this goose, who is not the most popular member of our household and would look better, most think, in the oven.

• *St. Elizabeth of Hungary (November 17)*. We have always loved this saint because she was so lovable, so beautiful, young, holy, and so much in love with her husband. It is refreshing to find a saint who made a fool of herself over her husband, and St. Elizabeth surely did (or so the court thought, at any rate). The legend that the bread in her basket turned to roses is probably not authentic, but it could have happened; so we like to tell it each year. Elizabeth is supposed to have been taking bread to the poor and met her husband King Ludwig on the way. He asked what was in her basket, lifted the napkin, and there underneath he found roses. Elizabeth, full of humility, was not exposed as the great benefactress of the poor. This is not consistent with her reputation for openly giving away to the poor everything she could get her hands on, but it is a charming story and gives us the cue for our St. Elizabeth's Day custom. We bake bread that afternoon so that it will be done by nightfall. It is shaped into large buns — or small loaves (if you prefer), wrapped carefully in linen napkins, and put into baskets. The children bundle up, get their flashlights, take notes explaining the day and the custom, and go off down the lane to the neighbors with hot bread for their suppers. It is given away for the love of Christ. Then, when you return home, the bread for your own supper tastes that much sweeter.

⁓

### Symbols to Stitch

For feasts such as *Corpus Christi*, the *Sacred Heart*, the *Immaculate Heart of Mary*, and others, we have a project that is easy, practical, and lots of fun, and provides us with a meditation on the lessons of the feast. On brightly colored construction paper chosen to go with the feast, we lightly sketch one of the appropriate symbols (Sacred Heart, Chalice and Host, Immaculate Heart with M, and so forth). Placing the paper on the couch or a hard pillow, we punch holes with a large nail every inch or inch and one-half around the outlines. With a large-eyed needle, the children outline the symbols with colored yarns in a sewing stitch (much as mothers have done with "sewing on cards" sets when they were little). The result is a bright banner for the wall or the center of the table on a feast day. Stephen has done them (very well, too), and he is only five; so it is a project the little ones will enjoy. It takes no time at all to assemble, and is a quiet, neat project — ideal for small apartments, crowded rooms, or "company times."

The saints, our Lord, and our Lady are our teachers, and they teach us in many delightful and beautiful ways. We should invite them into our homes every day of the year, joining our prayers to theirs, asking them to pray with us, now and then (when we have the time) creating a happy custom with which to celebrate their feasts. We are not without calculation in this matter. We look for profit and gain. A man is known by the company he keeps.

Chapter 17

 ⸺

# The Assumption

"Now what," I asked, "shall we do for the Assumption besides hav-ing a procession?"

"A tea!" That was Peter. He's for teas. It was Peter who thought up having the Mad Tea Party that time. And a tea seemed like a good idea this time, what with an afternoon procession and a bless-ing and flowers and mint and things. So we called the Hobsons.

"We're inviting you to a tea," we said, "in honor of our Lady's Assumption, with a procession and a *Blessing of Herbs and Flowers*."

"Oh, fine," said the Hobsons' mother. "We'll wear our organ-dies. We always wear our organdies to teas."

This promised to be very interesting since there are only two Hobson girls (their mother and Ginny) and the rest are boys. At least, at the time that was how matters stood. There are now three Hobson girls. Anne Marie has been added.

Then we decided that we should have something special for our procession during which we would give the *Blessing of Herbs and Flowers* (in the new ritual it is called simply the *Blessing of Herbs*). The blessing is traditionally given on August 15, perhaps because of the legend that the Apostles found flowers in the tomb where they had laid our Lady; or perhaps because the Church wanted to Christianize the pagan custom of gathering herbs for medicines at this time of year. At any rate, the legend about the flowers in her tomb and St. Thomas doubting is sufficiently popular to merit a telling, just so that everyone will get it straight that it is a legend. It goes like this (with many variations).

Our Lady fell asleep at last after the years of living with St. John and waiting for Heaven, and all the Apostles were gathered about her bed. Except St. Thomas. He was off in India preaching the Gospel and couldn't get back on time, although an angel is supposed to have told him to hurry. The other apostles carried her body to the tomb and laid it there, and sometime afterward they discovered that it was gone. They naturally concluded that it had been taken to Heaven (as indeed it had).

Then St. Thomas came home; and when they went out to meet him and to explain, he would not believe. He would not believe, the legend says, until he had seen for himself. So they took him to see where they had laid our Lady's body and in its place were flowers. Looking up, St. Thomas saw her going up to Heaven; and to convince him at last, an angel brought the girdle she had fastened about her robe and dropped it to Thomas.

It is a pretty story and parts of it are true, but frankly we doubt that St. Thomas had doubts *again*. You don't do that sort of thing twice, not after our very Lord said to you, "You are a doubting Thomas. Come *here*."

What is true is that our Lady fell asleep. The word *death* is not used for our Lady, because death is the consequence of Original Sin and a punishment for sin, and our Lady was without the slightest taint of sin. She would not, need not, have died, but merely waited for her divine Son to will that it was her time for Heaven, and then yield up her soul.

We would have accomplished it this way instead of through death if God's original plan had been permitted to unfold. But instead of God's original plan, we had Adam's Original Sin, and that is how death came in its stead.

# The Assumption

Mary was assumed into Heaven. At the end of Masses and after Benediction, when we say the Divine Praises, we add in praise of our Lady: "Blessed be her glorious Assumption," which is what we celebrate today.

Now back to our procession. With recollections of the magnificent banners and wall-hangings of our Grailville friends, a banner seemed in order — but one that we could design and execute in a reasonable time. One day, for a special project, we shall work out a more elaborate hanging, with wools and velvets, sateens, yarns, chain stitch, feather stitch, bands and borders; but this day we had little or no time to spare. So it was off to the linen trunk in the storeroom to see what treasures we could find.

We found a small linen guest towel of bachelor's-button blue, embroidered with cross-stitch roses, simple and nice. It made us think of the Mystical Rose. And we found a white linen cloth, heavy as a butcher's apron but fine as fine and bleached white with many washings and sunnings. Added to these were a length of white rickrack and a half-skein of white yarn, and our materials were complete.

We sewed a decorative M of the rickrack over the roses on the blue linen towel. We cut an oblong of the white linen large enough to double-hem the edges and leave a border of about one and a half inches of white around the blue. We mounted the blue towel on the white linen, sewing it across the top only. We divided the white yarn into three hanks, braided it into a rope and tacked it across the top of the banner with equal lengths to hang loose down either side.

Next, John went up to the woods and cut a new shoot of oak about an inch in diameter and skinned the bark off. He sawed a two-foot length for our cross-piece, and we bound the banner to this, with white yarn at four places across the top. Another length of oak about three feet long was the standard and we bound our cross-piece to it. There was our banner! It took about an hour, with children and Granny helping, before we had it finished and the threads and shreds swept up off the dining-room floor.

The next item was the *Ritual*, that slim black book the priest carries about when he gives the blessings, and a valuable addition to family life.

Then Stephen remembered something and ran into the study. Confetti! For over a year, we had saved a package of confetti, waiting for a feast of suitable magnitude before using it. Feast days had come and gone, of magnificent magnitude, but we forever forgot the confetti. This was the day for it! Then we sat down, more or less, to await the arrival of our guests in their organdies. As none of the Newland sprouts knows an organdy from a hole in the wall, there was wild anticipation.

At last they drove up, but in picture hats and blue espadrilles, in honor of our Lady. Also bearing with them a peach chiffon pie they had made to honor her and indulge all present, with a crown of sliced peaches decorating it.

We explained immediately that these were not organdies. Philip stood admiring them, nevertheless, as they dismounted from the station wagon. A three-year inventory of knowledge stored in his hard little head was clearly being examined for some clue to this apparel. Finally, he recognized the costumes. "'You look real nice in your cowboy hats and your bedroom slippers."

The Hobsons thanked him graciously.

After general clamor for a few minutes, customary as families assemble for any great event, we had a short discussion of our Lady's Dormition and Assumption with a clear explanation of the legend about the flowers at her tomb. Then we started out in this order:

Stephen with banner.

Mrs. Hobson with pewter mug of holy water and aspergill. Mother with *Ritual*. Ginny with confetti.

A quick shift of aspergill to Peter as Mrs. Hobson picks up John Archer, who is afraid of goose and goats.

Various additional children.

Arranged at last, we started with the flowerbed by the house where there is tansy, thyme, marigold, and an unidentified herb that will be a mystery until our herb lady comes back and identi-fies it.

The blessing begins beautifully with Psalm 64,[123] which has wonderful passages in it for children. As we had just recovered from the fringes of a hurricane which, in turn, had put an end to our drought, these lines had special and eloquent meaning.

*They shout and sing for joy.* Alas, our procession seems to be one part reading and blessing, and one part shouting and singing for joy. No loss: their joy is in the Lord, and if they are too little to stand still very long, psalms or no, let them shout and sing for joy. This is the making of many memories and impressions, a mixture of blessings and sun and sky and happiness and family and home and our Lady Mother Mary; this is one of the joys of being a Catholic.

After a *Gloria,* the blessing continues, the leader reading the versicles, the others responding:

*Leader:* The Lord will be gracious.
*All:* And our land bring forth its fruit.
*Leader:* Thou waterest the mountains from the clouds.
*All:* The earth is replenished from Thy rains.
*Leader:* Giving grass for cattle.
*All:* And plants for the service of man.
*Leader:* Thou bringest forth wheat from the earth.
*All:* And wine to cheer man's heart.

[123] RSV = Ps. 65.

*Leader:* He sends His command and heals their suffering.
   *All:*   And snatches them from distressing want.
*Leader:* O Lord, hear my prayer.
   *All:*   And let my cry come unto Thee.
*Leader:* The Lord be with you.
   *All:*   And with thy spirit.

Then follow three prayers of blessing, the first of which reads:

*Let us pray. Almighty, everlasting God, by Thy word alone
Thou hast made Heaven, earth, sea, all things visible and
invisible, and hast adorned the earth with plants and trees for
the use of men and animals. Thou appointest each species to
bring forth fruit in its kind, not only to serve as food for living
creatures, but also as medicine to sick bodies. With mind and
word, we earnestly appeal to Thine ineffable goodness to bless
these various herbs and fruits, and add to their natural powers
the grace of Thy new blessing. May they ward off disease
and adversity from men and beasts who use them in Thy
name. Through our Lord, Jesus Christ, Thy Son, who
liveth and reigneth with Thee in unity of the
Holy Spirit, God, forever and ever. Amen.*

We proceeded down to the vegetable garden and sprinkled the
dill, and thence off to the brook, where the wild mint flourishes,
singing "Mary, We Greet Thee" all the way (that is the *Salve Regina* in English).

Down along the brook is a magic place, with mint thick and
tangled and wild grape and small willows and a hidden bed of forget-me-not. We sprinkled that, and the flame flower far inside a
thicket by a private stream of its own. Then we went further down
to the place for sitting on banks and dangling feet. And here, with
a story while tasting mint and other wild leaves that were not

quite so delicious, everyone took off shoes and went wading, and the smallest ones sat down in the water in their clothes. Then at last we threw the confetti. It was a glorious sight floating on the brook, sun dappling the water, sounds of children, sounds of water, smell of mint, everyone laughing and splashing, all for the honor and glory of our Lady.

Then back home, to the pie with the Mary-crown on it and the spiced tea with orange and clove (because Holy Scripture says that Mary is like sweet spices and aromatic balm[124]): a lovely end to a day that had started with the whole family at Mass and Holy Communion. The fathers had pie saved for them in the refrigerator.

Processions like this are a particularly motherish kind of thing. These things that take fussing and patience and holding hands while walking with very little people with incredible slowness are things mothers were especially well made for. Lucky for mothers who have sunny afternoons to teach such beautiful truths and to make such beautiful memories as these of "her glorious Assumption"!

But suppose you live in the city, and there is no brook and no pasture, no wild mint or forget-me-not, or goose or garden or herbs to be blessed — what then? Still, I would not give in. Somehow I would find a way to make a family celebration and a happy memory of the Assumption. For some people, a trip to the nearby botanical gardens would be a lovely event for the afternoon. There are many more herbs there than in backyard gardens, and often there are also true Mary-gardens. You could take along the *Ritual*, or the words to the blessing copied out of it, and a little bottle of holy water; and when you were alone together for a while, read the blessing over some small patch of fragrance somewhere out of the way where you disturb no one.

[124] Cf. Ecclus. 24:20 (RSV = Sir. 24:15).

Or if there were friends in the country or the suburbs, I would plan a visit with them, a sharing of foods for a picnic supper and a procession to bless their flowers and herbs.

Or if there were no way to go anywhere, I would make it a celebration around the evening meal in the city apartment. I would buy a pot of flowers, or a few cut flowers from a pushcart, and go to the grocer's for some herbs. Celery, chives, parsley, endive, lettuce, and chicory are some of the common salad herbs we use all the time, without thinking of them as herbs. Mint for iced tea is another herb we use; so I'd find some of that. Then, when all the other dishes were ready, before mixing the salad or putting the mint in the tea, I'd have my family gather together around these lovely things and have the father or the oldest grown-up read the *Blessing of Herbs*, right in my own city apartment; or in my own room over my tray, if I lived all alone.

For dessert there would be spiced peaches or pears, and I would use cinnamon to spice them because Scripture says that our Lady is like the smell of sweet cinnamon. The juice drained off any canned or stewed fruit, brought to a boil and then left to simmer a while with a little extra sugar and a stick of cinnamon, quickly prepares spiced fruit. Do it the day before, then let it get nice and cold in the refrigerator.

I would bring out a book from the library with reproductions in it of the early Christian masters — Italian, French, Flemish — and explain to my family the meanings of the fruits they used as symbols and have my children search for them in pictures. Libraries, encyclopedias, and bookshops will help you find information on symbols.

To decorate a city apartment for the feast, a banner such as described can be used without the standard; or a group of the fruits may be arranged in a bowl, or cut out in simple patterns from bright fabrics or old felts, sewed in a garland around a decorative

M on heavy unbleached muslin or linen, or arranged in a group surmounted by an M and used as a center decoration on the table or a hanging on the wall behind it. Children may make such a banner of colored construction paper and paste, cutting the fruits from paper, silhouette-fashion, and mounting them. These symbolize only a few of the glorious virtues with which God adorned His Mother.

Perhaps it is the most obvious thing in this feast that evades us most successfully. We are so accustomed to understanding its meaning that we fail to understand it with impact: *we will see her womanly, motherly, virginal, presence in Heaven.* This is the great triumph. A creature, child of Adam and Eve, flesh and blood like ourselves, *not divine,* has so dignified our race by her obedience that we are now adopted sons of God and heirs of Heaven. And we will see her.

Children always put it so well. I asked them if they understood what *Assumption* — to be assumed into Heaven — meant.

"Yes. Her whole self went to Heaven. Not one crumb was left."

Only someone who lives with children and knows their language would understand. They will say, "I love you so much I could eat you up." That is why "not one crumb was left" has such eloquent meaning.

Another said, "You mean our Lady is really in Heaven. And when we see her, it will be more than just her soul, but her real face, and her real hands, and her really real smile!"

And it will be beautiful. There is a hint of it in her Mass: "The daughter of the King comes in, all beautiful: her robes are of golden cloth."[125]

[125] Cf. Ps. 44:10 (RSV = Ps. 45:9).

Chapter 18

# All Hallows Eve

One of the nicest surprises of living around the year with the Church is to find that Halloween is part of it. Not that the Mass of the day has mention of black cats, or the Divine Office of witches, but for so long, Halloween meant nothing but parties and vandalism that when someone first proposed that it came out of the liturgy, I asked, "Are you sure?"

You still hear people doubt it, even when you show them that Halloween is All Hallows Eve, which is the night before All Saints Day. Some tell me they understand that Halloween pranks were a post-Reformation contribution to plague Catholics who kept the vigil of All Saints. Now it is possible that Halloween was abused for such a purpose; nevertheless, during all the Christian centuries up until the simplification of the Church calendar in 1956, it was a liturgical vigil in its own right and thus has a reason for being. Learning this, one pious lady of our acquaintance was heard to say, "Oh, I'm so glad to know that. I was about to write my congressman and suggest the whole thing be outlawed."

A celebration much like our Halloween, with bonfires and feasting on apples and nuts and harvest fruits, was part of pagan worship for centuries. The Britons celebrated in honor of their sun-god with bonfires, a tribute to the light that brought them abundant harvest. At the same time, they saluted Samhain, their "lord of death," who was thought to gather together at last the souls of the year's dead which had been consigned to the bodies of animals in punishment for their sins. The Romans celebrated the same kind of festival at this time in honor of their goddess Pomona, a patroness of fruits and gardens.

Whether the Church "baptized" these customs or chose this season for her feasts of the dead independent of them, their coincidence shows again how alike men are when they seek God and His ways, give praise, and use the language of symbols to express the inexpressible.

It was in the eighth century that the Church appointed a special date for the feast of All Saints, followed by a day in honor of her soon-to-be saints, the feast of All Souls. She chose this time of year, it is supposed, because, in her part of the world, it was the time of barrenness on the earth. The harvest was in, the summer done, the world brown and drab and mindful of death. Snow had not yet descended to comfort and hide the bony trees or blackened fields; so with little effort, man could look about and see a meditation on death and life hereafter.

Apparently how you spent the vigil of All Saints depended on where you lived in Christendom. In Brittany the night was solemn and without a trace of merriment. On their "night of the dead" and for forty-eight hours thereafter, the Bretons believed the poor souls were liberated from Purgatory and were free to visit their old homes. The vigil for the souls, as well as the saints, had to be kept on this night because, of course, the two days were consecutive feasts — and a vigil is never kept on a feast.

Breton families prayed by their beloveds' graves during the day, attended church for "black vespers" in the evening, and in some parishes, proceeded thence to the charnel house in the cemetery to pray by the bones of those not yet buried or for whom no room could be found in the cemetery. Here they sang hymns to call on all Christians to pray for the dead and, speaking for the dead, they asked prayers and more prayers.

Late in the evening in the country parishes, after supper was over, the housewives would spread a clean cloth on the table and set out pancakes, curds, and cider. And after the fire was banked and chairs set around the table for the returning loved ones, the family would recite the *De Profundis*[126] again and go to bed. During the night, a townsman would go about the streets ringing a bell to warn them that it was unwise to roam abroad at the time of returning souls.

It was in Ireland and Scotland and England that All Hallows Eve became a combination of prayer and merriment. Following the break with the Holy See, Queen Elizabeth forbade all observances connected with All Souls Day. In spite of her laws, however, customs survived; even Shakespeare in his *Two Gentlemen of Verona* has Speed tell Valentine that he knows he is in love because he has learned to speak "puling like a beggar at Hallowmas." This line must have escaped the Queen.

⌒

### Tricks or Treats — Old Style

Begging at the door grew from an ancient English custom of knocking at doors to beg for a "soul cake" in return for which the beggars promised to pray for the dead of the household. Soul cakes, a form of shortbread — and sometimes quite fancy, with currants for eyes — became more important for the beggars than prayers for the dead, it is said. In her *Cooking for Christ,* Florence Berger tells a legend of a zealous cook who vowed she would invent soul cakes to remind them of eternity at every bite. So she cut a hole in the middle and dropped it in hot fat, and lo — a

---

[126] Ps. 129 (RSV = Ps. 130).

doughnut. Circle that it is, it suggests the never-ending of eternity. Truth or legend, it serves a good purpose at Halloween.

The refrains sung at the door varied from "a soul cake, a soul cake, have mercy on all Christian souls for a soul cake," to the later:

> Soul, soul, an apple or two,
> If you haven't an apple, a pear will do,
> One for Peter, two for Paul,
> Three for the Man who made us all.

Here they had either run out of soul cakes or plain didn't care. Charades, pantomimes, and little dramas, popular remnants of the miracle and morality plays of the Middle Ages, commonly rehearsed the folk in the reality of life after death and the means to attain it. It is probably from these that the custom of masquerading on Halloween had its beginning. The folly of a life of selfishness would be the message pantomimed by the damned; the torment of waiting, the message of the souls from Purgatory; the delights of the Beatific Vision, the message of the Heaven-sent. Together they warned the living to heed the means of salvation before it was too late. Doubtless the presence of goblins and witches with cats (ancient symbols of the Devil) were remnants of pagan times bespeaking to Christians of spirits loosed from Hell to keep track of their own and herd them back at cockcrow. Saint-Saëns' *Danse Macabre*, with death fiddling his eerie spell over the graveyard, fascinated us all the years of growing up. Waiting for the sound of cockcrow, which would send the souls scuttling back to their graves, was almost too much suspense to bear. Little did we know that it was inspired by old French customs and superstitions on All Hallows Eve.

The familiar harvest fruits, cornstalks, and pumpkins were seasonal. Although there is an old Irish legend about a miser named

Jack who was too stingy to go to Heaven and too clever to go to Hell, so that he had to spend eternity roaming the earth with a lighted pumpkin for a lantern, the appearance of jack-o'-lanterns has always seemed much more reasonable than that. These were ages when death was a serious and acceptable meditation. Christian art shows skulls and bones as a commonplace of interior decoration, at least in the cells of the convents and monasteries. Vigils were kept by the graves, and lights and bread left for the dead, all for the twofold purpose of recalling those dead and remembering that one day you would be dead. Surely it was some bright boy, stumbling over a pile of pumpkins by his father's barn, who hit on the notion of carving a grinning death's-head to carry, lighted by a candle, under his arm. If you know small boys, this is the most reasonable of all explanations.

*Prayers and Party Fun Together*

Our family's Halloween parties are now planned around the custom of begging for soul cakes. Among the neighborhood children who attend, Catholics together with non-Catholics, there is no one who is not intrigued to learn the stories of these customs and join in the prayers and the fun.

Frying doughnuts is a big undertaking, but this one time of the year we have a doughnut session — the day before Halloween. Soul cakes need not be doughnuts, but we like to tell Mrs. Berger's story; and this, of course, leads to much tasting to see if one does think of eternity at every bite. Other refreshments for the party are natural treats — apples, nuts, popcorn — all perfect companions to the soul cakes.

Next, costumes. Saint costumes have been much in vogue in our circle since the rediscovery of Christian Halloween. These are lots of fun to make, but if you are having non-Catholic children who do not know about patron saints, a full course on the subject is not possible before the party. You might suggest that these come as some departed soul, one of those from eternity who come to warn the living to mend their ways. This gives much leeway and justifies the inevitable cowboys and space cadets. Cowboys do eventually depart, I am confident, and space cadets look as though they already have.

A rhymed invitation tells everybody that this is a real party and keeps enough of the familiar Halloween ghostliness to enhance the rest, which sounds a bit unfamiliar. Our invitation goes like this:

> Come to keep vigil on All Hallows Even,
> With Monica, Jamie, Peter and Stephen,
> With John, Philip, Christopher, dressed up like souls;
> Bring berries of red to help warn off the ghouls.
> Come knock at the door and beg for soul cakes,
> Pray hard for the souls, for the prayers that it takes
> To speed them to Heav'n go too often unsaid,
> And who prays for poor souls will ne'er want for bread.

This hints at what is going to happen. Followed by a telephone call or a note to the mothers of the guests, it gives everyone time to get the "feel of it." This is important. If it isn't clearly explained how they will beg at the door and say a prayer for the dead, the party will disintegrate right there with the "gimmes."

The berries of red and their use have their origin way back when holly and evergreens bearing red berries were used to remind the Christians of the blood of Christ and the burning love of Mary for her Child. It is not hard for country children to find a spray of red berries, but even in the city, there is bittersweet on sale at the street corner; or if you live near a barberry hedge, you might prevail on the owner to let you have a sprig — and to show your goodwill, tell him that it is a wise way to ward off witches.

An old witch patrols the lawn at our house this night, riding a broomstick and fleeing in fright from the groups of guests, terrified at the sight of the berries. Barred from the house by these berries (some of which are combined with autumn leaves and fastened to the front door in a swag), she has to be content to hoot and screech, pop out from behind trees; and when the time comes, bade by what she knows is the truth, she gives directions for begging at the door:

> I am forced to tell ye this, miserable dearies, whether I would or no; so mark it well. If ye pray for the dead, they are released sooner from their torment of waiting in Purgatory and sped on the wings of light to their eternal reward. So go and knock and the woman will open to your knock, and sing as loud as ye can: 'A soul cake, a soul cake, a prayer for a soul cake!' She will bear on her arm a basket of cakes and tell ye for whom ye are to pray. And may ye all choke on every crumb and find praying and eating at one and the same time as miserable as the torment I endure forever riding hungry on my broomstick!

Everyone is delighted by her useless malice, and finds that simultaneous praying and eating is not difficult. Better yet, bade by the woman of the house, they pray before they eat (much more respectful). They pray for grandfathers and grandmothers and aunts and uncles and cousins and friends and all the souls in Purgatory. The Catholic children and the non-Catholic children say together for their dead the one prayer they share in common, the Our Father; and after the voices of the Catholic children have died away, the rest continue with "for Thine is the kingdom and the power and the glory forever." This, incidentally, was appended to the Our Father long before the so-called Reformation; it is one of those liturgical additions that was eventually dropped for the sake of purity. Knowing this helps eliminate some of the irritation Catholics feel when hearing it. It is not something the Protestants dreamed up just to be difficult.

Around the house to the various doors (because we live in the country, we must confine our party to one house), and then inside for the celebration. In the city, children could go to several houses close together, or to several apartment doors. The old witch, spying one door without red berries, makes a last appearance, cackling and greeting the guests from behind the puppet show. She shakes the children's hands with a wet glove and presses an ice cube in each unsuspecting palm, whereupon they shriek and scream and pile through the door into the living room to duck for apples, chase them on strings, eat popcorn and soul cakes, and drink cider.

If there are many small children, plan the party for them — and let the older children help give it. If there are more older children, it is best to plan the party for them. Sometimes it will work both ways, but more often than not, widely divergent age groups do not combine successfully for parties because the same games and entertainments do not appeal to both. If you have both small fry and older children, you might plan with the mothers of the neighborhood to hold two parties — one for little children at one house, one for older children at another.

For very small children, ducking for apples, apples on strings, refreshments, and the chance to make noise and antics in their costumes can be nicely gathered up and rounded off by reading one or two stories. If they have come in saint costumes, the outstanding game can be telling your saint's story — after the others have guessed who you are.

For older children or even adults, "A Trayful of Saints" is a good game. On a tray, place a dozen or more objects that symbolize familiar saints. For example: key — St. Peter; flower — Little Flower; rose — St. Rose of Lima; dog — St. Dominic; bird — St.

Francis of Assisi; cross — St. Helena; crown — St. Elizabeth of Hungary; eagle — St. John the Evangelist; shell — St. James; Sacred Heart — St. Margaret Mary Alacoque; kitchen utensil — St. Martha; half coat (paper cut-out) — St. Martin of Tours. Go slowly from one guest to another, giving them time to memorize what is on the tray. Then pass out paper and pencils and have them list what they remember, and what saint they think they symbolize.

Charades depicting outstanding events in the lives of the saints are always fun at such a party, and ghost stories are in order when the apple-ducking is done and people are sitting around the fire.

Chapter 19

⁓

# All Saints

The feast of All Saints is one of the greatest of all the feasts because it celebrates what could have been impossible. The Cross is a tree that bears fruit. This is the feast of its harvest. The celebrations of the mysteries in the life of our Lord are glorious, and there is no detracting from them. But He was God. This day we celebrate the perfecting of human nature, by grace pouring from the side of Christ on the Cross, through His Church and His sacraments, remaking men after their despoiling in the Garden.

Aside from all the lofty things to be said about the saints and to the saints on this day, we want our children to understand in the marrow of their bones what the principal idea is: "We are so glad for you. Now pray, so we'll be there too!" And they must add to this and to every feast an endless "Thank you, Lord Jesus, for making it possible."

Celebrating all its patrons this day, the family plans a procession to the dinner table, which will show them off splendidly. If there have been saint costumes from All Hallows Eve, nothing could be better than to wear them again in procession on All Hallows Day. Had someone suggested this to me as a child, I would have died of joy. I remember vain attempts to recapture Halloween magic by putting on a costume a second night, but the magic was gone. Only one night of the year did it really transform me, not because the night was really magic or that I knew why I wore it, but because it was the night for costumes. There was no reason to wear it a second time. Now that we understand there is a reason, it is a great incentive to be a saint on Halloween.

⌒

### A Procession of Hopeful Saints

We assemble for our procession.

St. Monica wears a veil, something black or grey, symbolic of widowhood. She might carry a monstrance with the Blessed Sacrament to tell of her devotion to the Holy Eucharist and her attendance at daily Mass (St. Augustine wrote about this in his *Confessions*), or she may carry a spindle, the symbol of all married ladies who were saints. The monstrance is a flat paste-up of yellow, gold, and white paper; the spindle is a stick with white cotton batting.

Jamie carries as many of the symbols of pilgrims as he can find, because St. James the Great (the tall) is always dressed as a pilgrim. His best friend gave him a keychain with little shells on it one year, for his feast day, because the scallop shell is the most common symbol of pilgrims. A staff is another, and a pilgrim's hat (broad brimmed), and a purse (like a shoulder-strap bag).

John has difficulty deciding which St. John to be, but usually ends up as St. John the Baptist. One Halloween we had a charade of St. John the Baptist. A mysterious maiden came dancing in with a jack-o'-lantern on a platter — representing what? Some people are shocked to think that we would disport so, but we think it is apropos. Losing one's head for the love of God and going right to Heaven is something to grin about. A cruciform staff is one of his symbols, and the paste-up puzzle of St. John has several symbols on it (described in chapter 3). (We keep forgetting to buy a comb of honey.)

Peter rattles keys and carries the paste-up puzzle of St. Peter — or, if he can manage it, a rock — and the fishing pole with the yellow fish dangling (see chapter 18).

Stephen wears a gorgeous crown made of two crowns. A high red paper crown has a smaller silver paper crown stapled over it. It is really very handsome. In this he represents St. Stephen, King and Confessor, of Hungary. He also carries a rock to show his devotion to St. Stephen, Deacon and Martyr. He always says, "This is for St. Stephen of Hungary, and this is for the St. Stephen what got rocks thrown at his head, and when I get there, I'll be St. Stephen Newland."

Philip carries a basket of bread to recall that St. Philip doubted that the five thousand (not counting women and children) could be fed. That evening, after the Sermon on the Mount, he literally had to eat his own words. He also carries a branch with green leaves. Although this is a little obscure, it reminds us of Philip's friend Nathanael, sitting under the fig tree when Philip told him they had found "Him of whom Moses and the prophets spoke." It was Jesus, son of Joseph, of Nazareth, he said. Nathanael muttered, "Can anything good come out of Nazareth?" And Philip, to his everlasting credit, answered, "Come and see."[127]

Christopher is still to be initiated to carrying anything but his faded dolly stuffed with shredded nylons and his little doggy. Perhaps this year he will get in line if we give him a flashlight, a modern counterpart of St. Christopher's lantern. Grandma Reed will carry our Lady, because her name is Ann; Granny Newland will carry a rosary because her name is Catherine and she is a Dominican tertiary.

There are plenty of St. Williams for daddies named William, but not all their stories are told in detail. The symbols of St.

---

[127] Cf. John 1:45-46.

William of Monte Virgine are a trowel (because he built a monastery), a lily for chastity, and a passion flower (to indicate that he was devoted to the Passion of our Lord).

But there is another St. William, of Perth, a Scottish saint who is mighty appealing to fathers bearing his name. He was a baker in private life, then turned his feet toward God and set out on a pilgrimage with his apprentice to do penance for his sins. Somewhere along the way, the apprentice murdered him. This is not the feature that appeals to fathers. For lack of a symbol, a tray of hot rolls would do nicely, luring even the most self-conscious father into a procession. (Not all fathers go for processions. It is fatal to try to drag them in. Never use force on them or on older children who may feel it is an awkward idea. You can always think of some happy but unobtrusive way to recall the triumphs of their saints. Often just to tell their stories at dinner is enough. Your own good sense will guide you.)

The banner for the Assumption is carried by the mother in this household, because her name is Mary and she was baptized on the feast of the Assumption.

It is beautiful to have each one carry a lighted candle — his baptismal candle, if he has one. This to remind us that we and the saints together have life in Christ. In the Mystical Body, we are all one. They are in Heaven; we are on earth; the holy souls are in Purgatory: one Church extending into eternity. If you have enough room and time for a long procession, it is nice to sing the Litany of the Saints. If this isn't practicable, save it for night prayers.

⌒

### Why We Should Know the Saints

The Gospel of John tells us, "But as many as received Him, to them gave He power to become the sons of God: to them that believe in His name: who were born, not of blood, nor of the will of the flesh, nor of the will of man, but of God."[128]

Each succeeding feast gives us a new understanding of this. We have been "born of God." We must know the saints because we can learn from them how to receive His will, to love it, to act on it, to use the power He has given us *to become the sons of God*. Here, we are His adopted sons separated from Heaven by life in the flesh. That part of us that He made in His own image and likeness is detained a while, in the body. It is being tried. The saints went through the trials too, and with the help of His grace, they overcame them. They are in glory now, sons united at last with their Father. This is the greatest of His mercies. He loved us before the creation of the world and planned for us to be in eternity with Him. When sin spoiled the plan, He perfected it — if one can say that — with the Incarnation. He became a man and spent Himself to devise the means for our perfection. The saints used it. We must too.

The antiphon from Vespers for this feast says what we want to say:

*O ye Angels and Archangels, Thrones and Dominions, Principalities and Powers, Virtues of Heaven. Cherubim and Seraphim, ye Patriarchs and Prophets, holy Doctors of the Law, Apostles, all Martyrs of Christ, holy Confessors, Virgins of the Lord, Hermits and all Saints: Intercede for us.*

[128] John 1:12-13.

Chapter 20

⁀

# November and the Holy Souls

The children had never been to a funeral before, nor attended a wake, nor had any personal acquaintance with death. Then in November, the month of the dead, someone dear to our neighborhood left this life to go to God.

They had prayed for her through a long illness. Their first concern was: "Did she go right to Heaven?"

Children always give you the point at which to start. A subject may have a dozen approaches, but the best one is by way of their questions.

We would like to have said, flatly, yes, she went right to Heaven. She had suffered much, uniting it to Christ's suffering. She had lived a life of prayer and sacrifice, had received the last sacraments and the final blessing with its plenary indulgence. Her last few months had been an excruciating trial, and she had lain weeks longing for death, accepting suffering, but ready to welcome death. She wanted to die on Saturday because it was our Lady's day, and our Lady granted her wish. It would be easy to say yes, she is surely in Heaven. But even when you think so, you can never say that you know. It is God's secret, and no one here *knows*.

But there is comfort for the living in what we do know: how the Church prepares us for death; how she prays for us after death, and the real possibility that we may "go right to Heaven" if we try very hard. Haven't we just celebrated the feast of All Saints, the glory of those who did? True, some among them entered by way of Purgatory, but they are there in Heaven nevertheless, and they confirm us in high hope.

Death is a touchy subject. People who do not know the Church (and some who think they do) accuse her of being "too mournful about death." Perhaps this is because she is so candid about man and his origin — dust. She knows he will return to dust. She knows that he inherited Original Sin and is weak, that the Devil is clever; and she does not admit the impossibility of going to Hell. She knows that Purgatory exists, and hurts, and that man was created for Heaven but may refuse to go there. She admits what everyone must admit: that wherever he is going, there is only one way to go there: to die. Death is a doorway we must go through. How else can the spirit leave the body behind and enter eternity?

For Catholics, the idea of death ought not to be mournful. There is natural grief and loneliness for the bereaved families and friends, of course, but God mellows these with time. If death is otherwise mournful as an idea, as something to think about — or avoid thinking about — it is because we look at it from the wrong direction. We should be seeing it as the middle step, not the final step: life, then death, then God. It is God for whom we are created. By way of death. He is where we are bound.

This was the spirit of our neighbor's death. It accounted for the tranquility of her family's grief, their hopefulness, their ready resignation. Entering their home, where her body was returned until time for the funeral, our children saw death for the first time as they knelt beside her and prayed.

"But, Mother" — this was in a whisper — "you said she might even be in Heaven with God. But she's not. She's here asleep."

You see? You are sure you have made it clear about the body and the soul, and not until such a time do you discover that you haven't. Not until such a time, either, do you see how truly the Church speaks of us as creatures with souls that will not die. Our bodies are the least of us. We could not talk about this at the moment, but we did when we got home.

"That wasn't *her,* dear. That was just her body. She has really and truly gone to see God and, we hope, to be with Him immediately in Heaven." How to explain this once and for all and put confusion to rest?

"You close your eyes." He did. "Now think a thought about yourself."

He closed his eyes very tightly, and thought, and said, "I'm thinking about myself."

"That is you, dear, that part that can think about itself, know who he is, say to me, 'I'm thinking about myself.' That is truly you, the you that will not die. Your body will die one day, and it will be carefully put in the ground, and the people will say, 'He has gone to see God.' They will be right. When our bodies finally die, the part of us that is soul and lives forever goes off to see God."

⌒

### The Sacrament of the Sick Examined

After this experience with death, we were glad we had read through the prayers for the sick and the Sacrament of the Sick several months before. Their attitude toward death had always been wholesome, even cheerful, and it was a happy discovery to find that the Church in her prayers for the dying is nothing if not persistently cheerful. God was good to let them find this reaffirmed at the home of our neighbor, among her family, at her Mass and burial.

The prayers of the Last Sacraments are most appropriate additions to family prayer for the month of November. In the discussions that follow them, the family will find that it is not difficult to speak in the most practical way of specific customs, attitudes, requests, each in regard to his own death. What has seemed to be morbid and distasteful, almost unmentionable, is brought into the daylight, and we agree that it is only common sense to make arrangements and requests ahead of time for that final journey to the highest of all the "states of grace," eternal glory.

Never had I read the prayers of the Sacrament of the Sick in English before the summer of 1955 (and you know how old I am). That is a lot of years for a Catholic to brush with death every so often and not know what the sacrament for the dying is all about. I did not know that *Viaticum*, which is the Holy Eucharist administered to the dying, means "provisions for a journey." I would never have dreamed that a sick call could be such a heartening experience, more so than ever now that much of it is in English.

The first thing a priest on a sick call says, as he enters the house, is: *Peace be unto this home and unto all that dwell herein.* He hears the confession of the sick person in private, administers Holy Communion if the patient is able to receive it, then makes this great petition (Father Weller's translation):

> *Let us pray. O Holy Lord, almighty Father, everlasting God,*
> *full of trust we beseech Thee that the most holy Body of our*
> *Lord Jesus, Thy Son, which our brother (sister) hath now*
> *received, may be unto him (her) an eternal remedy both in*
> *soul and body. Who livest and reignest with Thee in the*
> *unity of the Holy Spirit, God, forever and ever. Amen.*

To postpone calling a priest to administer these sacraments to our seriously sick is hardly Christian solicitude. Yet many do, out of ignorance of what this rite implies, imagining that it will "frighten her." This is a failure to understand not only the wording of the prayers used, but the *use* of these sacraments. They are not merely forms it is customary to enact over Catholics when they are dying. They are Christ Himself coming to the patient. The Divine Physician is asked to come and heal the body as well as the soul.

The frequent use of these prayers in our families will quickly dispel such misunderstanding, for when their content is examined, we see that they contain marvelous petitions for the living as well as the dying, for the entire household where there is illness. Nowhere in them is there the dread sound of cracking doom. Even at the end, in the prayers before death, tenderness, charity, holy hope, sweet resignation, and powerful faith are recommended to the soul, and the saints and angels are called upon to conduct the soul to the Most High. Here is the beginning prayer.:

> *Let us pray. Along with our lowly coming, O Lord*
> *Jesus Christ, let there enter into this home unending*
> *happiness, divine blessing, untroubled joy, charity which*
> *is fruitful, continual health. Drive forth from this place*
> *the spirits of evil, let Thine angel of peace come hither,*
> *and banish all harmful dissension from this house. O Lord,*
> *extol Thy holy name in our esteem, and bless what we are*
> *about to do. Sanctify the coming of Thine unworthy servant,*
> *for Thou art holy, Thou art kind, Thou art abiding with*
> *the Father and the Holy Spirit through all eternity. Amen.*

My, we should have these said for us every day. This prayer is *especially* for the living. But perhaps the next one will be about death:

> *Let us pray to our Lord, Jesus Christ, and beseech Him to*
> *bless with His abundant benediction this home and all who*
> *dwell herein. May He appoint over them a good angel as a*
> *guardian, and assist them to serve Him, to contemplate the*
> *grandeur of His law. May He turn away all powers that would*
> *harm them, free them from all anxiety and distress, and keep*

*them in well-being within their home. Thou who livest
and reignest with the Father and the Holy Spirit,
God, for all eternity. Amen.*

*Free them from all anxiety and distress:* This seems a petition for
our times, for those ridden with neuroses and fears.

A passage from the Gospels is read, but not — as you might expect — the story of Lazarus, or Jairus' daughter, or the widow of
Naim, or "what doth it profit a man,"[129] but the magnificent story
of the cure of the Centurion's servant, emphasizing our Lord's
healing power and our need to have faith in it. "Lord, my servant is
lying sick in the house, paralyzed, and is grievously afflicted." Jesus
said to him, "I will come and cure him. . . ."[130]

Shortly after this come the anointing prayers (in Latin) from
which the sacrament receives its name. *Extreme Unction*[131] means
"last [extreme] anointing with oil [unction]." Last, not because
death is inevitable, but because it is the last of the anointing sacraments. The anointing sacraments are Baptism, when the newly
baptized is anointed first on the breast and between the shoulders
and later on the crown of the head; Confirmation, when the
bishop anoints the candidate's forehead; and Holy Orders, when
the bishop anoints the hands of the newly ordained priests. The
oil used for the Sacrament of the Sick is the blessed Oil of the
Sick, which is also used for the blessing of bells. (The other sacred
oils are the Oil of Catechumens, used for Baptism and at ordina-
tion, and for the blessing of baptismal fonts, baptismal water, altars, altar stones, consecrations of churches, and at the coronation
of Catholic kings and queens; and Holy Chrism, an oil scented

[129] Matt. 16:26.
[130] Cf. Matt. 8:6-7.
[131] The Sacrament of the Sick is the term more commonly used
now. — ED.

with balsam and used at Baptism and Confirmation, at the consecration of bishops and churches, and for the blessing of chalices,
patens, baptismal water, and church bells.)

If we have faith in the efficacy of holy water, properly used,
consider the efficacy of the use of the sacred oils. All things considered — the three sacraments together, the powerful petitions,
the use of this great sacramental — it is no wonder people regain
their health and doctors ask priests, "What do you *do* to them?"

The sick person is anointed with the oil on his eyes, ears, nos-
trils, mouth, hands, and feet, if possible, and the prayer adapted to
each anointing is: "Through this holy anointing and through His
tender mercy, may the Lord forgive thee whatever sins thou hast
committed by the sense of sight (hearing, taste, etc.). . . ." The oil
is wiped away with the six balls of cotton provided on the sick-call
table.

Now, in Latin, a truly marvelous plea for recovery taken in part
from the letter of St. James the Apostle:

*Let us pray. O Lord God, who didst say through Thine apostle
James, "Is any man sick among you? Let him call in the priests
of the Church, and let them pray over him, anointing him with
oil in the name of the Lord. And the prayer of faith shall save
the sick man, and the Lord will raise him up; and if he be in
sins, they shall be forgiven him," cure, we beseech Thee,
O our Redeemer, by the grace of the Holy Spirit, the ailment
of this sick man (woman), heal his (her) wounds, and forgive
his (her) sins. Deliver him (her) from all miseries of body
and mind, and mercifully restore him (her) to perfect health
inwardly and outwardly, that, having recovered by an act of
Thy kindness, he (she) be able to take up anew his (her)
former duties. Thou who, with the Father and the self-same
Holy Spirit, livest and reignest, God, forevermore. Amen.*

*Let us pray. Look down with favor, O Lord, we beseech
Thee, upon Thy servant (handmaid) N., failing from
bodily weakness, and revive the soul which Thou hast
created, that reformed by Thy chastisement, he (she)
may acknowledge himself (herself) saved by Thy
healing. Through Christ our Lord. Amen.*

A third prayer, and still no mention of death. Actually the only reference to death occurs in a shorter prayer used in emergencies, and even then the word is not used.

The Church does not agree with those who don't believe in Hell because "you get your Hell on earth." She does agree that the pains of Purgatory can be hellish, and that suffering here on earth can seem to be hellish; so in her wisdom she begs our Father to let us bear them here in reparation for the sins which, otherwise, we will be purged of by the pains of Purgatory. The saints have said that it is a far easier way to pay for sin than in Purgatory. Part of the training of a Christian must include instruction in the use of suffering: we may accept and use it in payment for our sins, and for the sins of others. Suffering is to be considered one of our most precious possessions.

⌒

### Indulgences

With the apostolic blessing following the Sacrament of the Sick, one of the powers given to St. Peter is used in a final act of divine mercy. Before reading this prayer, and becoming involved with our children in a discussion of indulgences, we should open the Gospels and find the passages where this power is given by our Lord Himself. It is unnecessary for Catholics to be embarrassed or apologetic about indulgences. The power to bind and loose is referred to in Scripture by our Lord.

And I tell thee this in my turn, that thou art Peter, and it is upon this rock that I will build my church; and the gates of Hell shall not prevail against it; and I will give to thee the keys of the kingdom of Heaven; and whatever thou shalt bind on earth shall be bound in Heaven, and whatever thou shalt loose on earth shall be loosed in Heaven.[132]

Here He has given St. Peter both the authority and the concept, to bind and to loose. Later He speaks to the disciples: "I promise you, all that you bind on earth shall be bound in Heaven, and all that you loose on earth shall be loosed in Heaven."[133]

Children will ask immediately about indulgences; so we must explain. Indulgences obtained for ourselves by ourselves depend on our disposition. They are not mechanically granted. It would do no one any good to spend his life reciting indulgenced prayers if he made no real attempt to avoid sin, if he failed in the first requirement — true sorrow for sin — if he did not try to live a good Christian life. (Franz Werfel's novel *Embezzled Heaven* treats this subject.) God is not to be tricked into letting anyone into Heaven.

The indulgences we gain for departed souls depend as well on our disposition. We must make the intention to gain them, and we must fulfill the requirements of the indulgence (for example, Confession and Communion with certain prayers, or the Rosary in the presence of the Blessed Sacrament); but we must also remember that the final word rests with God. He alone knows the state of the soul, at the moment of death, of the one for whom we pray. It will do no good to obtain a plenary indulgence for a soul in Hell. But God is merciful, and accepts such riches to apply to some other soul, as He decrees. Lucy dos Santos asked our Lady at Fatima

[132] Cf. Matt. 16:18-19.
[133] Cf. Matt. 18:18.

about two village girls who had died not long before the apparitions, and was told that one was in Heaven and one would be in Purgatory until the end of the world. Indulgences are a manifestation of God's love and mercy, but He is the Master all the same.

Children and grown-ups, too, will ask if an indulgence of, say, one hundred days means "you get one hundred days off your Purgatory." Someone said not long ago, "How can your Church teach something as silly as that?"

She doesn't. If a doctrine is really silly, you may be sure that the Catholic Church does not teach it. The Church has never defined anything with regard to the meaning of an indulgence of so many days or years. The origin of this terminology arose out of the remission of penances imposed for certain periods of time: for so many years, or so many quarantines (Lents). Even the common theory that an indulgence of one hundred days would benefit a sinner to the same extent as the performance of a hundred days' penance in the past, has no foundation. The arithmetical aspect of penance is not our first concern, but rather the conviction that we are sinners, and need to do penance. God is merciful to give us indulgences as one of the means of fulfilling our penance.

The apostolic blessing after the Sacrament of the Sick obtains for the person a plenary (full) indulgence at the moment of death:

> *May our Lord, Jesus Christ, Son of the living God,*
> *who hath given to His blessed apostle Peter the power of*
> *binding and loosing, mercifully receive thy confession, and*
> *restore unto thee the pristine robe of Baptism. And I, by the*
> *power given to me by the Apostolic See, grant thee a Plenary*
> *Indulgence and remission of all sins. In the name of the*
> *Father, and of the Son, and of the Holy Spirit. Amen.*
>
> *Through the most sacred mysteries of mankind's restoration,*
> *may the almighty God remit unto thee the punishment of the*

*present and of eternity, open to thee the gates of Paradise,
and lead thee to everlasting happiness. Amen.*

*May Almighty God, the Father, the Son,
and the Holy Spirit, bless you. Amen.*

We must begin immediately to become familiar with this sacrament. Booklets with the English words can be obtained at little cost, and for the month of November, it is a worthwhile investment to obtain one for each member of the family, so that the children may by turns read the prayers aloud for the family, thus attending closely to what they say. Several of the prayers are ideally suited for family prayer when someone in the house or the neighborhood, or some other relative or friend, is ill, or as a frequent intercession for any and all "in all the world" who are ill.

*Applying the Prayers to Our Senses*

The anointing prayers also offer an excellent means of teaching children to ponder the right use of the senses. For example, the day after we had read these prayers together for the first time, John and I were in the drugstore. He came over from a rack of paperback mysteries with his eyes popping.

"Mother! Come here — wait till you see." We went back to the display, and he pointed to a cover showing a voluptuous lady in hardly any clothes. "Look! Isn't that awful! Not half enough clothes on."

"Yes, it's terrible. It's too bad. God makes people and gives them fine bodies, and they do such things as this with them. You know, don't you, that it isn't a body that is bad, but what you do *with* one, or *to* one, or how you *look* at one or *think* about one that can be bad. It makes you think of those anointing prayers, doesn't it?

"This is a good example of how you use your sense of sight. You see things with it — both good and bad, and what you must do is make the decision what to look at and what not to look at. You see, it is quite possible that if you stood looking at these books long enough, you'd no longer be shocked to see the immodest ladies on the covers. The Devil would try very hard to make you more curious, and if you continued to gaze at them, you could begin to like seeing them. You could then start to have immodest thoughts, and in time say it isn't wrong at all to stand around and look at them. That is how the Devil tries to make you abuse your sense of sight. In the end, if you were not careful, you could commit serious sin with it. You have committed no sin today because you happened to see them accidentally and you know they are improper. But remember now that such things are wrong, that you must walk away and refuse to look at them."

It is not too soon to begin teaching him to think about how he uses his eyes. He is living in a world where pictures of sexy ladies are on most of the magazines on the newsstand, on paperback mysteries in the drugstore, most of the movie posters, many of the television shows, hanging on the walls of barracks (and he may be there sooner than one likes to think). He needs years of practice to learn a Christian "custody of the eyes."

When we got home and were all together again in the evening, we talked some more about it.

"It helps you to remember how great your body is if you remember how the Church feels about it. When you were baptized, your body was anointed. Father made the Sign of the Cross on your forehead and above your heart, and prayed that you might be a fitting temple of God. After he poured the water over your head and Original Sin was washed from your soul, he made another Sign of the Cross on the crown of your head, because you were now a Christian and shared a royal kingship with Christ, our King. He asked Almighty God to make that anointing a blessing unto 'life everlasting.'

"When you know that at the end of your life, each of your senses will be anointed and the priest will ask God to forgive your abuses of them, it makes you think about how carefully you should use them."

Having had a practical example of the possible abuse of sight, the day before, we tried to think of examples of the abuse of the others. For instance, what wrongs could you commit with *touch?*

*Taking* things is obvious, but not always common. It has not been one of our problems so far. But that famous childhood curiosity, possessed by the Newlands' child as well as the Elephant's, is relative to this. No sin, this: it seems as nothing to adults removed from the world of children. But out of its temptations resisted can grow obedience, patience, and the allaying of curiosity — and it demands reciprocal virtues from parents: that they understand the torments of the young and curious. These small struggles with obedience ("Now *please*, dear, do not *touch!*"), related with simplicity and love to the right use of the sense of touch, do not hint at the serious sins of touch, but help awaken a sense of the proper custody of the gift.

What of smell? I cannot imagine there are childhood abuses of this lovely gift, but we can talk about abuses to which it can lead. Part of gluttony is an unholy anticipation, perhaps whetted for some by the delicious smells of foods and beverages. We should rejoice when our food smells good, but never forget that eating is a habit of humans, so that they may stay alive and do God's work; it is not the purpose of living. It must always be kept under control.

The delights of cosmetic smells can easily become a form of sensuality for women, spinning a web that can trap a soul deep in self-indulgence. I remember walking into one of the great beauty salons — into that startling other-world of scent, powder, handsome decor, delicate mannerism — and sensing the danger there. One could so easily be persuaded this "world of loveliness" was the reality. Lovely scents can praise God and lift our thoughts to Him; after all, we use incense in our worship and flowers praise Him with their scent. But evil can smell lovely, too, and sanctity can sometimes smell so evil.

Girls and mothers find many opportunities to ponder the right use of smell, especially when there are babies in the house who sometimes smell so bad. Yet the loving attendance on them can be the most exquisite prayer. How many times we have thought, when asking with the Church that our prayers rise to Him as a sweet odor, that many's the "sweet odor of prayer" that goes up from a houseful of children!

To be clean and sweet and smell good is to be socially acceptable, and we all try to teach our children the habits of good grooming; but we must be very sure they understand that sweetness within is more important than sweetness without, and that they must use their sense of smell, and all the good things to smell, to give glory to God.

The sense of taste, of course, is companion to the sense of smell. It is easy to find examples of this.

The sense of hearing is not such a subtle offender, and with it goes the power to speak. A fragment of a telephone conversation gives an example.

"Did you hear what ____ said? No? Neither did I, but I know because I was told by ____, who heard it and told me, and I said I thought it was awful. Don't you think it's awful?"

But if ____ is awful for saying something, what about ____, who heard ____ say it, and repeated it to ____, who listened and then repeated it to ____ and asked if it wasn't awful?

Perhaps this is not a serious sin this time, or the next time, or the time after that, but doing it can become a habit, possibly serious, potentially sinful. Gossip and giving scandal have no place on the list of Christian accomplishments. We have no right to circulate and thereby multiply the revelation of secrets that are the concern of some single soul and God.

What of the power of motion?

"My goodness, what sins can you commit with your feet?"

"I know — kicking!"

"If you kicked someone on purpose, it would probably be a sin. Certainly a dreadful imperfection. But there is more to the power of motion than kicking. We do know someone who, this day, went to you-know-who's house when he was told not to. That was disobedience and it had to be punished. What got him there?"

"Feet!"

"Right. Many times we use our power of motion in disobedience. When you grow up, there will be places you must not go to because they are occasions of sin. While you are little, you practice making the right kind of decisions about going and coming by being obedient to your parents and using your power of motion in obedience. Think of where you are going when your feet take you somewhere. If it is not good to go there, say to them, 'Feet! Turn around and go back!'" They are great gifts, these powers. The right use of them is part of the battle for perfection.

⁀

### No Discrimination

November is the month of praying for the dead; so this proposes further discussion. We want the children to pray generously, boldly, not only for "our dead" but for all the world of the dead. Strangely enough, this is their way if they are left to themselves. Rarely are they content with our conventional phrasing, "relatives and friends and all the souls in Purgatory." They care about so many and want to name them by name.

I was icing a cake one day, and one of the boys was watching hungrily.

"Who's he?" he asked, pointing to Paul Revere on the sugar package.

So I told him the story of Paul Revere.

"Boy. He was pretty brave to do that. Is he dead?"

"Yes. That happened a long time ago."

That night at prayers we listed our intentions and our dead, and he added, "And Paul Revere, in case he's in Purgatory."

Yes, Paul Revere, and Rudyard Kipling, because he wrote the *Jungle Book,* and the *Just-So Stories,* and Kenneth Grahame because he wrote *Wind in the Willows*, and Beatrix Potter for Jemima Puddleduck and Peter Rabbit. They pray for Stephen Foster because they sing his songs, and all the ones who wrote their favorite music; for the Brothers Grimm, of course, and Hans Andersen. Then there is Abraham Lincoln, and George Washington, and all the dead in the cemeteries (for whom we pray when we drive by cemeteries), and the dead in the newspapers, and the accident victims. Add to these the bad dead, like Stalin and Hitler (whom they do not even know except from history books or, now and then, grown-ups' conversation), and the dead who have died without Baptism, "because we hope they got baptism of desire," also the dead of the terrible persecutions, and the bad Indians who martyred the Jesuits, the dead in our floods, and of course the dead who have no one to care about them or pray for them.

The listings could go on all night, just as the lists for All Souls Day could go on all day. But this is good, because we don't know about the dead. If they are in Heaven, our prayers will be used for someone else, and if they are beyond saving, our prayers will be used for someone else. Always, we must remember how much God loves souls and how dearly He paid on the Cross in order to save them.

Charity is not just for this world. It extends to the world where so many we have loved, and God has loved, must wait and endure purification, "as though by fire."[134] Masses, prayers, sacrifices — all must be encouraged for the dead. Blessed John Massias[135] used to sprinkle holy water on the ground, saying that it was an efficacious devotion together with prayers for the souls in Purgatory. His story *Warrior in White*, by Mary Fabyan Windeatt, is a good read-aloud story for November.

In the Canon of every Mass, there is a special memento for the dead, so we can remind our children the night before and on the way in the morning to make their Mass intention for the dead. We can encourage them to sacrifice in order to give an offering for a Mass for the dead. We can remind them after they have been to confession that for the few moments it takes them to make the Stations of the Cross or to recite the Rosary before the Blessed Sacrament and pray for the intention of the Holy Father, there is a plenary indulgence applicable to the souls in Purgatory. We can faithfully attend Forty Hours' devotion, parish Holy Hours, or whatever devotions our parish holds by which we may give praise and honor to God and succor to the dear dead.

Above all, let us not fail to teach our children that death is one of the punishments of Original Sin. It was not part of God's original plan. If Adam had not committed Original Sin, we would have gone to God in some other way. Now we go through death.

We receive the gift of human life from God at conception and the gift of sacramental life from Christ at Baptism. Death is our

---

[134] Cf. 1 Cor. 3:15.

[135] St. John Massias (1585-1645), Dominican tertiary and visionary known for his service to the poor and his devotion to the souls in Purgatory; canonized in 1975. — ED.

opportunity to give life, our life; not merely to lie helplessly and let it be taken from us, but to offer Him with a willing heart this life we received from Him. We are free to make it our own surrender, in order to go to Him and glory.

Chapter 21

⤳

# Thanksgiving

It looks like a happy coincidence that our American feast of
Thanksgiving should come at the end of the Church year where
properly a thanksgiving ought to come, but actually it is no coincidence at all. The Pilgrims' feast was another manifestation of the
sense of God that is common in all men, and the need they have
for giving thanks to Him. Everywhere men have had thanksgiving
feasts to whatever gods they worshiped, celebrating their har-
vests, the end of their journeys, and their protection under a divine providence. For thousands of years before, a rite and feast of
thanksgiving was dictated in the law of Moses, their forms appeared everywhere, out of the instinct of man. After the Exodus,
the One True God made it a law for the Jews.

> Three times every year, you shall celebrate feasts to me:
> Thou shall keep the feast of the unleavened bread . . . and
> the feast of the harvest of the firstfruits of thy work. . . . The
> feast also in the end of the year, when thou hast gathered in
> all thy corn out of the field.[136]

Perhaps Elder Brewster held this in mind when he and Governor Bradford and the others planned the Pilgrim prayer meeting

[136] Exod. 23:14-17.

and the feast of thanks to follow. God gave explicit instructions to
the Jews.

> Thou shalt celebrate the solemnity also of tabernacles seven
> days, when thou . . . make merry in thy festival time, thou,
> thy son, and thy daughter, thy manservant and thy maidser-
> vant, the Levite also and the stranger, and the fatherless,
> and the widow that are within thy gates. Seven days shalt
> thou celebrate feasts to the Lord thy God in the place
> which the Lord shall choose; and the Lord thy God will
> bless thee in all thy fruits, and in every work of thy hands,
> and thou shalt be in joy.[137]

For the Pilgrims, the "stranger within the gates" was Massasoit
and some ninety of the Wampanoags who had helped the Pilgrims
clear ground, plant crops, and hunt game that first difficult year.
There were fatherless and widows, you may be sure: of the original
102, only fifty remained, twenty-nine of them women and children, some with familiar names, some with strange. There were
the Carvers and the Bradfords and the Allertons, Priscilla Mullins
who would marry John Alden, and Myles Standish in charge of
their military affairs. The Hopkins children were Constantia,
Damaris, and Oceanus, and among the other children were Desire
Minter, Resolved White, Humility Cooper, Love Brewster, and a
baby named Peregrine White who was born on the Mayflower and
probably never knew he bore the name of a half-dozen martyrs.
Governor Bradford and Elder Brewster had been with the original
group who left Scrooby in England, went to Leyden in Holland,
and finally set out for the new England.

They were Bible-living Christians, no more tolerant of the religious convictions of others than the Church of England was of

[137] Deut. 16:13-15.

their own, but neither is that new under the sun. Even with the ancient form of worship unrecognizable after its truncation, limping after its dismemberment, the instinct to worship is still common; if there is a meeting point left anywhere, this is it. This is the beginning point of the struggle for unity among men who two hundred years before would have offered in thanksgiving "from among Thy gifts bestowed upon us, a victim perfect, holy and spotless, the holy bread of everlasting life and the chalice of everlasting salvation."

We must not think of ourselves as islands of "tolerant" men, worshiping in the way that is most pleasing to each. There is a true way, taught by one who said, "I am the Way, and the Truth and the Life."[138] We must go all the way in our desire to bring all men to His Way, meeting them where we can meet them, sharing warmly with them at least the desire to give some kind of praise, some kind of thanks.

They marched to the fort to the roll of drums, held prayer meeting, sang Psalms in thanksgiving, then gathered around the festive tables. Massasoit and his people brought five deer as their offering. Governor Bradford sent Pilgrim men to the forest with Indians to hunt wild turkey, and they brought down wild geese, duck, and water fowl as well. The women cooked cod and shellfish, prepared barley loaves, cornbread, and vegetables from the harvest of their tiny fields.

These are the things our children learn in school about this great national feast of Thanksgiving, and they love to hear the stories that go with the preparations. It is part of our history. Tell them, if they do not know, that George Washington made it a national feast by proclamation in 1789, with words of homage to the One True God:

[138] John 14:6.

Whereas it is the duty of all nations to acknowledge the providence of Almighty God, to obey His will, to be grateful for His benefits, and humbly implore His protection, aid and favors. . . . Now, therefore, I do recommend and assign Thursday, the 26th day of November next, to be devoted by the people of these States to the service of that great and glorious Being, who is the Beneficent Author of all the good that was, that is, or that will be; that we may then all unite in rendering unto Him our sincere and humble thanks for His kind care and protection of the people of this country, and for all the great and various favors which He has been pleased to confer on us.

And in 1867 Abraham Lincoln reaffirmed the observance by another Thanksgiving proclamation.

If they should visit Plymouth one day, they would find the William Harlow house there, built in 1677 from the timbers of the old fort, where, in the springtime, Plymouth schoolchildren follow the Pilgrim custom and plant in the yard corn and flax, "when the oak leaves are the size of a mouse's ear." The corn is fertilized with alewives from Town Brook, three to the hill. In April or May or whenever the oak leaves peek out, mouse-like, in your countryside, let your children plant some corn and flax of their own. They may not spin the flax, but it has a beautiful blue blossom, exactly the color for bouquets for our Lady; and once they know the plant, they will begin to notice how often flax and fine linen and linen cloth are mentioned in their favorite stories from Holy Scripture.

☞

*Preparing for the Feast*
Pinecone turkeys are made for Thanksgiving by almost every schoolchild in America. Although no novelty, they are one of the

symbols of the feast. Our children never tire of making them. They are decorative as place favors, or all together (if you have a large family with a turkey for each) they are an amusingly large flock of turkeys. Pinecones, pipe cleaners, cupcake papers, and crayons are the materials. The pinecone is used "sideways," with the top for the turkey's head, the flat bottom part for his tail. A pipe cleaner is twisted around the top. The end sticking out as the turkey's neck is daubed with lipstick for red wattles. Another pipe cleaner is twisted around the bottom, with two ends sticking out and turned under for feet. A cupcake paper is folded in half, colored bright colors in the little ridged sections, and this is slipped between the petals of the cone for the turkey's tail.

Several years ago, we typed out individual copies of a "long" *Grace before Meals*. Monica decorated them with little figures praying, and we have used these each year as our special Thanksgiving Grace. They are a bit greasy now, what with all those turkey dinners rubbed off on them, but they have become so traditional a part of our Thanksgiving that we are loath to make new copies. Since it may be used at any time, it is not accurately called *Grace before Thanksgiving Dinner* — but that is what it is for our family.

GRACE BEFORE THANKSGIVING DINNER

*Leader:* Bless you.

    *All:* Bless you.

*Leader:* The eyes of all hope in Thee, O Lord.

    *All:* And Thou givest them their food in due season. Thou openest Thy hand, and fillest with blessing every living creature.

*Leader:* Glory be to the Father, and to the Son, and to the Holy Spirit.

    *All:* As it was in the beginning, is now, and ever shall be, world without end. Amen.

*Leader:* Lord, have mercy on us.

*All:* Christ, have mercy on us. Lord, have mercy on us. (The Our Father, silently.)

*Leader:* And lead us not into temptation.

*All:* But deliver us from evil. Amen.

*Leader:* Let us pray. Bless us, O Lord, and these Thy gifts, which we are about to receive. Through Christ, our Lord.

*All:* Amen.

GRACE AFTER THANKSGIVING DINNER

(Suggestion: Say this as soon as all are finished with dessert; then the children may leave to play, and the grown-ups may stay and talk.)

*Leader:* Do Thou, O Lord, have mercy on us.

*All:* Thanks be to God.

*Leader:* Let all Thy works, O Lord, praise Thee.

*All:* And let all Thy saints bless Thee.

*Leader:* Glory be to the Father, and to the Son, and to the Holy Spirit.

*All:* As it was in the beginning, is now, and ever shall be, world without end. Amen.

*Leader:* We give Thee thanks, O Almighty God, for all Thy benefits, who livest and reignest world without end.

Now we are prepared for our feast. Dinner is planned; the silver is polished; the linen is ready; the Grace is copied for each one. The turkeys are made for decorations; the cranberry sauce is molded; the stuffing is prepared, and the sauce for the onions; and the celery is crisping ahead of time. When the morning of our feast day has come, let us offer Him in Thanksgiving.

⌒

*The Mass:*

*The Perfect Thanksgiving*

Men have not only prayed in thanksgiving, but have offered in thanksgiving: something that was a sign of themselves, to show they were thankful for life, were sorry for their sins against the Giver of life, would give their lives in return, if they might, to the One they owe so much. They made offerings in thanks for the things that sustain life, for the preservation of life.

"Abel also offered of the firstlings of his flock, and of their fat."[139] . . . "So Noah went out, he and his sons, his wife and the wives of his sons — all living things went out of the ark. And Noah built an altar unto the Lord: and taking of all cattle and fowl that were clean, offered holocausts upon the altar. . . ."[140]

They made bloody offerings, because the offering is a symbol of the offerer, and blood is the essence of life. Blood is life.

There were other offerings: "Melchidesech, the king of Salem, bringing forth bread and wine, for he was the priest of the most high God, blessed him and said, 'Blessed be Abram by the most high God, who created heaven and earth.' "[141] . . . Because bread maintains life, and wine enhances life.

God told them what to sacrifice and how to sacrifice; but especially He told them to make the sacrifice of the Pasch, because it was a memorial to their freedom and their protection, a memorial of thanksgiving to the God who loved them: ". . . and it shall be a lamb without blemish, a male, one year . . . and the whole multitude of the children of Israel shall sacrifice it in the evening." . . . "And this day shall be a memorial unto you: and you shall keep it a

[139] Gen. 4:4.
[140] Cf. Gen. 8:18-20.
[141] Gen. 14:18-19.

feast to the Lord . . . for with a strong hand the Lord hath brought you out of this place."

He brought them through water, led them by fire, fed them with manna, and when they sinned against Him, He chastised them and accepted their sacrifices of expiation. He made it part of their Law, their Covenant, that they were to offer sacrifice: of reparation, of petition, of praise, of thanksgiving.

Then Christ came.

When it was time for the thing to happen for which He came, He said to the Apostles, "This is my body, which is being given for you; do this, in remembrance of me."

And He said: "This cup is the new covenant in my blood, which shall be shed for you."

This was the *new* covenant, the new Pasch . . . "in *my* blood," He said. From that moment on, they were to make sacrifice "in *my* blood."

The offering is a symbol of the offerer. Blood is the essence of life. This is our gift to offer: His Body and Blood, every day.

Think of all the things the Redemption accomplished, and do not forget this last: to put into our hands the perfect Gift, the pure Victim — "holy and spotless, the holy bread of everlasting life and the chalice of everlasting salvation." With the sacrifice of Holy Mass, Catholics make their thanksgiving.

# Biographical Note

Mary Reed Newland was a wife, mother of seven, artist, social advocate, gourmet cook, and biographer of saints. She wrote many books for Catholic families, including *How to Raise Good Catholic Children*.

# Sophia Institute Press®

Sophia Institute® is a nonprofit institution that seeks to restore man's knowledge of eternal truth, including man's knowledge of his own nature, his relation to other persons, and his relation to God. Sophia Institute Press® serves this end in numerous ways: it publishes translations of foreign works to make them accessible for the first time to English-speaking readers; it brings out-of-print books back into print; and it publishes important new books that fulfill the ideals of Sophia Institute. These books afford readers a rich source of the enduring wisdom of mankind.

Sophia Institute Press® makes these high-quality books available to the general public by using advanced technology and by soliciting donations to subsidize its general publishing costs. Your generosity can help Sophia Institute Press® to provide the public with editions of works containing the enduring wisdom of the ages. Please send your tax-deductible contribution to the address below. We welcome your questions, comments, and suggestions.

*For your free catalog, call:*
**Toll-free: 1-800-888-9344**

Sophia Institute Press®
Box 5284, Manchester, NH 03108
www.sophiainstitute.com

Sophia Institute® is a tax-exempt institution as defined by the Internal Revenue Code, Section 501(c)(3). Tax I.D. 22-2548708.